United Arab Emirates

WORLD BIBLIOGRAPHICAL SERIES

General Editors:
Robert G. Neville (Executive Editor)
John J. Horton

Robert A. Myers   Hans H. Wellisch
Ian Wallace   Ralph Lee Woodward, Jr.

John J. Horton is Deputy Librarian of the University of Bradford and was formerly Chairman of its Academic Board of Studies in Social Sciences. He has maintained a longstanding interest in the discipline of area studies and its associated bibliographical problems, with special reference to European Studies. In particular he has published in the field of Icelandic and of Yugoslav studies, including the two relevant volumes in the World Bibliographical Series.

Robert A. Myers is Associate Professor of Anthropology in the Division of Social Sciences and Director of Study Abroad Programs at Alfred University, Alfred, New York. He has studied post-colonial island nations of the Caribbean and has spent two years in Nigeria on a Fulbright Lectureship. His interests include international public health, historical anthropology and developing societies. In addition to *Amerindians of the Lesser Antilles: a bibliography* (1981), *A Resource Guide to Dominica, 1493-1986* (1987) and numerous articles, he has compiled the World Bibliographical Series volumes on *Dominica* (1987), *Nigeria* (1989) and *Ghana* (1991).

Ian Wallace is Professor of German at the University of Bath. A graduate of Oxford in French and German, he also studied in Tübingen, Heidelberg and Lausanne before taking teaching posts at universities in the USA, Scotland and England. He specializes in contemporary German affairs, especially literature and culture, on which he has published numerous articles and books. In 1979 he founded the journal *GDR Monitor*, which he continues to edit under its new title *German Monitor*.

Hans H. Wellisch is Professor emeritus at the College of Library and Information Services, University of Maryland. He was President of the American Society of Indexers and was a member of the International Federation for Documentation. He is the author of numerous articles and several books on indexing and abstracting, and has published *The Conversion of Scripts and Indexing and Abstracting: an International Bibliography*, and *Indexing from A to Z*. He also contributes frequently to *Journal of the American Society for Information Science*, *The Indexer* and other professional journals.

Ralph Lee Woodward, Jr. is Professor of History at Tulane University, New Orleans. He is the author of *Central America, a Nation Divided*, 2nd ed. (1985), as well as several monographs and more than seventy scholarly articles on modern Latin America. He has also compiled volumes in the World Bibliographical Series on *Belize* (1980), *El Salvador* (1988), *Guatemala* (Rev. Ed.) (1992) and *Nicaragua* (Rev. Ed.) (1994). Dr. Woodward edited the Central American section of the *Research Guide to Central America and the Caribbean* (1985) and is currently associate editor of Scribner's *Encyclopedia of Latin American History*.

VOLUME 43

United Arab Emirates

Revised Edition

Frank A. Clements

Compiler

CLIO PRESS

OXFORD, ENGLAND · SANTA BARBARA, CALIFORNIA
DENVER, COLORADO

British Library Cataloguing in Publication Data

Clements, Frank A.
United Arab Emirates – Rev. Ed. – (World bibliographical series; v. 43)
1. United Arab Emirates – Bibliography
I. Title
016.9'5357

ISBN 1–85109–274–9

ABC-CLIO Ltd.,
Old Clarendon Ironworks,
35A Great Clarendon Street,
Oxford OX2 6AT, England.

———————

ABC-CLIO Inc.,
130 Cremona Drive,
Santa Barbara,
CA 93117, USA.

Designed by Bernard Crossland.
Typeset by Columns Design Ltd., Reading, England.
Printed in Great Britain by print in black, Midsomer Norton.

THE WORLD BIBLIOGRAPHICAL SERIES

This series, which is principally designed for the English speaker, will eventually cover every country (and some of the world's principal regions and cities), each in a separate volume comprising annotated entries on works dealing with its history, geography, economy and politics; and with its people, their culture, customs, religion and social organization. Attention will also be paid to current living conditions – housing, education, newspapers, clothing, etc. – that are all too often ignored in standard bibliographies; and to those particular aspects relevant to individual countries. Each volume seeks to achieve, by use of careful selectivity and critical assessment of the literature, an expression of the country and an appreciation of its nature and national aspirations, to guide the reader towards an understanding of its importance. The keynote of the series is to provide, in a uniform format, an interpretation of each country that will express its culture, its place in the world, and the qualities and background that make it unique. The views expressed in individual volumes, however, are not necessarily those of the publisher.

VOLUMES IN THE SERIES

Contents

Contents

Contents

Introduction

The Federation of the United Arab Emirates came into being in 1971 following British withdrawal from the Arabian Gulf. It comprises the seven states of Abu Dhabi, Dubai, Sharjah, Ajman, Umm al-Qaiwain, Ras al-Khaimah and Fujairah. It was originally thought that Bahrain and Qatar would also join the federation but various difficulties presented themselves during the negotiations and the two states decided to retain their independence and withdrew from discussions. However, the region as a whole has responded to external problems and pressures by the formation in 1981 of the Gulf Co-operation Council (GCC) to which these states now belong, as well as Kuwait, Oman and Saudi Arabia, and this regional co-operation will certainly continue to affect inter-state relationships. Significantly, at the end of the Iraq–Iran war an invitation to membership of the GCC was not extended to Iraq, nor to the Yemen, though the former omission was to have a far greater impact on regional events.

Prior to 1971 the external affairs of the seven states were looked after by the United Kingdom through a series of treaties and undertakings built up over a period of nearly 300 years. The treaties and engagements were originally designed to protect the trade routes of the East India Company and the passage to the Indian Empire, and to prevent what were regarded by the British as acts of piracy in the Gulf, primarily by the Qawasim tribe from Ras al-Khaimah. This was regarded as a justification for imperial expansion in the Gulf region but this conventional view has now been challenged and presented as a myth created by the East India Company for commercial reasons. It is argued that the East India Company was determined to increase its share of trade with India at the expense of the traditional Arab traders from the lower Gulf.

The Company, based in Bombay, did not have warships to tackle the Qawasin fleet and had to involve the Royal Navy in any actions which required orchestration of events to secure intervention by the

British Government. A campaign was mounted to misrepresent, so it is claimed, the Qawasim as pirates threatening all maritime activity in the Gulf and the Indian Ocean and any misfortune to any vessel was attributed to pirate activity. The end result of this campaign was the storming of Ras al-Khaimah by British forces in 1809 and the final destruction of the Qawasim in 1819. The British view is represented by *Pirates of Trucial Oman* by H. Moyse-Bartlett, and the Arab view by *The myth of Arab piracy in the Gulf* by Sultan Muhammad Al-Qasimi.

It is not disputed, however, that the Royal Navy also became heavily involved in attempting to suppress the slave trade in the region and a number of the earlier understandings and engagements with the various tribal sheikhs were intended to put an end to that trade. The succession of agreements and understandings, and the signing of a Treaty of Perpetual Maritime Peace, led to the present-day Emirates and the Sultanate of Oman being known as the Trucial States or Trucial Oman. Because of this, the reader will find reference to the United Arab Emirates as the Trucial States in addition to the names of the individual states.

The situation regarding the area is also complicated by the fact that its affairs were handled by the Indian Government, from the earliest days of British involvement in the Arabian Gulf until Indian independence when they were transferred to the Foreign Office. This was primarily due to the impact and influence of the East India Company which was based in India, and whose interests dominated the region. However, the Foreign Office had control over affairs in the remainder of the Arabian Peninsula and its policies for that area were often in conflict with Indian Government policy regarding the Gulf States. This serves to explain the presence within this bibliography of official documents and records from both sources.

The federation has now survived for twenty-seven years, a period far in excess of the pessimistic forecasts made at its birth. Initially it was felt that this bonding could not survive because of the disparities between the seven states and because of the historical rivalries and territorial disputes which had endured for centuries. Although Britain had resolved a number of these before withdrawal from the Gulf, some were unresolved; these included particularly the offshore borders, which had assumed greater significance because of the anticipated presence of hydrocarbon reserves. The situation has been further complicated by Iranian claims to sovereignty over certain islands in the Gulf, such as Abu Musa and the Tunbs, and these problems too are reflected in the literature covered.

As each problem has arisen, observers have looked for signs that the union was in the process of disintegration, but despite various traumas, some of them serious, it has survived. In the initial stages the main problem was the traditional rivalry between Abu Dhabi and Dubai, together with the fact that only these two states and Sharjah had discovered oil and gas in commercially viable quantities, though Ras al-Khaimah has now become a producer. But the bulk of the federal budget still comes from Abu Dhabi and, to a lesser extent Dubai, and the remainder of the states are dependent upon these two states financing the federal infrastructure and development programmes. This fact is reflected in the bibliography in the sections covering finance, banking, economics and industrial diversification, and these sections have, of necessity, a predominance of items relating to Abu Dhabi and Dubai.

At the time when the federation was established the area could still be considered underdeveloped in nearly all respects. There was a shortage of hospital beds, provision being at the rate of one per 1,000 of population; schooling was restricted to the towns, with only 35,000 children at school, a figure which had grown to 193,633 by 1983-84. These few figures are merely illustrative of the whole pattern of underdevelopment which also included a lack of housing, power supplies and a communications network, no industry and only subsistence agriculture. All of this set against a backcloth of rising oil income, most of which, until the industry entered into participation agreements with the governments, was in the hands of the international oil companies who controlled the means of production, transportation, refining and marketing. An enormous amount of development took place during the federation's first decade, using income from oil – income which had risen dramatically following the 1973-74 oil embargo imposed through OPEC as a means of exerting political pressure in the Arab–Israeli dispute.

Decades of change were compressed into this relatively short period and the federation was forced to mature quickly. The rapid expansion of the infrastructure and the resultant economic boom brought additional problems as the pace of development was not matched by the capacity of the newly created infrastructure to handle the volume and speed of development and change. Errors were made, and at times the economy was overstretched, resulting in severe, if temporary, financial crises. One specific example of this was the banking crisis caused by a rapid boom in the economy, lack of sophistication in the banking system and a lack of controls. The reader will find this reflected in the section entitled 'Finance and Banking'. Problems were also experienced in the construction industry which was proceeding at a frantic rate, but the port facilities were not capable of handling the importation of raw material, resulting in ships anchored in the Gulf waiting to unload deteriorating cargoes.

The major problem during the first five years of federal development was the lack of an overall development strategy to deal with the structural characteristics of the economy and its social, political, geographical and environmental traits. The absence of such a strategy during this period is understandable as a result of the underdevelopment in the federation and the need to make rapid progress. Provision of the basic infrastructure and services constituted a priority, at a time when no national strategy existed and the state institutions charged with their management lacked experience and co-ordination. Despite these problems a plan should have been drawn up to control the overall development process, but nothing was done and the absence of a federal strategy brought unwelcome consequences.

Initially, development concentrated on prestigious projects such as imports, government buildings, conference facilities, university and school buildings, hospitals, ports and palaces. Some of these projects were necessary but more were developed without an overall plan. In addition, project costs were abnormally high, 30 to 60 per cent higher than in other developing countries, a fact which reflects the inadequacy of the base for projects, lack of technical and managerial expertise, and a lack of co-ordination within the federation and with other Gulf States.

The development plans and programmes which were initially issued were little more than lists of projects representing national aspirations. They were not based on a realistic evaluation of achievable objectives, in line with available resources, nor were they related to the characteristics of each of the emirates.

Evidence of the lack of co-ordination within the federation can be illustrated by examining the field of petrochemicals, with Abu Dhabi and Dubai competing with each other in this area of industrial diversification. Dubai in 1976 announced plans to develop an industrial complex and harbour at Jebel Ali and, at the same time, Abu Dhabi announced plans for an industrial complex at Ruwais. Each had similar industrial activities and objectives. Other examples can be found across the economy with cement plants being built in each emirate, four international airports constructed to serve the federation, and duplicated port complexes along a relatively short coastline. This total lack of co-ordination was a reflection of the unplanned development of economic resources and a wasteful use of the revenues from oil.

The federation is still dependent upon oil as the main source of revenue with no real prospects of significant diversification. Despite the various development plans, the non-oil sector's contribution to GDP remained relatively static. It rose by only 4.2 per cent to 36.7 per cent between 1975 and 1980, a small increase in a period of intense development. Development in the federation was not balanced across sectors or across emirates largely because responsibility for development rested with each emirate, and because regional governments wielded significant power over local decisions in areas of activity where control was supposed to have been ceded to the federal government. Oil revenues flowing to the producing emirates was supposed to contribute to the federal budget, but only Abu Dhabi fully discharged its obligations.

The wealth of the individual emirates also led to the strengthening of their independence which led, in turn, to their drawing up and implementing individual development projects. It was not until 1977 that the federation set up a Ministry of Planning, but even then authority was limited to the level of co-operation allowed by individual state governments. It is considered that the lack of co-ordination and planning contributed to a development slump between 1977 and 1979 and a further slump between 1982 and 1986, the second exacerbated by a decline in world oil prices. A further contributing factor was the lack of reliable data at both public and private sector level, a situation which also detracting from the effectiveness of the central planning authority.

A secondary strand has been the development of the agricultural sector which has received a high priority in order to try to reduce the enormous volume of imports in this sector. The problems here are mainly environmental – only 0.2 per cent of the land is capable of supporting agriculture, and there are problems associated with the availability of sufficient water resources. As a consequence, investment is high in relation to yields and subsidies had to be paid to farmers to persuade them to remain active in this sector of the economy.

Agriculture was the most neglected sector in the pre-independence era but also had the highest percentage of employment for nationals. By the mid-1980s the proportion of nationals in farming was 50 per cent, in animal husbandry 80 per cent and in fishing 75 per cent, and development of the sector would enable a significant percentage of the national workforce to participate in economic development. It was also planned to move towards self-sufficiency in basic foods, but by the mid-1980s the sector catered for only 20 per cent of the total food needs of the population despite the face that this objective should be regarded as one of the most important facing the federation and the other Gulf States.

Development of the sector was in two stages. The first decade of the federation saw the laying down of an infrastructure with the expansion of reclaimed land, the digging of wells and an audit of the underground water reserves. This was accompanied by the provision of machinery and equipment, the construction of model farms and the building of a fishing fleet. The government also distributed free seeds and seedlings.

In the 1980s the sector moved into the actual production and marketing of products but the return on government investment has been modest, rising from 0.7 per cent of income from non-oil resources to 1 per cent after the first decade of investment. Some gains were made with production increases because of the expansion of arable land and higher productivity resulting from mechanization and the introduction of modern methods. Animal husbandry also improved through the provision by the government of veterinary services and the establishment of a poultry industry. Fishery production has also improved through government provision of boats and fishing equipment.

The main problems facing the sector are the dearth of arable land and the lack of water; groundwater depletion was continuous in the absence of conservation measures. In the mid-1980s research was still lagging behind usage and lacked co-ordination and synchronization across the federation. In recent years there has been increased usage of treated wastewater for irrigation purchases and more control over consumption and conservation. Additionally, agricultural labour has been a problem; nationals are attracted to other sectors with easier and larger profits, resulting in immigrant labour, often with no experience, being employed in the sector. The situation has again been dominated by lack of co-ordination between the federal authorities and the municipalities of the various emirates.

Rapid development in the oil industry and downstream activities, together with ambitious infrastructure projects, led to the federation becoming attractive to migrant labour on account of the small indigenous population. This is illustrated by an examination of the figures just prior to independence and at the end of the first decade of the federation. In 1968, the population of the seven states amounted to 180,000 of which 63 per cent were nationals; by 1979 the population had risen to 1,015,000, with nationals accounting for only 22 per cent of the population. The increase was largely in the emirates of Abu Dhabi, Dubai and Sharjah which, at that time, were the major oil producers and accounted for 85 per cent of the total population of the federation.

The need for a large immigrant workforce was caused by a

combination of factors; the most significant of these are the demands caused by modernization and the lack of an indigenous labour supply. The latter was worsened by both the reluctance of the urban and the nomadic population to participate quickly in development projects, and the fact that women do not take an active part in production work. The second major problem was the lack of an educated workforce, a fact which heightened the demand for skilled and trained labour from abroad to bridge the gap until the education system could catch up and produce well-trained, skilled personnel.

The United Arab Emirates has been a magnet for migrant labour from the Arab non-oil-producing states, but workers have come primarily from the Indian subcontinent and South East Asia, some of them illegally. Again the lack of planning and co-ordination caused continuing problems for the federation as delays in implementing legislation left loopholes which allowed companies to import limitless amounts of labour from cheap markets abroad and then, at the end of contracts, to dismiss large groups, some of whom moved into the black economy. Work sponsorship permits were also uncontrolled and an absence of a legal framework encouraged a trade in permits. The impact of oil wealth on the standards of living of nationals also led to an explosion in the employment of domestic servants such that by the mid-1980s the overall number of migrant domestic workers had risen to 150,000.

Lack of control and the planning of employment against identified needs was further affected by downturns in oil prices and the economy in the mid-1980s, and the growth of an illegal workforce continued. The situation was considered to be critical mainly in terms of the employment sector, but also with regard to the effects on society and the welfare services; clampdowns were instigated and severe penalties imposed on illegal workers. The government granted a three-month amnesty for illegal workers between July and September 1996 and it has been estimated that 200,000 illegal workers left the country under the terms of the amnesty. However, such has been the reliance on illegal migrant labour that it was feared that every aspect of the economy would be affected by the resultant labour shortage and that labour costs would inevitably rise thanks to effective regulation of the market.

At its establishment, the federation gave immediate priority to the provision of education and by 1972 a number of laws and regulations had been enacted to guarantee a competent level of education. Significantly, Section 120 of the constitution made educational legislation, educational planning and implementation, and regular education the sole responsibility of the federal government. The

Introduction

various legislative measures covered compulsory education at primary level, guaranteed free education at all levels, targeted the system at the eradication of illiteracy, allowed the development of private education under the control of the public authorities, and by 1976 legislation covered the provision of university education.

Growth in provision has been significant both in quantitative and qualitative terms and special attention has also been given to evening schools and centres for adults, particularly in the drive against illiteracy. But the take-up of vocational and technical education has been slow, as has that in the agricultural sector, despite the need for trained manpower in these areas. Lack of interest is also the result of the low status given to jobs in that area of employment. Problems still exist in the education sector: a continuing imbalance between the sexes, as many families still do not see the need for female education; and only a modest take-up in the illiteracy programme. The enforcement of compulsory education has also been difficult, especially in the rural areas and in the mountainous and nomadic regions where children are an integral part of the economy from an early age.

In the initial stages of development the sector was heavily dependent upon expatriate teachers from other Arab countries, primarily Egypt and Jordan. The acquisition of a qualified national teaching force has been a major development problem and even in the 1990s the sector has still been heavily reliant on expatriate teachers and concerns were still being voiced about quality.

Other significant areas of development have been in the health, welfare and housing sectors. In terms of the health service there was a major investment in the provision of hospital services, clinics, and specialist centres aimed at schools, mother-and-child care centres, and dental facilities. Initially development was targeted on quantitative development in all sectors and in both the rural and urban environment but from 1975 the emphasis changed to qualitative improvements and the regulation of the sector. The whole system had been under extreme pressure, affecting efficiency and standards in all areas, largely as a result of the influx of expatriate workers and their dependants – employing companies were not forced to make provision for their workers either in the private sector or through contributions to the federal budget. This factor was addressed in 1985 when low medical charges were introduced to reduce unnecessary demands upon the services.

Social welfare was a further area of provision covered by the constitution; the stress was on equality, social justice and a guarantee of equal opportunities, together with legislation to preserve the rights of workers and the interests of employers. The immediate income was under the control of community development centres, to deal with family problems and to provide training programmes in household skills, domestic science and other programmes aimed at women. In addition, care is provided for the handicapped and social benefits are paid to target groups which include widows, orphans, old people, the disabled and the destitute. This sector has shown considerable expansion over the years but without the application of criteria for the granting of benefits and the appropriate nature of assistance.

The housing sector was also an area which experienced a high rate of growth; in the period 1976-80 130,000 units were built, whilst 1980-85 saw the construction of 218,000 units. The decade of the 1970s was one of boom in the construction industry, with a demand for accommodation which could not be satisfied. This resulted in extremely high rents, the attraction of investment from banks, finance houses and individuals fuelled by the possibility of high returns, and the sector flourished. However, the bubble burst in the late 1980s when supply outstripped demand, rents fell and investments were not covered by housing equity. Yet again the situation was complicated by lack of planning and co-ordination between the federal government, local authorities in the seven emirates and the private sector. In addition, the absence, and then inadequacy, of rent laws failed to guarantee the stability of tenancies or the rights of landlords.

The main problem faced by the federation is the reliance on oil and allied products. Oil is a finite resource and there is a need to pursue diversification. One possible growth sector is in the area of tourism, and that is receiving considerable investment, particularly in the Emirate of Dubai. The emirate has a well-developed infrastructure, good weather, and a competitive pricing policy with high hotel occupancy; the scale of investment is evidenced by the Chicago Beach and Jumairah beach developments. The industry is still on a small scale but Abu Dhabi and Dubai are now being extensively marketed throughout Europe as winter destinations.

In terms of regional development, the main feature was the establishment of the Gulf Co-operation Council in 1981 – after a period of about five years of consultation and negotiation. The GCC also incorporates the states of Bahrain, Kuwait, Qatar, Saudi Arabia and Oman and has made progress in unification in economic terms with the creation of an internal free-trade market, common external tariffs, and the creation of common institutions such as the Gulf Investment Corporation and the Gulf Organization for Industrial Consultancy. The political agenda of the GCC has three main thrusts: the enhancement of social and economic conditions within the member states; the promotion of stability in the Arabian Peninsula and Gulf region; and the direction of resources towards Arab and Muslim causes, as well as the resolution of inter-Arab differences. Collective attention has therefore been directed to securing stability in the Gulf waters to protect the transportation of oil; problems associated with the Iraq–Iran war; relations between Oman and the People's Democratic Yemen Republic; the rights of the Palestinians; and the crucial role of Islam in all the Gulf States.

However, the political agenda of the GCC has not resulted in a surrender of sovereignty by the member states but has served as a means of implementing consensus policies where they arise. The main problem within the region is instability, as evidenced by the Iraq–Iran war and the Iraqi invasion of Kuwait. Although not primarily a defensive organization, some commitments were made with regard to military co-operation with the creation of a Rapid Defence Force and joint military exercises, but there are still major differences in policy particularly with regard to relations with Western states. Kuwait, prior to the Iraqi invasion pursued a policy of non-alignment whereas, at the other extreme, Oman maintained very close military relations with the United Kingdom and the United States. Despite the instability in the region it is clear that efforts at military integration are certain to continue at an extremely cautious pace. It is also clear that the GCC does not have the ability to maintain its territorial integrity without outside assistance, as was evidenced by the Iraqi invasion of Kuwait and the inability of the GCC to respond effectively. The GCC is a significant regional development to which the United Arab Emirates is totally committed and in economic terms it is important to the future development and long-term survival of the federation.

The bibliography

This bibliography makes no claim to completeness, but the information listed should provide a comprehensive picture of the United Arab Emirates for the general reader, librarian, information professional or researcher. Arrangement is by broad subject heading, and within that breakdown alphabetical by author or title. Cross-references have been used where necessary to refer the user back to the main annotated entry. As is the case with all bibliographers my main aim has been objectivity but, inevitably, a subjective element is present. The annotations are designed primarily to illustrate the content of the material but also represent my interpretation as to the nature of the contribution.

As a deliberate policy, all the general trade and national bibliographies have been excluded, and only English-language and a small selection of translated items have been listed. A large amount of material on the Gulf in general could have been included because of the inter-relationships between states, the impact of the Iraq–Iran and Gulf wars, and the strategic significance of the area, but this material was deliberately excluded to maintain a correct balance. The user should also be aware that not all of the material included in the first edition has been carried forward into this work. In terms of transliteration, the most accepted forms have been adopted, but there may be variation in a title where I have retained that used by the author. For ease of use diacritics have not been included in this work or its indexes.

The Country and Its People

1 **The United Arab Emirates: a modern history.**
Muhammad Morsy Abdullah.   London: Croom Helm; New York:
Barnes & Noble, 1978. 365p. maps. bibliog.

An authoritative and indispensable illustrated study of the federation by the director of
the Centre for Documentation and Research in Abu Dhabi. The first part of the work
discusses the Trucial States in relation to British imperial interests and includes an
examination of internal changes during the period. The second part deals with the
development of nationalism in the region, the relations between the UAE and her
neighbours, and the growth of Iranian interests in the Gulf. The final part of the book
provides the background to the historical development of the emirates, the evolution
of the political boundaries between the states and their political geography. The author
also deals with the formative years of the federation and sets out the political, social,
economic and cultural heritage of the new state.

2 **Historical and cultural directory of the Sultanate of Oman and the
emirates of eastern Arabia.**
John Duke Anthony.   Metuchen, New Jersey: Scarecrow Press, 1976.
136p. bibliog. (Historical and Cultural Dictionaries of Asia, no. 9).

A useful publication which provides, in dictionary form, a brief account of the issues,
personalities and events of significance to the area. A handy publication for the begin-
ner, because a large number of the other available publications assume prior
knowledge, while this dictionary helps provide a background.

1

3 **Kuwait, Qatar and the United Arab Emirates: political and social evolution.**
Glen Balfour-Paul. In: *Arabia and the Gulf: from traditional society to modern states*, edited by Ian Richard Netton. London: Croom Helm, 1986, p. 156-78.

The author considers that the seven states which form the United Arab Emirates were a prime example of the political fragmentation of the Arabian Gulf which was confirmed, though not caused, by the treaty system adopted by Britain. The federation is seen as being essential because of the maldistribution of oil and the special need for a new sort of protection, though the Emirates were characterized by a complex series of inter-Emirate and inter-tribal jealousy, often over who owned which well, palm-tree or grazing rights. These jealousies have survived the union but the union has also survived despite the differences. One major development problem identified here is a demographic one: nearly 90 per cent of the labour force are expatriate labour and 85 per cent of the armed forces are mercenary. The development of the state institutions and infrastructure has been a feature of the oil era and there is little to do in quantitative terms but maintenance is costly. However, Balfour-Paul considers that as long as oil lasts, despite price reductions, there should be ample revenues to maintain the public services and to invest for the post-oil era. A major problem is the desired objective to achieve self-sufficiency in food, but this aim is hampered by a serious and growing inadequacy of water for irrigation, and production at a cost well above world prices cannot be sustained even by wealthy governments. In terms of political evolution, Western-style democracy has not taken root in the UAE and four observations are made in assessing the contemporary situation. Firstly, democracy has not taken root where socialist revolutions have taken place or in traditional states; secondly, in the West authoritarianism causes neuroses but in the Arab world it prevents them; thirdly, the emerging middle class were more concerned with profiting from the existing order than in subverting it; finally, the sheikhdoms survived British withdrawal, a fact which seems to illustrate that the system survives because it is more readily understood by the indigenous population rather than any alternative mode of government which Westerners declare would be better.

4 **Britain's withdrawal from the Persian Gulf and the formation of the United Arab Emirates, 1968-1971.**
Nelson R. Beck. *Towson State Journal of International Affairs*, vol. 12, no. 2 (1978), p. 77-98.

Analyses the reasons for British withdrawal from the Persian Gulf between 1969 and 1971. The reasons were largely economic but there was also a realization that land bases were an anachronism and, in fact, posed a threat to oil refineries in the area. Britain encouraged the United Arab Emirates as a means of collective survival following the withdrawal of British military protection.

5 **The Gulf: a portrait of Kuwait, Qatar, Bahrain and the UAE.**
John Bulloch. London: Century Publishing, 1984. 224p. maps. bibliog.

This illustrated examination of the Gulf region, a useful introduction for the general reader, was written by a journalist working with the *Daily Telegraph* who, at the time of writing, was their Middle East correspondent. The work covers the history of the region; superpower interests in the area; problems of mass labour migration; the oil industry; the banking sector; architecture; culture and future development potential.

Britain's withdrawal from the Gulf is also considered in the context of the establishment of the United Arab Emirates and the resolution of the various boundary disputes. Bulloch then considers the area following the exploitation of oil. There are references to the United Arab Emirates throughout the text and also to the individual Emirates.

6 The seven sheikhdoms.
Ronald Codrai.   London: Stacey International, 1990. 176p. maps.

A well-illustrated account of the way of life in the United Arab Emirates as it was before the discovery of oil in the 1960s.

7 Abu Dhabi: a portrait.
John Daniels.   London: Longman, 1974. 102p. map.

One of the earliest books about the wealthiest state in the federation; it serves as a useful introduction. Daniels's concise illustrated study deals with the early history of Abu Dhabi, the importance of pearl fishing, the discovery of oil, and the creation of the federation in 1971 following British withdrawal, with the oil wealth of Abu Dhabi providing the bulk of the finance. Also examined are developments in health, education, development projects, and the culture and customs of the people.

8 Ras al-Khaimah, flame in the desert.
Michael Deakin, Robin Constable.   London: Namara Publications, 1976. 144p. map.

A lavishly illustrated book on the Emirates whose traditions were very much rooted in the past and whose future was very much tied to agriculture with only the minimal prospect of oil revenues. The authors provide a basic introduction for the general reader, and the illustrative material is well presented.

9 War and peace in the Gulf: domestic politics and regional relations into the 1990s.
Anoushiravan Ehteshami, Gerd Nonneman.   Reading, England: Ithaca Press, 1991. 287p. maps. bibliog.

A detailed study of the Arabian Gulf during the decade 1980-90, with particular reference to the roles of Iran and Iraq, and the effects of the Iraq–Iran war and the Iraqi invasion of Kuwait on the region's politics. The work also examines domestic politics and the changing regional political relations together with issues of defence, the military balance and arms transfers. The authors provide a chronology of Gulf events from 1980 to 1991, and documents from the 1975 Algiers Agreement to the 1990 UN Security Council resolutions on the Kuwait crisis. References to the UAE are scattered throughout the text, but with particular relation to oil policies, relations with Iran, relations with Iraq, and military expenditure. The text is supplemented by tables and notes.

10 Emirates are bonding as never before.
Middle East Economic Digest, vol. 40, no. 49 (1996), p. 33-35.

A review of 25 years of the United Arab Emirates, which is seen to have been a success story in terms of economic development. Each Emirate retains a high degree of autonomy within the federation which is largely dominated by Abu Dhabi and Dubai, the two richest Emirates. However, they are coming closer together economically with

Abu Dhabi supplying gas to the Jebel Ali industrial complex in Dubai, and investment by the Emirate in the Dubai Cable Company. The competition of previous years is now being replaced by synergy within the development process and there is a recognition within the two Emirates that each needs the other; Abu Dhabi has the energy resources but needs the business flair of Dubai. The federal government is also gaining some power as it is assuming a more active role in terms of establishing a regulatory framework which is being adopted throughout the federation.

11 United Arab Emirates: special report.
Kathy Evans (et al.). *The Guardian* (London), (2 Dec. 1992) p. 10-11.

A special report on the United Arab Emirates on the occasion of its twenty-first anniversary. The authors survey the economy and explain that it is heavily reliant on oil – accounting for 40 per cent of production and 60 per cent of exports – but point out that tourism is being actively promoted.

12 Arabian profiles: the Arab Gulf Cooperation Council.
Edited by Ian Fairservice, Chuck Grieve. Dubai: Motivate Publishing, 1991. 167p.

A lavishly illustrated profile of the various states of the Gulf Co-operation Council with the United Arab Emirates being covered from page 136 to page 166. Amongst the topics covered are: the historical background; geography; archaeology; culture and traditions; oil industry; industrial diversification; economic growth; social services; agriculture and fisheries; and leisure and recreation facilities. This is a useful introductory work for the general reader, largely descriptive in nature, though with a wealth of relevant colour plates.

13 The United Arab Emirates: an economic and social survey.
Kevin Fenelon. London: Longman, 1976. 2nd ed. 164p. maps. bibliog.

An extremely valuable work on the Emirates, which, although not as detailed as that by Morsy Abdullah, is more general in its coverage and tends not to be as academic or as scholarly. The author, who was statistical adviser to the Abu Dhabi government, begins by outlining the historical background to the area and the founding of the federation. The bulk of the book is concerned with economic and social developments, and comprises chapters on economic development, trade and commerce, industry, banking and finance, transport and communications, the tradition of pearl fishing, and agricultural activities. On the social development front, there are chapters devoted to education, health and housing. It concludes with an examination of culture, customs and sporting activities.

14 United Arab Emirates: *Financial Times* Survey: Section III.
Michael Field. *Financial Times* (24 March 1988), p. I-IV. maps.

The Gulf War did not have a major impact on the United Arab Emirates and concern was focused more on the spread and impact of Iranian propaganda. Amongst the topics considered are: the political situation, the economy and oil prices, banking, tourism, the long-term need for evolution towards a modern nation, and relations with the Soviet Union. The text is enhanced by illustrations and tables.

15 **Phoenix rising: the United Arab Emirates; past, present and future.**
Werner Formen.   London: Harvill, 1996. 256p. maps.
Formen's illustrated description of the federation after twenty-five years of existence
provides an account of the state, its history, social life, traditions and customs. He also
deals with the oil-based economy, and the development process brought about by oil
revenues.

16 **Oil monarchies: domestic and security challenges in the Arab Gulf
States.**
F. Gregory Gause III.   New York: Council on Foreign Relations, 1993.
237p. maps.
Examines a number of themes relating to the Gulf States but focuses in particular on
Saudi Arabia and Kuwait. The author argues that the strength of the monarchical
states has been underestimated as their systems of development and patronage are
sufficient for the management of their societies. The United Arab Emirates figure
extensively throughout the text, with a consideration of the armed forces, civil service,
finance, demography, the significance of Islam, tribalism, the effects of the Iraq–Iran
war, women's issues, and statistical data. Amongst other relevant topics considered
are US thinking and policies towards the Gulf States, transformation of Gulf society
through oil, Gulf States' foreign and defence policies, and future challenges to the
Gulf region.

17 **The turbulent Gulf: people, politics and power.**
Liesl Graz.   London and New York: Tauris, in association with the
Gulf Centre for Strategic Studies, 1992. rev. ed. 311p. bibliog.
Graz's survey of the Gulf States in the post-Cold War era takes into account the Gulf
War and its immediate aftermath. She provides an analysis of social, economic, commercial and political developments, with particular reference to the effects of the oil
boom in the 1970s and the post-1982 decline in the economies of the oil-producing
states. The United Arab Emirates is covered in Chapter 8 (p. 181-213), with the main
attention being devoted to Abu Dhabi and Dubai, and only brief coverage of the other
Emirates. The main subject, apart from the topics cited, concerns the future of the federation, particularly in any post-Sheikh Zayed era. The introductory section is also
relevant for a consideration of the British historical presence in the Gulf, the withdrawal in 1970, and the effects of Iranian and Iraqi aspirations in the region.

18 **Dubai – strategic centre.**
Hilary Gush.   *Far Eastern Economic Review*, vol. 157 (15 Dec. 1994),
p. 33-44.
A special advertising section on Dubai which considers the Emirate's strategic position in the Gulf, the significance of the finance and banking sector, trade,
manufacturing industry, and tourism.

19 **The Trucial States.**
Donald Hawley.   London: Allen & Unwin, 1970. 379p.
An extremely valuable work, dealing with the seven states from their early history,
and concluding with the decision to form the federation of the United Arab Emirates
following British withdrawal from the region. Initial coverage is of the prehistory of

the area followed by the arrival of the Arabs and the spread of Islam, including the Ibadhi sect in Oman. The second part of the book deals with the arrival of the British and the development of the treaty relationship, which resulted in the area being known as the Trucial States. In this section also, Hawley deals with the internal history of the area in the 19th and early 20th centuries, including the problems of the Buraimi Oasis and the dispute with Saudi Arabia and Oman over the demarcation of the borders. The work concludes with a study of the economy, the importance of oil, development projects, and the future of the federation. The appendices are particularly useful, giving notes on the geography of the area, tribal structures, flora and fauna, history, notes on each state, and the trade statistics of Dubai.

20 The towers of Ras al-Khaimah.

Derek Kennet.   Oxford, England: Tempus Reparatum, 1995. 237p. maps. (British Archaeological Report S601).

The work was produced for the Government of Ras al-Khaimah Department of Antiquities and Museums and details the defensive towers of the Emirate. These are located in both the occupied areas of the fertile plains and in the hilltops overlooking the wadi beds in the south of the country. The towers, all of which are defensive in nature, are abandoned and slowly falling into disrepair. Although the department has undertaken restoration of the most important towers, this report is designed to document all of the remaining towers in order to record and understand them before they are lost forever. The towers were for the defence of a village, smallholding, a resource, or of an entire region, and their form and function is the core of this work. The first two chapters (p. 3-13) deal with the geography of the Emirate and the historical background to the development of military architecture in Ras al-Khaimah from before the 16th century to the early 19th century. Chapters 3 and 4 (p. 14-30) detail the typology and function of the towers and the building techniques and architectural features. The remainder of the work is a catalogue of the 75 known standing towers and defensive structures recorded between December 1991 and January 1992.

21 The United Arab Emirates: unity in fragmentation.

Ali Mohammed Khalifa.   London: Croom Helm; Boulder, Colorado: Westview Press, 1979. 235p. maps. bibliog.

This study is based on the premiss that the UAE came into being because the various states realized that they could not survive as separate entities after over a century of dependence upon a foreign power. The development of the federation is seen as being hindered by the fact that it emerged from a primarily tribal structure based on paternalism, with unresolved border disputes and relying heavily on migrant labour. But, as a balance to these, the author regards the quest for survival, the raising of living standards, the existence of a core unit built around the state of Abu Dhabi, geographical and cultural links, and a sense of mission as being integrative factors. The study is divided into three parts. The first part deals with the foundation of the federation and the institutional setting, and includes an analysis of the administration at state and federal level, the laws and constitution, and the financial and developmental base of the federation. The second part deals with the hindering and integrative factors outlined above, and the work concludes with an examination of the federation in a regional and global context.

22   **Abu Dhabi: birth of an oil sheikhdom.**

Clarence Mann. Beirut: Khayat, 1969. rev. ed. 153p. maps. bibliog.

In this account of the sheikhdom from the 18th century, a brief introductory chapter examines the land and its inhabitants, followed by an account of the creation of the sheikhdom between 1761 and 1833. The work goes on to consider a period of turbulence in the emirate from 1834 to 1854 – characterized by a resurgence of piracy in the area and conflicts with the Wahhabis, particularly over the Buraimi Oasis – and this section concludes with a consideration of the anti-slavery agreements, the maritime truce with the other Gulf States, and the crucial role of the British Resident in the area. The role of Sheikh Zaid from 1855 to 1909 was marked by petty wars throughout the Gulf and the political acumen of the ruler in securing the status of Abu Dhabi in the region. The period after his death saw a decline in the status of Abu Dhabi, with succession being determined by assassination, and with economic problems caused by the decline of the pearl trade. The work as a whole concludes with a consideration of the impact of oil on the sheikhdom, the resurgent dispute over the Buraimi Oasis, and the pace of development brought about by oil revenues. The British position in the area is also examined (but at a time before any consideration of withdrawal), as are the impact of labour migration on the social structure of the sheikhdom and the need for carefully planned development. The appendices provide a genealogy of the ruling family, a chronology of events, and the various peace treaties and agreements with Great Britain.

23   **Arabia and the Gulf: from traditional society to modern states.**

Edited by Ian Richard Netton. London: Croom Helm, 1986. 259p. map.

A series of contributions examining the transformation of the Gulf States from traditional societies to modern states in the space of a few decades and using revenues from oil. However, this transformation has been paralleled by continuity in political institutions, social organization and religious beliefs. The work considers the roots of the traditional societies; the political, social and cultural evolution of the Gulf; human resources in the Gulf; the oil industry; and the role of women in the UAE. The text has numerous references to the UAE, covering the armed forces, education, its formation, the legal system, oil, demography, migrant labour and the role of women. There are also references to individual emirates and to their early history under the Trucial States. Separate annotations are provided for contributions dealing specifically with the United Arab Emirates.

24   **The desert reformist marks 30 years rule.**

Christine Osborne. *Middle East*, no. 258 (July 1996), p. 22-24.

An examination of the developments that have taken place in the United Arab Emirates under the Presidency of Sheikh Zayed, with particular reference to his environmental policies.

25   **The Gulf States and Oman.**

Christine Osborne. London: Croom Helm, 1977. 208p. maps.

The section on the United Arab Emirates (p. 61-129) begins by dealing with the birth of the federation. Each state is then considered separately, dealing, where appropriate, with the oil industry, economy, development projects, education and welfare, agriculture, industry and investment. The prospects for tourism are also considered. The volume is illustrated.

26 **UAE – 25th anniversary report: sands of fortune.**
Christine Osborne.   *Middle East*, no. 262 (Dec. 1996), p. 18-20.
Takes a retrospective look at development in the United Arab Emirates (UAE) from
its founding in December 1971 when Sheikh Zayed became President. Osborne con-
siders that twenty-five years of development has transformed the UAE into one of the
Gulf's most impressive political and economic success stories.

27 **The Emirates by the first photographers.**
William Pacey, Gillian Grant.   London: Stacey International, 1996.
128p. maps. bibliog.
This pictorial record of the early history of the seven sheikhdoms – now known as the
United Arab Emirates – covers all aspects of society and architectural heritage.

28 **The United Arab Emirates: a venture in unity.**
Malcolm C. Peck.   Boulder, Colorado: Westview Press; London:
Croom Helm, 1986. 176p. map. bibliog.
This illustrated work provides a full profile of the United Arab Emirates which is seen
as having successfully defied the predictions of failure made at its birth in 1971. The
federation is regarded as an intrinsic case-study of interaction between integrative and
disintegrative factors and its success makes the country an interesting study. Oil has
also transformed the country with a development process not repeated elsewhere, and
this has challenged the basic stability and continuity of society, especially because of
its heavy reliance on migrant labour. The work provides a comprehensive coverage of
the federation, dealing with the land and the people; the historical background; society
and culture; the economy; domestic politics; regional security; and international
strategic interests in the region.

29 **Tribes and politics in eastern Arabia.**
E. Peterson.   *Middle East Journal*, vol. 31, no. 3 (Summer 1977),
p. 297-312.
Peterson discusses the evolution of the present UAE from tribal areas into sheikhdoms
under British protection and thence into independent states. This change is seen in
relation to the split between the desert and urban settlement, which inevitably resulted
from contact with the outside world. It was this contact which brought about the
British presence in the area through the 1853 Treaty of Perpetual Maritime Peace and
the pattern of further treaties which led to the area being known as the Trucial States.
The author examines the discovery of oil and its effects, the various boundary disputes
and the eventual independence of the area following British withdrawal.

30 **The United Arab Emirates.**
Khalida Qureshi.   *Pakistan Horizon*, vol. 26, no. 4 (1973) p. 3-27.
A review of the history of the United Arab Emirates, which was founded in 1971, and
the problems faced by the federation if it is to survive as a political entity. The federation has significance because of the international importance of its oil reserves.

31   **Dubai: life and times.**
     Noor Ali Rashid.   London and Dubai: Motivate Publishing, 1997. 144p.
A lavishly illustrated account of the historic blueprint of Sheikh Rashid for the development of the Emirate. The development has been the result of major infrastructure programmes which have turned Dubai into an important regional trade centre, with a growing tourist industry based on excellent facilities at the international airport, shopping facilities, and hotel complexes. The non-oil sector is significant to the future of the Emirate and an example of development in this area is the Jebel Ali free-trade zone and port facilities.

32   **Dubai, Arabia.**
     Janet Robinson.   Bognor Regis, England: New Horizon, 1981. 179p.
     maps.
An illustrated study of society in Dubai, covering all aspects of everyday life, culture, traditions, commerce, trade, and development as a regional business centre.

33   **The Emirates: Abu Dhabi, Dubai, Sharjah, Ras Al-Khaimah, Fujairah, Umm Al-Qaiwain, Ajman.**
     Photographs by Helene Rogers with a text by Kevin Higgins.   Reading, England: Garnet Publishing, 1995. 147p. maps.
This work is primarily a collection of photographs designed to celebrate the 25th anniversary of the federation, with coverage of the various development programmes instigated by the federation, including cultural aspects such as museums and mosque decorations. There is a brief introductory text followed by photographs on each individual Emirate, and a conclusion covering the federation as a political entity.

34   **Dubai's wealth and the greening of the Emirates.**
     Hameeb Salloum.   *Contemporary Review*, vol. 267 (July 1995),
     p. 28-32.
Discusses the economy of Dubai, the main trading centre in the Arabian Gulf. Dubai handles about one-third of the region's non-petroleum trade, and has transferred its trading pattern into re-export throughout the Middle East, the republics of the former Soviet Union, East and South Africa, and the Indian subcontinent. The article also examines the federal government's policy of investment in agriculture, largely based on oil revenues and Dubai's commercial activities. The expansion of productive land is significant as, in 1971, only 6250 acres were cultivated but by the 1990s this had increased to 1,161,370 acres. The main result of this investment has been the achievement of self-sufficiency in fruit and vegetables and 60 per cent sufficiency in other agricultural products.

35   **Die Scheiktumer am Arabisch-Persischen Golf: Geschichte und Gegenwartsprobleme.** (The sheikhdoms on the Arab-Persian Gulf: history and current problems.)
     F. Scholz.   *Geographische Rundschau,* vol. 45, no. 1 (1993), p. 24-31.
     map.
This German-language article examines the United Arab Emirates with particular relevance to structural deficiencies and problems. The Oasis Agricultural Farm Dhaid in

Sharjah and the Jabal Ali industrial zone of Dubai are used as case-studies for an analysis of economic geography. Scholz considers that sudden progress strengthens the need for settlement and the extension of agricultural land, but also stresses that the Bedouin tradition is still strong within the UAE.

36   The establishment of the United Arab Emirates, 1980-85.

R. O. Taryam.   London and New York: Croom Helm, 1987. 290p. maps. bibliog.

A detailed examination of the establishment of the United Arab Emirates in response to the proposed British withdrawal from the Gulf which was announced in 1968 and planned for 1971. The announcement caused the rulers of the Gulf States a great deal of alarm as the area was not stable, it was plagued by border disputes, and there were suspicions about Iranian intentions in the region. The area had been under British dominance for centuries, a state of affairs which had suppressed mutual suspicion and rivalries and provided a security guarantee against outside threats. It was against this backcloth that discussions began amongst the various states with a view to forming a federation. These began in 1968 with a union between Abu Dhabi and Dubai, followed by three years of discussion between nine states which resulted in the withdrawal from the proposed federation of Bahrain and Qatar. In the case of Bahrain, withdrawal was due to claims to her territory from Iran that resulted in her wishing to resolve these problems before entering into any agreement, whilst Qatar withdrew because she could not achieve a dominant position. The other states continued negotiations until 1971, ending with the formation of the United Arab Emirates. The study considers the internal and external pressures on the Emirates from 1950, including: educational development; the commercial development of Dubai; the Buraimi Oasis dispute with Saudi Arabia and Oman; and the internal unrest within Oman. The impact of oil on the various states is also considered and this is linked to the local, regional and international reactions to British withdrawal because of the strategic significance of oil. The work examines the Abu Dhabi–Dubai agreement, the negotiations between the nine states, Iranian and Saudi Arabian attitudes to the negotiations, the failure of the talks, and the success of the seven Emirates union. The concluding part of the work deals with the constitutional aspects of the federation and the relative position of the regional authorities, together with the bid towards the establishment of a strong federal structure. A final chapter deals with the evolution of social and economic development within the UAE, and gives brief information on education, health, social welfare, agriculture and fishing, power, water resources, communications and transport, the oil industry, trade, finance and banking, manpower problems and migrant labour, and the development planning bodies within the UAE.

37   The United Arab Emirates.

Abu Dhabi: United Arab Emirates Ministry of Information, 1973. 143p. map.

This work provides a heavily illustrated account of the United Arab Emirates with a text in English and French. It begins with a brief account of the establishment of the federation, followed by the historical background, then a brief consideration of the various sectors of the economy, society, traditions, culture, and the potential for the future in terms of development. The bulk of the work consists of the coloured plates illustrating those aspects. There are sections on each of the Emirates.

38   United Arab Emirates.
Financial Times (12 June 1990), p. 32-36.
A survey article which examines the benefits to business of the end of the Gulf War
but also highlights the weakness of the federal structure. It is also considered that the
majority of problems relate to a mismatch between economic progress, a large
per capita income, and political progress. Both illustrations and tables are included.

39   United Arab Emirates – MERI Report.
London; Dover, New Hampshire: Croom Helm, for the Middle East
Research Institute, University of Pennsylvania, 1985. 198p.
This report is divided into a number of sections and provides: background information; a political analysis of the UAE which deals with internal development, regional
developments, external developments, and future prospects; an economic analysis
which covers contemporary developments, planning policies, finance, the oil industry,
industry, agriculture, manpower, foreign trade, and demography. The final section
(p. 121-98) consists of a series of tables and statistics covering defence, demography,
the economy, banking and finance, energy, industry, agriculture and fishing, trade,
labour, transport and communications, health, education, and welfare.

40   Arab gold: heritage of the UAE.
Peter Vine, Paula Casey.   London: Immel, 1989. 160p. bibliog.
The gold referred to in the title relates to oil and the revenues and wealth that it has
brought to the federation. This illustrated book reviews the natural history, folklore,
art, and the modern development of the United Arab Emirates.

41   Practical problems of boundary delimitation in Arabia: the case of the United Arab Emirates.
Julian Walker.   In: *Territorial foundations of the Gulf States*, edited by
Richard Schofield.   London: UCL Press, 1994, p. 109-16.
At the time of publication the author of this contribution was working at the British
Foreign Office Research Department on outstanding territorial problems within the
United Arab Emirates. Walker was also involved in the contemporary territorial
framework that now exists in the UAE and because of this, and the strict confidential-
ity rules, the contribution has no references and notes. The article begins by
examining the basic conceptual difficulties behind the question of frontier settlement,
and then goes on to outline the practical differences. These include the absence of
maps, problems of transportation, personal safety, and the local British bureaucracy.
Walker concludes with an outline of the methods used to determine boundaries, and
the tactics which attempted to ensure that the local way of life, and the situation on the
ground, were altered as little as possible.

42   The origins of the United Arab Emirates.
Rosemary Said Zahlan.   London: Macmillan, 1978. 278p. map.
bibliog.
Deals largely with developments between the two world wars, providing an essential
background to the politics and social framework of the present-day federation whose
creation is dealt with in the form of an epilogue. The work makes extensive use of the

Records of the Persian Gulf Territories and the India Office, which had just become available, and these form part of an extensive section of references and bibliographical citations.

Dissertation

43   **United Arab Emirates (UAE): regional and global dimensions.**
Nigel Abdullah Al-Nabeh.   PhD thesis, Claremont Graduate School, California, 1984. 208p. (Available from University Microfilms, Ann Arbor, Michigan, order no. AAD84-07445).
A study of the background and development of the United Arab Emirates (UAE), following British withdrawal from the Gulf, as a federal entity in an essentially tribal culture. The political dynamics of the region are also discussed, as are the regional and global factors affecting the federation. The question of regional economic policies is examined in relation to the establishment of the Gulf Co-operation Council which is regarded as an essential step toward comprehensive economic development.

UAE in General Works on the Middle East

44 Politics in the Gulf.
  M. S. Agwani.   New Delhi, India: Vikas Publishing House, 1978.
  199p. bibliog.
A study of the process of internal politics in the Arabian Gulf, the implications of superpower interests in the region, and the interests of India in the Gulf States. The political landscape of the various states is covered and this section deals with the creation of the Federation of the United Arab Emirates which was motivated by Britain's decision to withdraw from the Gulf in 1971. The main problem identified with the UAE is the dilemma of reconciling the conflicting claims of stability and change and the integration of self-asserting tribal politics into a nation-state. Additionally, the states have been successful in avoiding internal unrest through three factors: the swift pace of economic growth; public acceptance of the continuance of traditional rule; and the use of foreign nationals in the defence and internal security forces.

45 Britain, India and the Arabs.
  Briton Cooper Busch.   Berkeley, California: University of California
  Press, 1971. 522p. maps. bibliog.
Although primarily concerned with the Arab Revolt, the peace settlements, and the consequences, this work also deals with the question of the Gulf States. The interest is largely related to British involvement in the area, in particular the conflicting interests and policies of the British Foreign Office and the Indian Government, which are crucial to an understanding of developments in the area.

46 Military forces in the Persian Gulf.
  Alvin J. Cottrell, Frank Bray.   Washington, DC: Georgetown
  University, Center for Strategic and International Studies, with Sage
  Publications, 1978. 71p. map. (Washington Papers, vol. VI, no. 60).
Pages 52-56 outline the composition and strength of the United Arab Emirates armed forces, the types of military equipment in service and the sources of supply.

47 Money rush.
Andrew Duncan. London: Hutchinson, 1979. 384p. map.
The work deals with the United Arab Emirates (p. 241-312) in the discussion of the general effect of increasing oil revenues on the economies and societies of the area. Although primarily an examination of the economic boom, Duncan also deals with the problems facing the federation in achieving a measure of unity and the deployment of resources to this end. Also examined are the position of the expatriate community in society and the role of women. The problems of social change in relation to Islam and, in particular, *sharia* (Islamic law) are also briefly considered.

48 A handbook of Arabia.
Great Britain. Admiralty, Naval Intelligence Division. London: HM Stationery Office, 1917. 709p. maps. (Geographical Handbook Series).
One of a series of illustrated handbooks designed for military purposes and, although dated, extremely valuable. In particular, some of the detailed geographical material and observations on flora and fauna are still relevant.

49 Iraq and the Persian Gulf.
Great Britain. Admiralty, Naval Intelligence Division. London: HM Stationery Office, 1944. 682p. maps. (Geographical Handbook Series).
Another volume in the series of illustrated handbooks designed to provide material for the discussion of naval, military and political problems, and although dated, extremely useful, especially for the detailed geographical observations, and the material on flora and fauna. The historical background material presents a precise picture of the political situation of the period and the tribal structure of the Gulf region.

50 The affairs of Arabia.
Great Britain. Foreign and Commonwealth Office, edited by Robin L. Bidwell. London: Cass, 1971. 2 vols.
An indispensable reference source and a basic tool for any consideration of British involvement in the area. The reprint has a valuable introductory section by the late Robin Bidwell, which discusses the text, gives biographical outlines of people mentioned, and provides an overview of the events and items covered in the volumes. However, a large amount of the correspondence is not relevant to the United Arab Emirates, and specific documents can be located only if their full details are known.

51 Dictionary of the Middle East.
Dilip Hiro. London: Macmillan, 1996. xiii+367p. map.
A general-purpose dictionary of the Middle East, covering a full range of topics and including country entries for each of the relevant states. In addition to the country entry which provides basic reference material about the United Arab Emirates, there are relevant entries under the Gulf Co-operation Council, the oil and gas industry of the UAE, oil reserves, OPEC, and the military, with brief entries under the constituent members of the federation.

52 The Gulf: Arabia's western approaches.

Molly Izzard. London: Murray, 1979. 327p. map.

An excellent illustrated introduction to the Gulf area, with Part 3 of the book (p. 205-67) largely taken up with a consideration of the United Arab Emirates. Amongst topics dealt with are the early history of the states, the arrival of the British, and the growth of Dubai as a centre for trade. The author also considers developments in the area, the growth of agriculture, and the social structure of the Emirates, including that of the expatriate community.

53 Arabia, the Gulf and the West.

John Barrett Kelly. London: Weidenfeld & Nicolson, 1980. ix+530p. maps. bibliog.

An analysis of the oil policy of the Arabs which is considered to be mistaken in its concept. The work is also highly critical of British withdrawal from the Gulf, considering it not to have been in the best interests of the West in strategic terms, or for the long-term future of the Gulf States.

54 Britain and the Persian Gulf, 1795-1880.

John Barrett Kelly. London: Oxford University Press, 1968. 911p. maps. bibliog.

An indispensable work for any consideration of Britain's role in the Gulf during the period under consideration. The detail provided in this excellent study is of particular relevance to a consideration of the historical background to the present-day United Arab Emirates, British interests in the area through a series of treaty negotiations, the Royal Navy's role in the suppression of the slave trade, and the commercial growth of the region.

55 Saudi Arabia and the Gulf States.

John Barrett Kelly. In: *The Middle East: oil, conflict and hope*, edited by A. L. Udovitch. Lexington, Massachusetts: Lexington Books, 1976, p. 427-62. (Critical Choices for Americans, vol. 10).

This contribution begins by examining the stability of the Gulf States, including the United Arab Emirates, in the period following British withdrawal from the Gulf, and studies the elements which make for change and instability. Social and economic conditions are examined in the light of the changes to traditional society and culture, and the effect that migrant labour has had on the character of the urban areas, especially in Abu Dhabi and Dubai. The economic benefits of oil are assessed in relation to the benefits accorded to the indigenous population through the provision of a sophisticated, heavily subsidized welfare state, and on relations between the indigenous population and the migrant communities. The political situation is examined in brief, dealing with the federal government of the United Arab Emirates, the continuing strains within the federation due to traditional rivalries, and the potential problems of the allegiance of the Union Defence Force and the Abu Dhabi Defence Force. The question of relations with Saudi Arabia, Iraq and Iran are also considered in relation to border disputes, Iraq's perceived role in the Arabian Gulf, and Western interests in the region.

56 **The Persian Gulf: an introduction to its peoples, politics and economics.**
David E. Long.   Boulder, Colorado: Westview Press, 1976. 172p. maps.

An examination (with tables) of the political situation, economy, and social structure of the Gulf, including the United Arab Emirates, specifically in relation to United States policy in the area.

57 **Gazetteer of the Persian Gulf, Oman and central Arabia.**
J. G. Lorimer.   Farnborough, England: Gregg International, 1970. 4,693p. maps. bibliog. (6 vols. Reprint of original published in 2 vols, Calcutta, 1915).

Although dated, this is an invaluable work and a basic research tool. It should, however, be borne in mind that this was an official work for use by officials and the viewpoints expressed are seen through British eyes. The first three volumes deal with the history of the area as an entity, then by individual states, with appendices on the slave trade, gun-running, etc. Designed originally as a working tool, the gazetteer has excellent indexes which make it easy to use.

58 **The Arab state.**
Edited by Giacomo Luciani.   London: Routledge, 1990. 454p. bibliog.

A series of essays on the Arab state, which investigates the roots of the nation-state in the Arab world, with particular emphasis on the economic bases of individual states. Luciani discusses the evolution of Arab societies and examines the problems of domestic and international integration from the Arab viewpoint. There are various references to the United Arab Emirates in the text; amongst other topics, these cover: the nature of the state; expatriate labour; industry; and migration. The UAE is included in most of the statistical tables.

59 **The Arabs.**
Peter Mansfield.   London: Penguin, 1978. rev. ed. 572p. map.

A major contribution to a study of the social, political and historical aspects of the Arab World, with the United Arab Emirates being considered as part of 'The Gulf: the Eldorado States', p. 371-84. References are also found with regard to border disputes with Saudi Arabia, and in a general section dealing with the position of oil in the world economy.

60 **The Middle East: a political and economic survey.**
Edited by Peter Mansfield.   Oxford, England: Oxford University Press, 1980. 5th ed. 448p. maps.

A significant work divided into an introductory section, a series of thematic studies, and a country-by-country survey. The introductory section provides a useful insight into the region as a whole covering, in outline, history, politics, religion, and an economic and social survey. The country section deals with the Trucial States as an entity and each Emirate in turn, and covers recent history and economy.

61   **The Middle East and North Africa.**
London: Europa Publications, 1948- . annual.
One of the standard reference books on the area. Divided into four parts, the first is a
series of general survey articles and the second covers the work of various organizations in the area, such as the specialist agencies of the United Nations. The third
section is a country-by-country survey covering physical and social geography, history, economics, statistics, and providing a directory and a short bibliography. The
final section covers other reference material and includes a brief biographical section,
details concerning calendars, weights and measures, research bodies, and a listing of
general bibliographies.

62   **Middle East Review.**
London: World of Information, 1974- . annual.
Contains a large introductory section dealing with various aspects of the Middle East
as a region, including economics, society, and prospects for development. The second
part is a country-by-country survey, with an essay on each state covering all aspects
and giving basic facts and figures.

63   **Middle East Yearbook.**
London: Middle East Magazine, 1977- . annual.
The four sections of this reference book cover background features, the Middle East in
relation to the rest of the world, the economy of the area, and a country-by-country
survey. The country survey makes up the bulk of the volume and is prefaced by an
introductory article giving an outline of the history, economy, etc. Brief facts are then
given on such topics as geography, climate, population, and public services, with statistics provided on production, oil and budgets. The work is enhanced by numerous
maps showing oil production and refining, agriculture, population, etc. The specialist
articles are also of value.

64   **The countries and tribes of the Persian Gulf.**
Samuel Barret Miles.   London: Harrison & Sons, 1919. 2 vols.
Reprinted, Garnet Publishing, 1994, in 1 vol. with an introduction by
Robin Bidwell. xi+644p.
An important work on the area particularly for the early history of the region, including the present-day United Arab Emirates (though the bulk of the work is on Oman).
The author was British Consul at Muscat from 1872 to 1887 and provides an insight
into the tribal structure of the region, the tribal spheres of influence, and the historical
development of the area. Miles travelled widely throughout the area as part of his
official duties and carefully observed and recorded everything of relevance. Amongst
a number of topics, he covers: history, social conditions, architecture, agriculture,
fishing, shipbuilding and the pearl fisheries. In his introduction to this reprint Bidwell
points out that Miles was a scholar as learned as any academic of his day and preceded
other scholars by 70 years in linking classical texts to the contemporary situation
through fieldwork.

65 **Saddamania.**
P. J. O'Rourke, L. Smith. *Rolling Stone* (18 Oct. 1990), p. 51-54.

An illustrated report on the writers' travels through Jordan and the United Arab Emirates whilst covering the United States military response to the Iraqi invasion of Kuwait. The article describes the city of Abu Dhabi and its architecture in an uncomplimentary manner, though the gardens are admired and well received. The markets of Abu Dhabi and Dubai are also described, where, it is pointed out, everything is imported, and everything available, for the consumer.

66 **Historical dictionary of the Gulf Arab States.**
Malcolm C. Peck. Lantham, Maryland: Scarecrow Press, 1987. 324p.

This work covers the Arab Gulf States, including the United Arab Emirates, and is divided into an introductory section; an A–Z dictionary section, forming the bulk of the work; the United Arab Emirates are dealt with between pages 200 and 208; and a bibliographical section. The work is aimed at academics, researchers, diplomats, and business people.

67 **The Arab Gulf and the Arab World.**
Edited by B. R. Pridham. London: Croom Helm, 1988. 302p. bibliog.

A series of essays (with tables) on the Gulf States. They cover early history, migrant labour, demographic changes, aid and investment programmes, and aspects of regional security. Pridham also examines the changes in the post-independence period, resulting from the impact of the oil-based economies and the numerically dominant migrant workers. Essays of relevance are annotated within the appropriate sections of this bibliography.

68 **The Arabian Gulf: winds of change.**
Riad N. El-Rayyes. London: Riedel-Rayyes Books, 1987. 96p.

A work which traces the developments in the region, including the United Arab Emirates, from the days of British Protectorate status, through independence, to the creation of the Gulf Co-operation Council (GCC). The role of intellectuals and the ruling élites are discussed in relation to these developments, as are the effects of the Iraq–Iran war, Islamic fundamentalism, and the prospects for the region when oil runs out. The eventual conclusion is that the survival of the present regimes and the GCC can be guaranteed only through more popular participation and democracy.

69 **The future of the Gulf: politics and oil in the 1990s.**
Philip Robins. Aldershot, England: Dartmouth Publishing Company, for the Royal Institute of International Affairs, 1989. 145p.

This study of the Gulf States provides an assessment of the stability of the ruling regimes, particularly in relation to foreign policy and foreign relations, and superpower interests in the region. The significance of oil is also assessed against a possibility of flat oil prices creating a recession in the 1990s. The work has placed significant emphasis on primary sources, with visits to the Gulf States and interviews with diplomats, decision-makers, businessmen, local intellectuals, and other influential figures. The United Arab Emirates is dealt with in Chapter 3, 'The Gulf Cooperation Council States' (p. 57-81), providing an overview of its formation and successes but not forgetting the historical tensions amongst the member states, the question of Gulf security, and the political and economic significance of oil reserves.

70   **The kingdom of oil: the Middle East, its people and its power.**
Roy Vicker.   New York: Scribner, 1974; London: Hale, 1975. 264p.

This work deals with the Middle East, country by country, and attempts to portray for
the interested reader the oil-producing nations, and the part they play in world affairs.
The United Arab Emirates is considered in two chapters entitled 'Gulf dwellers' and
'Gulf politics', which deal with the questions of economics, social structure, prospects
for development, and political disputes, such as the border dispute between the United
Arab Emirates and Saudi Arabia over the Buraimi Oasis.

71   **The Middle East in the coming decade: from wellhead to**
well-being?
John Waterbury, Ragaei El Mallakh.   London and New York: McGraw
Hill, 1978. 217p. bibliog.

This study is designed to chart the likely future course of economic and political
development in the Middle East. In the case of the United Arab Emirates consideration is given to the economy, relations with non-oil-producing Arab states, oil
production and pricing structures, migrant labour, and the aid programme of the Abu
Dhabi Fund for Arab Economic Development. Tables are included.

72   **The making of the modern Gulf States.**
Rosemary Said Zahlan.   London: Unwin Hyman, 1989. 180p. maps.

A study of the history of the Gulf States which examines the period during which they
were under colonial dependency, independence, oil development and oil wealth, inter-
regional relationships, and superpower interests in the Gulf region. The United Arab
Emirates is dealt with extensively throughout this work under the federation, individual states, and as the historical Trucial States. Amongst topics covered are: relations
with Great Britain, Kuwait, Saudi Arabia, and the Soviet Union; the impact of the
Iraq–Iran war; the federal infrastructure; the ruling families; state sector employment;
and historical and contemporary relations between the member states.

Exploration and Travel

73 **Travellers in Arabia.**
    Robin L. Bidwell.   London: Hamlyn, 1976. 224p. maps.

A work which brings together the major explorations of Arabia, covering the United Arab Emirates as part of the sections 'Travellers in eastern and northern Arabia' and 'Travellers in Oman'.

74 **Far Arabia: explorers of the myth.**
    Peter Brent.   London: Weidenfeld & Nicolson, 1977. 239p. maps.
    bibliog.

An extremely readable study of exploration in Arabia. Discusses the effects of explorers' accounts on the Western image of Arabia, which was often far removed from reality.

75 **Some excursions in Arabia.**
    Percy Z. Cox.   *Geographical Journal*, vol. 66, no. 3 (1925), p. 193-227.

Although primarily concerned with Oman, the first recorded journey was from Abu Dhabi to Buraimi which is part of the al-Liwa oasis area. The article is illustrated.

76 **Across the Empty Quarter.**
    Wilfred P. Thesiger.   *Geographical Journal*, vol. 111, no. 1 (1948),
    p. 1-21.

Although primarily concerned with the Sultanate of Oman, the author visited al-Liwa as part of his travels before returning across the Empty Quarter to Salalah.

77   **Desert borderlands of Oman.**
Wilfred Thesiger.   *Geographical Journal*, vol. 116, nos. 4-6 (1950),
p. 137-71. map.
An illustrated description of Abu Dhabi, as seen during an exploration of Oman made
in 1948-49, with Abu Dhabi as the starting point. As part of the journey, Thesiger
explored the Liwa oases and describes the sport of falconry and the customs of the
tribes.

78   **A further journey across the Empty Quarter.**
Wilfred Thesiger.   *Geographical Journal*, vol. 113, no. 1 (1949),
p. 21-46. map.
This journey was centred in the western part of the Empty Quarter and ended in the
region of al-Liwa and Buraimi. As with all his other works, this illustrated article contains a wealth of information conveyed in an engaging manner.

79   **From Hasa to Oman by car.**
Desmond Vesey-Fitzgerald.   *Geographical Review,* vol. 41, no. 4
(1951), p. 544-60. map.
An interesting, illustrated account of a journey from Saudi Arabia to Oman passing
through Abu Dhabi. The author includes geographical descriptions and observations
on the flora and fauna.

Geography

Regional and physical

80 **Sedimentological interpretation of the Albanian Nahr Um formation in the United Arab Emirates.**
A. S. Alsharhan. *Sedimentary Geology*, vol. 73, nos. 3-4 (1991), p. 317-27.

Describes a series of varicoloured shales, siltstones and mudstones with an increasing carbonate content in the north of the formation. The clay minerals in the shoals range from 62 per cent to 73 per cent whilst the non-clay fraction is dominated by calcite, quartz and some traces of dolomite, feldspar pyrite, glauconite and phosphate.

81 **Nature and distribution of porosity and permeability in Jurassic carbonate reservoirs of the Arabian Gulf basin.**
A. S. Alsharhan, K. Mayara. *Facies*, no. 32 (1995), p. 237-53.

Describes the geology of the Jurassic sections of the Arabian Gulf basin which consists of source facies, reservoir facies and seal facies. Their characteristics are detailed. The Jurassic reservoirs of the oil-fields in the region, including the United Arab Emirates, have extremely high porosity up to 30 per cent, and depths of burial which range between 1,200 and 2,700 metres. The existence of such high porosity and permeability is examined in relation to the probable geological, physical and chemical factors.

82 **Sedimentological and geochemical interpretation of a transgressive sequence: the late Cretaceous Qahlah formation in the western Oman Mountains, United Arab Emirates.**
A. S. Alsharhan, S. J. Y. Nasir. *Sedimentary Geology*, vol. 101, nos. 3-4 (1996), p. 227-42.

Discusses the geology of the Qahlah formation which ranges from a few metres to more than seventy metres in thickness. The sedimentary sequence can be divided into four facies: ophiolitic breccia; ophiolitic conglomerate; lateritic ferruginous siltstone; and lithic sandstone.

83   **Facies and sedimentary environment of the Permian carbonates (Khuff formation) in the United Arab Emirates.**
   S. Alsharan.   *Sedimentary Geology*, vol. 84, nos. 1-4 (1993), p. 89-99.
   The shallow-water carbonates are 625-970 metres thick and can be subdivided into ten facies units distinguished on the basis of their depositional textures. Four distinct settings can be recognized: supratidal (sabkha), lagoon, shoal and shallow shelf.

84   **Sedimentary facies analysis of the subsurface Triassic and hydrocarbon potential in the United Arab Emirates.**
   S. Alsharhan.   *Facies*, no. 28 (1993), p. 97-108.
   Examines the development of reservoirs in the Triassic sediments. Although no oil has been discovered in these sediments pronounced gas shows have been located in offshore fields.

85   **Sedimentology and depositional setting of the late Cretaceous Fiqa formation in the United Arab Emirates.**
   S. Alsharhan.   *Cretaceous Research*, vol. 16, no. 1 (1995), p. 39-51.
   The Fiqa formation in the United Arab Emirates ranges in thickness from about 60 to 1,220 metres in thickness and consists of argillaceous limestone, shales, marls and marly shale with abundant benthonic and planktonic foraminifera. The sediments were laid down in a shallow to deep open-marine shelf setting. The petroleum source-rock potential of the formation is fairly low, primarily because of a lack of organic maturation owing to relatively shallow burial in most areas.

86   **Holocene shoreline variations in the Persian Gulf: example of the Umm al-Qawayn Lagoon (UAE).**
   P. Bernier (et al.).   *Quaternary International*, nos. 29-30 (1995), p. 95-103.
   The lagoons in the United Arab Emirates are characterized by generations of successfully settled coastal spits, with the volume of sediment along the coast attesting to climatic change.

87   **Organic matter distribution, water circulation and dolomitization beneath the Abu Dhabi sabkha.**
   F. Boltzer (et al.).   In: *Dolomites: a volume in honour of Dolomieu*, edited by B. Purser (et al.).   Oxford: Blackwell, 1994, p. 409-27.
   An examination of the northeastern section of the Abu Dhabi sabkha (salt flat), including its geological composition, and the effects of decaying organic matter below the surface resulting in acidic conditions and the dissolution of aragonite.

88   **Internal structure of aeolian dunes in Abu Dhabi determined using ground-penetrating radar.**
C. Bristow, J. Pugh, T. Goodall.   *Sedimentology*, vol. 43, no. 6 (1996), p. 995-1003.

An examination, using ground-penetrating radar, of the internal structure of aeolian dunes in the Al-Liwa area of Abu Dhabi. The results were subsequently confirmed by trench excavation in the study area.

89   **Les variations récentes de la ligne de rivage dans le Golfe Persique: l'exemple de la lagune d'Umm Al-Qawayn (Emirates Arabes Union).** (Holocene variations of the shoreline in the Persian Gulf: example of the Umm al-Qawayn lagoon, UAE.)
R. Dalongeville (et al.).   *Bulletin Institut de Géologie du Bassin d'Aquitaine*, nos. 53-54 (1993), p. 179-92.

The lagoons of the United Arab Emirates represent several generations of littoral spits, and enable shoreline modifications to be reconstituted through the Holocene period from the end of the last marine transgression. The sedimentary stock has suffered many variations which may have a climatic significance.

90   **The arid peritidal complex of Abu Dhabi: a historical perspective.**
G. M. Friedman.   *Carbonates and Evaporites*, vol. 10, no. 1 (1995), p. 2-7.

Provides a narrative for a series of photographs taken in 1969 from the air and the ground to show arid peritidal settings around Abu Dhabi. The photographs show peritidal settings including sabkhas, microbial mats, and supratidal anhydrite, but it is pointed out that the area of study has suffered since 1969 from urban sprawl.

91   **Rapid emplacement of the Oman ophiolite: thermal and geochronologic constraints.**
B. R. Hacker (et al.).   *Tectonics*, vol. 15, no. 6 (1996), p. 1230-47. map.

This study of the emplacement of oceanic lithosphere on to continents uses data from the United Arab Emirates and Oman, leading to the proposal that the ophiolites were young at the time of intra-oceanic thrusting.

92   **Geochemistry of some ultramafic and gabbroic rocks from the northern Oman Mountains, United Arab Emirates.**
M. A. Hassan.   *Journal of the University of Kuwait*, vol. 6, no. 1 (1979), p. 243-70.

Ultramafic and gabbroic rocks of the ophiolite in the Oman Mountains in the United Arab Emirates crop out in the Emirate of Al-Fujairah. This article details the geochemical characteristics of these rocks.

93   Holocene marine cement coatings on beach rocks of the Abu Dhabi
     coastline: analysis for cement fabrics in ancient limestones.
     C. G. St. C. Kendall, J. L. Sadd, A. S. Alsharhan.   *Carbonate and
     Evaporites*, vol. 9, no. 2 (1994), p. 119-31.
Marine carbonate cements are coating and binding some intertidal sedimentary rock
surfaces in coastal Abu Dhabi, some of which can be 3 cm thick, especially in the area
of Jebal Dhana. It is suggested that the marine cements precipitate from the agitated
hypersaline Arabian Gulf water as a result of repeated cycles of exposure, evaporation
and immersion.

94   Sedimentation, distribution and diagenesis of organic matter in a
     recent carbonate environment, Abu Dhabi, UAE.
     F. Kenig (et al.).   *Organic Geochemistry*, vol. 16, nos. 4-6 (1990),
     p. 735-47.
The results of a study of recent sedimentary processes and cross-sections through the
sabkha sediments, leading to the definition of organo-sedimentary facies based on
geochemical and sedimentological criteria.

95   Interpretation of recent gravity profiles over the ophiolite belt,
     northern Oman mountains, United Arab Emirates.
     M. M. Khattab.   *Journal of African Earth Sciences*, vol. 16, no. 3
     (1993), p. 319-27.
A discussion of the geological composition and evolution of the ophiolite belt which
covers northern Oman and the United Arab Emirates. Khattab identifies the existence
of three partially separated serpentized nappes, one of which is in the United Arab
Emirates.

96   Hydrologic framework of a sabkha along the Arabian Gulf.
     R. J. Patterson, D. J. J. Kinsman.   *American Association of Petroleum
     Geologists Bulletin*, vol. 65, no. 8 (1981), p. 1457-75.
A detailed examination of the development of sabkhas along the Arabian Gulf and,
particularly, of the characteristics of the water table in the sabkhas of the Abu Dhabi
lagoons. Evolution of sabkhas began 4,500 years ago through deposits of sediment and
a relative fall in sea level. The water-table beneath the sabkha always slopes seaward
and is part of a regional seaward-flowing groundwater regime.

97   Stable isotope studies and the hydrological regime of sabkhas in
     southern Kuwait, Arabian Gulf.
     B. W. Robinson, A. Gunatilaka.   *Sedimentary Geology*, vol. 73,
     nos. 1-2 (1991), p. 141-59.
The authors examined the sulphate content of the sabkhas in the Abu Dhabi delta and
conclude that it may be recycled particulate sulphate distributed by major sandstorms
in the area. The values of sulphate are compared with those found at Al-Khiran in
Libya.

98   **Untersuchungen zur Morphogenese der Oman Mountains im**
      Emirat Ras Al-Khaimah. (Investigation on the morphogenesis of the
      Oman mountains in the Ras Al-Khaimah Emirate.)
      J. Schmidt.   *Zeitschrift für Geomorphologie*, no. 74 (1989), p. 45-55.

A German-language study of the geological structures of the Oman Mountains
between 25 degrees and 26 degrees north in the Emirate of Ras Al-Khaimah. The
northern part of the mountains experienced greater subsidence or less uplift than the
southern part of the mountains. An asymmetrical uplift of the mountains during the
Quaternary is also indicated by the different systems of terraces developed in the
larger wadis.

99   **Structure of the Musandam culmination (Sultanate of Oman and**
      United Arab Emirates) and the Straits of Hormuz syntaxis.
      M. P. Searle.   *Journal of the Geological Society*, vol. 145, pt. 5 (1988),
      p. 831-45.

Searle defines the structural geology and evolution of the Musandam Mountains and
the link with the Oman Mountains in the southeast and Zagras Mountains to the north-
west. The Musandam Peninsula and Dibba zone in Oman and the United Arab
Emirates were investigated over a period of three years and the western part mapped
at a scale of 1:20,000.

100   **Thrust tectonics of the Dibba zone and the structural evolution of**
      the Arabian continental margin along the Musandam Mountains
      (Oman and United Arab Emirates).
      M. P. Searle.   *Journal of the Geological Society*, vol. 145, pt. 1
      (1988), p. 43-53.

This geological study of the mountains of northern Oman and the United Arab
Emirates deals with the incidence of several major thrust sheets of Tethyan oceanic
rocks.

101   **Partially disordered dolomite: microstructural characterization of**
      Abu Dhabi sabkha carbonates.
      H. A. Wenk (et al.).   *American Mineralogist*, vol. 78, nos. 7-8 (1993),
      p. 769-74.

Records three carbonate phases in the Abu Dhabi sabkhas or salt flats: aragonite,
ordered dolomite and a mostly disordered calcium magnesium carbonate with sub-
micrometre-size ordered domains.

102   **Dolomitization and chertification of the early Eocene Rus**
      formation in Abu Dhabi, United Arab Emirates.
      G. L. Whittle, A. S. Alsharan.   *Sedimentary Geology*, vol. 92, nos. 3-4
      (1994), p. 273-85.

A geological examination of carbonates which were cyclically deposited in a shallow-
water environment and are characterized by extensive dolomitization and
chertification.

103   **Observations on the diagenesis of the Lower Triassic Sudair Formation, Abu Dhabi, United Arab Emirates.**
      G. L. Whittle, A. S. Alsharan.   *Facies*, no. 33 (1995), p. 185-94.
The Lower Triassic Sudair Formation in the United Arab Emirates consists of three units: interbedded limestone; argillaceous limestone; dolomite and anhydrite. Diagenesis in the Sudair includes extensive leaching of grain-supported carbonates, partial-to-complete dolomitization, evaporite formation, and a number of other processes which have had the effect of reducing the secondary porosity.

Climatology

104   **Wind speed and temperature profiles in the lower atmosphere of the Arabian Gulf region.**
      Y. A. C. Abdalla.   *Wind Engineering,* vol. 18, no. 6 (1994), p. 305-15.
A detailed study of wind speed, its speed–height power, temperature, and relative humidity during the period 1984-87. Abu Dhabi is used as a case-study. Abdalla found that the rate of increase with height for winter months is higher than for summer months. He also presents data on humidity, temperature variations in relation to height, and on the vertical relative humidity profiles for winter and summer months.

105   **Tornadic waterspout at the Jebel Ali sailing club.**
      B. J. Davey.   *Meteorological Magazine*, vol. 116, no. 1378 (1987), p. 129-37.
An account of a tornadic waterspout which struck the boat park of the Jebel Ali sailing club near Dubai. The article describes the situation leading up to the storm, its devastating effects, and attempts to provide indicators to assist with the forecasting of severe storms and associated waterspouts.

106   **Meteorological network expansion using information decoy concept.**
      T. Husain (et al.).   *Journal of Atmospheric and Oceanic Technology*, vol. 3, no. 1 (1984), p. 27-35.
The authors of this article used a generalized network design methodology to select potential sites for meteorological network expansion purposes throughout the Arabian Gulf, including the United Arab Emirates.

107   **Vortex phenomena in the United Arab Emirates.**
      C. C. E. Jackson.   *Weather*, vol. 42, no. 10 (1987), p. 302-8.
An account of the incidence of waterspouts and twisters during 1982 and 1995, with an assessment of the pertinent meteorological conditions. Jackson also provides a descriptive account of the geography of the Emirates, its rainfall and temperature.

108   **A unique August cyclonic storm across Arabia.**
D. A. Membery.   *Weather*, vol. 40, no. 4 (1985), p. 108-14.

Describes a storm which crossed the Arabian Sea, the Gulf of Oman and the United
Arab Emirates in August 1983.

109   **Storm surges in the Arabian Gulf.**
M. I. El-Sabh, T. S. Murty.   *Natural Hazards*, vol. 1, no. 4 (1989),
p. 371-85.

The Arabian Gulf and the coast of the United Arab Emirates is mainly influenced by
extra-tropical weather systems and storm surge phenomena, with the winter characterized by a *shamal*, or strong winds. The authors discuss the development of a
mathematical model to predict storms, and data collected between 1 and 17 January
1973 are analysed.

110   **How wet is wet? Precipitation constraints on late Quaternary
climate in the southern Arabian Peninsula.**
Warren W. Wood, Jeffrey L. Imes.   *Journal of Hydrology*, vol. 164,
nos. 1-4 (1995), p. 263-68.

It is accepted that the southern Arabian Peninsula, including the United Arab
Emirates, had two wet periods in the late Quaternary. The study used a model to
assess the climate during these periods, suggesting that 1.4 mm a year was necessary
to support the water-table. The climatic relations between rainfall and recharge indicate that rainfall in the area would have been five times higher than the present rate.

Water resources

111   **Integrated approach to water resource development and
management in the GCC countries.**
Mohamed J. Abdulrazzak.   Paper presented at a symposium on *Water
and Arab Gulf development: problems and policies,* held at the
University of Exeter, England, 10-12 September 1996. 25p. (Available
from the Centre for Arab Gulf Studies, University of Exeter, Prince of
Wales Road, Exeter, Devon EX4 3RY).

The Gulf Co-operation Council states have natural water supply problems due to the
arid climate and increasing demands caused by the pace of development and high population growth. Demands on water resources have exceeded supply because of a lack
of effective planning and management, and it is anticipated that a number of problems
will arise, including: over-exploitation of renewable and fossil groundwater reserves;
large monetary investment in desalination plants; urban water pollution; and the deterioration of water quality.

112 Review and assessment of water resources in Gulf Cooperation Council countries.
M. J. Abdulrazzak. *International Journal of Water Resources Development*, vol. 10, no. 1 (1994), p. 23-37.

A review of water resource problems in the Gulf Co-operation Council, including the United Arab Emirates, identified: intermittent or no surface run-off; depletion of fossil groundwater; over-consumption; salt-water intrusion and pollution of shallow aquifers; lack of trained personnel; deficient institutional arrangements; and poor resource management. The available water resources are described, utilization in each country is detailed, and future demands for water are considered, together with the need for efficient planning, long-term water plans, and institutional arrangements and research.

113 Water supply versus demand in countries of Arabian Peninsula.
M. J. Abdulrazzak. *Journal of Water Resources Planning and Management*, vol. 121, no. 3 (1995), p. 227-34.

A survey of water supply and demand problems for all of the countries of the Arabian Peninsula, including the United Arab Emirates. Rapid economic development, agricultural programmes, and a lack of conservation measures will lead to demand outstripping supply unless action is taken. Suggestions are made for water planning measures, conservation techniques and optimum allocations within, and between, countries.

114 Quality of water in relation to irrigating sandy soils.
A. Arar. *Food and Agriculture Organization Soils Bulletin*, no. 25 (1975), p. 73-83.

In the UAE, forestation projects have taken place in sandy soils using drip irrigation with saline groundwater. Results have varied, but it is found that the effects are greater during germination than at later stages of growth.

115 Wastewater reuse for irrigation in the Near East region.
A. Arar. *Water Science and Technology*, vol. 23, no. 10 (1991), p. 2127-34.

Intrusion and direct reuse of wastewater is being practised in a number of countries in the Middle East, including the United Arab Emirates, because of the limited water supply available. However, the health and environmental hazards associated with the reuse of wastewater means that formalization of wastewater treatment is an urgent requirement.

116 The hydrochemistry of the spring at Ain bu Sukhanah, UAE.
F. Elschami. *Arab Gulf Journal of Scientific Research*, vol. 8, no. 1 (1990), p. 33-49.

An analysis of the artesian spring at Ain bu Sukhanah. It is brackish with the type CA sodium chloride; the water reaches the spring along fractured beds of the underlying Miocene gypsum sequence.

29

117 **Water type variation during pumping test – Al Jaww Plain southeast of Al-Ain in the United Arab Emirates.**
F. Elschami. *GeoJournal*, vol. 25, no. 4 (1991), p. 383-86.
The results of a pumping test at Al Jaww Plain that indicated the presence of calcium bicarbonate, calcium sulphate, sodium sulphate, and sodium chloride water families from top to bottom within the water-bearing formations.

118 **Electromagnetic mapping of buried paleochannels in eastern Abu Dhabi Emirate, UAE.**
D. V. Fitterman (et al.). *Geoexploration*, vol. 27, nos. 1-2 (1991), p. 111-33.
Fitterman describes the use of transient electromagnetic soundings and terrain conductivity meter measurements to map palaeochannel geometry in the Al Jaww Plain. It was undertaken as part of an integrated hydrogeological study of the Quaternary alluvial aquifer system.

119 **Maintenance activity for partial intervention of retubing on four distillers multi-flash double-deck (capacity 3 mgd for each unit) of Abu Dhabi power station after eighteen years of operation activity.**
V. Franchini. *Desalination*, vol. 108, nos. 1-3 (1997), p. 295-313.
A description of a maintenance programme carried out on the distillation sections of five power stations in Abu Dhabi to cure leakage in tube bundles and a consequent loss of production efficiency. The programme of refurbishment is described with the objective of not taking the plants completely out of production whilst the work was undertaken. The paper was first presented at the Annual Meeting of the European Desalination Society held at Genoa, Italy, 20-23 October 1996.

120 **Water resources in the GCC countries: a strategic option.**
K. R. Al-Hajri, L. A. Misned. *Renewable Energy*, vol. 5, nos. 1-4 (1994), p. 524-28.
Highlights the water resource problems of the members of the Gulf Co-operation Council and examines possible solutions to the ever-growing consumption. Currently, desalination plants make up the shortfall but they use depletable fossil fuels and it is considered that only by developing solar energy as a major fuel source can water supplies be guaranteed for the future.

121 **Economical and thermal comparative study of flat plate collectors and parabolic concentrators for sea water desalination.**
A. Hanafi. In: *Proceedings of the First World Renewable Energy Congress*, held in Reading, England, 23-28 September 1980. Edited by A. A. M. Sayigh. Oxford, England: Pergamon, 1990, p. 1302-8.
An analysis of two plans for a solar desalination system of the multi-stage flash type. The first is a flat plate collection system, while the second uses parabolic concentrators. Comparisons are also made with data from other solar desalination plants in the United Arab Emirates.

122   **Petrophysical analysis of geophysical logs of the National Drilling
       Company – US Geological Survey ground-water research project
       for Abu Dhabi Emirate, United Arab Emirates.**
       D. G. Jorgensen, M. Petricola.   Washington, DC: US Geological
       Survey, 1994. 35p. (Water Supply Paper, no. 2417).

A description of the use of geological logs to: determine lithology; correlate lithogical
and permeable zones; calibrate seismic reprocessing; calibrate transient-electromag-
netic surveys; and to calibrate uphole-survey interpretations. The logs were used at the
drill site to: determine permeability zones and dissolved-solid content – a function of
water resistivity; and to design wells accordingly.

123   **Gulf agricultural policies and water scarcity.**
       Kamil Mahdi.   Paper presented at a symposium on *Water and Arab
       Gulf development: problems and policies*, held at the University of
       Exeter, England, 10-12 September 1996. 10p. (Obtainable from the
       Centre for Arab Gulf Studies, University of Exeter, Prince of Wales
       Road, Exeter, Devon EX4 3RY).

This paper deals with the present state of and potential for agricultural development in
the member states of the Gulf Co-operation Council, with particular reference to the
constraints of water. Agriculture in the United Arab Emirates amounts to 2 per cent of
Gross Domestic Product and as such is a small component of the oil-exporting economy. However, in terms of water consumption, agriculture utilizes a large proportion
of the water supply and of investment expenditure in that area of provision. The need
for a policy which considers long-term implications is stressed, because it is considered that the present level of activity remains unsustainable, both economically and
environmentally.

124   **Abu Dhabi solar distillation plant.**
       A. M. El-Nashar, K. Ishvi.   *Desalination*, vol. 52, no. 3 (1985),
       p. 217-34.

Describes the design and construction of a small seawater desalination plant powered
completely by solar energy and designed to run on a 24-hour basis.

125   **Techniques of ground water recharge estimates in arid/semi-arid
       areas, with examples from Abu Dhabi.**
       W. R. Osterkamp (et al.).   *Journal of Arid Environments*, vol. 31,
       no. 3 (1995), p. 349-69.

Estimates groundwater recharge in Oman and Abu Dhabi using the water-balance
method for ungauged basins, a technique which is explained in detail. Water recharge
was estimated by routing an index storm down channel, accounting for channel losses,
and adjusting for interchannel recharge during low-frequency precipitation.

126 **Large seawater reverse osmosis plant: design considerations.**
M. A. A. Soleman (et al.). *Desalination*, vol. 46, nos. 1-2 (1983),
p. 163-70.
A discussion of the technical specifications required for desalination plants in the
Middle East as a result of the high degree of salinity and the temperature of the seawater. The desalination plant at Ajman in the United Arab Emirates is used as a
case-study.

127 **Reduction of power requirements for MSF desalination plants:
the example of Al Taweelah B.**
C. Sommariva (et al.). *Desalination*, vol. 108, nos. 1-3 (1997),
p. 37-42.
An examination of the Al Taweelah desalination plant aimed at determining the
design factors necessary to achieve optimum electric power consumption in the MSF
(multi-stage flash) desalination process. Problems result from the high usage in relation to the distillate produced.

128 **Ship-mounted seawater 2500 m^{3}d flash evaporation plant for Abu
Dhabi. Economical drinking water for arid regions.**
K. Wangnick. *Desalination*, vol. 41, no. 2 (1982), p. 171-80.
Describes the specification for, and operation of, a self-propelled desalination plant
built for commercial use and designed to supply islands, coastal towns, and major construction sites in Abu Dhabi with drinking water. It is also intended to use the facility
as a source of emergency supply in the event of a breakdown of stationary desalination plants.

129 **Water in the desert: ground-water studies in the United Arab
Emirates.**
In: *U.S. Geological Survey Yearbook*, edited by Craig B. Hutchinson,
Anna M. Lennox. Reston, Virginia: US Geological Survey, 1995,
p. 93-95.
A report on a survey of the United Arab Emirates, particularly of the aeolian sand
dunes, with the aim of assessing groundwater capacity and recharge rates, and to pro-
duce proposals for conservation.

130 **Application of uphole data from petroleum seismic surveys to
groundwater investigations, Abu Dhabi (United Arab Emirates).**
D. Woodward, C. M. Menges. *Geoexploration*, vol. 27, nos. 1-2
(1991), p. 193-212.
The authors use data from uphole seismic petroleum surveys to map the water-table in
Abu Dhabi, as part of a joint National Drilling Company–United States Geological
Survey groundwater research project in Abu Dhabi. The data used were from a seis-
mic survey for petroleum exploration in the east of Abu Dhabi from 1981 to 1983.

131 **Towards the establishment of a total water cycle management and
re-use programme in the GCC countries.**
Waleed K. Al-Zubari.   Paper presented at a symposium on *Water and
Arab Gulf development: problems and policies*, held at the University
of Exeter, 10-12 September 1996. 12p. (Obtainable from the Centre
for Arab Gulf Studies, University of Exeter, Prince of Wales Road,
Exeter, Devon EX4 3RY).
The Gulf Co-operation Council states suffer from a shortage of water. This paper considers the economic use of water and the appropriate level of water for the activity in
question, which is particularly relevant to the agricultural sector in Abu Dhabi with its
high demand for water when matched against the available groundwater. This paper
deals with the use of treated wastewater for both agriculture and industry, with about
35 per cent currently being recycled and so contributing 2.2 per cent to total water
supply. Al-Zubari considers that if 50 per cent of domestic water supply could be
recycled, at least 11 per cent of total water demand could be satisfied, as could 14 per
cent of agricultural demand. If these targets could be achieved, fossil groundwater
withdrawal could be reduced by 15 per cent by the year 2020, though it is stressed that
there are significant social and technical handicaps that need to be overcome: psychological repugnance; religion; microbiological pollutants; heavy metals accumulation in
irrigated soils; and industrial waste mixing.

The desert blooms with power and water from Al Taweelah B.
See item no. 479.

Agriculture and water resources in the United Arab Emirates.
See item no. 533.

Maps, atlases and gazetteers

132 **Use of remote sensing and geographic information systems in
mapping geomorphologic formations and coastlines in semi-arid
environments, Saudi Arabia and the United Arab Emirates.**
John D. Althausen (et al.).   In: *Proceedings of the Tenth Conference
on Geologic Remote Sensing; exploration, environment, and
engineering.*   Ann Arbor: Environmental Research Institute of
Michigan, 1994, vol. 10, part II, p. 551-57.
Describes the use of remote sensing techniques and geographical information systems
to map the geomorphological features of the United Arab Emirates and the coastlines
of both Saudi Arabia and the UAE. In the case of the coastal areas, the mapping was
used to identify oil spills in the Arabian Gulf and other pollutants, and the environment of the various lagoons.

133 **Oman and the Emirates in Ptolemy's map.**
   N. Groom. *Arabian Archaeology and Epigraphy*, vol. 5, no. 3 (1994),
   p. 198-214.
Examines Ptolemy's mapping of southeast Arabia in relation to the migrations of the
Azds to the area, and in the light of related archaeological discoveries over the last
few decades.

134 **Measurement of surface roughness in desert terrain by close range**
   photogrammetry.
   R. P. Kirby. *Photogrammetric Record,* vol. 13, no. 78 (1991),
   p. 855-75.
A report on desert terrain characteristics in the United Arab Emirates resulting from
close-range vertical stereographs of various natural surfaces taken by Hasselbled
MK70 metric cameras. The technique is described and the various types of terrain are
illustrated. The report was made in association with a study of airborne radar.

135 **The Oxford map of the United Arab Emirates – Abu Dhabi,**
   Ajman, Dubai, Fujairah, Ras al Khaimah, Sharjah, Umm al
   Qawain.
   Beirut: GEOprojects, 1974. Scale 1:750,000. (GMAP 11279/4).
This full-colour map is largely administrative in coverage.

136 **The Gulf coast of the United Arab Emirates in the Homem-Reinels**
   atlas of 1519.
   D. T. Potts. *Arabian Archaeology and Epigraphy*, vol. 7, no. 1
   (1996), p. 119-23.
A study of the Homen-Reinels atlas of 1519 in terms of place-names. Many remain
unidentified, although firm indications can be advanced. However, despite the
Portuguese distortion of Arabic names, many of them have not changed too much
from the local nomenclature. Many local names appear to be extremely durable, a fact
which has implications for historical geography. In terms of the centuries of European
impact on the region the names preserved in Portuguese and Dutch charts are likely to
be accepted because of the scarcity or non-existence of Arabic sources.

137 **Persian Gulf pilot: comprising the Persian Gulf, Gulf of Oman and**
   the Makran coast.
   United States. Navy Hydrographic Office.   Washington, DC:
   US Government Printing Office. irregular.
Descriptive data supplement the various nautical charts which are frequently revised
and updated.

138   **Sailing directions for the Persian Gulf: includes Gulf of Oman and**
       northern shore of Arabian Sea eastward to Ras Muari.
       United States. Oceanographic Office.   Washington, DC:
       US Government Printing Office, 1960. 351p. (loose-leaf). maps.
Designed to serve the mariner, this illustrated publication reviews the coastal areas,
offshore areas, port facilities and the settlements that can be seen from a ship. As this
is a working tool for mariners the detail is continually being revised, hence the loose-
leaf format.

139   **Production procedures for an oversize satellite image map.**
       E. W. Vickers.   *Photogrammetric Engineering and Remote Sensing*,
       vol. 59, no. 2 (1993), p. 247-54.
The United States Geological Survey had developed guidelines and standards for the
production of maps based on remotely sensed image data captured by Landsat satel-
lites. These techniques were applied to the production of two 44 × 65 inch coloured
image maps of the United Arab Emirates.

Flora and Fauna

140   **Chemical composition of important range plant species in United Arab Emirates. 1. Trees and perennial plants.**
O. M. Abdalla.   *Emirates Journal of Agricultural Sciences*, vol. 7, no. 1 (1995), p. 65-86.

A detailed report on the chemical composition and nutritive value of eight tree species. It gives the various results of the analysis, including species of *Acacia arabica*, *Acacia tortillis*, mimosa and *Prosopsis*.

141   **Analysis of amoxycillin in bustard plasma by high-performance liquid chromatography after administration of a long-acting formulation.**
T. A. Bailey (et al.).   *Journal of Veterinary Pharmacology and Therapeutics*, vol. 19, no. 4 (1996), p. 313-15.

A study of fifteen bustards in the United Arab Emirates which showed that amoxycillin could be used for the treatment of birds suffering from microbial infections, with doses repeated at 5- to 7-day intervals.

142   **Causes of morbidity in bustards in the United Arab Emirates.**
T. A. Bailey (et al.).   *Avian Diseases*, vol. 40, no. 1 (1996), p. 121-25.

Presents the results of 1,746 clinical examinations on six species of bustards and discusses the different causes of morbidity as between imported adult, captive adult, and captive juvenile bustards. Trauma was evident across all species, but infectious viral diseases were almost exclusively confined to imported adults.

143 Lead toxicosis in captive houbara bustards (*Chlamydotis undulata macqueenii*).
T. A. Bailey (et al.). *Veterinary Record*, vol. 137, no. 8 (1995), p. 193-94.

An investigation into lead toxicosis in a flock of captive houbara bustards on a private farm in the United Arab Emirates. The problem was eventually found to be caused by flaking paint peeling off metal in the aviary. Some birds died as a result of the lead poisoning, but further losses were prevented by removing all paint debris and by covering the painted areas with netting.

144 Post-mortem findings in bustards in the United Arab Emirates.
T. A. Bailey (et al.). *Avian Diseases*, vol. 40, no. 2 (1996), p. 296-305.

Describes the various causes of death in six species of captive and imported bustards in the United Arab Emirates for the period 1979-94. The most common causes of death were Newcastle disease, aspergillosis, and deaths related to transportation trauma. Detailed results of 236 post-mortem examinations are presented.

145 Serological survey for avian viruses in houbara bustards.
T. A. Bailey (et al.). *Veterinary Record*, vol. 139, no. 10 (1996), p. 238-39.

Results from a survey aimed at finding antibodies against common avian viruses in houbara bustards in the United Arab Emirates. Tests were carried out on birds in private collections, quarantined birds imported from Pakistan, and free-ranging birds. The authors provide details of the bodies which were identified, and of those viruses for which no antibodies were found.

146 Flora Arabica.
E. Blatter. *Records of the Botanical Survey of India*, vol. 8, nos. 1-6 (1919-36). 519p.

This official publication of the Government Printing Office of Calcutta includes records of the flora and fauna of the present-day UAE as part of its survey.

147 Mangal-associated Brachyura (Ocypodidae, Portunidae, Majidae, Xanthidae and Leucosiidae) from the north-eastern coastal islands of Abu Dhabi, United Arab Emirates.
R. T. Cooper. *Crustaceana*, vol. 70, no. 2 (1997), p. 155-79.

A collection of thirteen different crab species from the listed families was made from the mangrove swamps of Abu Dhabi. Information is given as to habitat, distribution, and morphology.

148 Brachyura (Grasidae, Ocypodidae, Portunidae, Xanthidae and Leucosiidae) of Umm Al Qaiwain mangal, United Arab Emirates.
S. M. Al-Ghais, R. T. Cooper. *Tropical Zoology*, vol. 9, no. 2 (1996), p. 409-30.

This paper presents findings on a collection of crabs from the Umm Al Qaiwain mangal made during 1993 and 1994 from a mangrove with seagrass and salt marsh vegetation. The flora of this area is not well known and an account is given of the various species found in the mangrove, together with their habitat, geographical distribution and identification.

149 *Haemoproteus* **in the houbara (***Chlamydotis undulata macqueenii***)**
   and the rufous-crested bustard (*Eupodotis ruficresta***) in the United**
   Arab Emirates.
   J. C. Howlett (et al.). *Avian Pathology*, vol. 25, no. 1 (1996), p. 49-55.

Reports on the results of microscopic examination of blood smears from 52 houbara bustards and eight rufous-crested bustards, all of which had been imported into the United Arab Emirates. *Haemoproteus tenderoi* was found in 61.5 per cent of the houbara bustards, and 50 per cent of the rufous-crested bustards were also infected.

150 **Birds of the Arabian Gulf.**
   Michael C. Jennings. London: Allen & Unwin, 1981. 167p. (Natural
   History of the Arabian Gulf).

Part of a series on the natural history of the Gulf, this illustrated volume lists the local bird population, its characteristics and locations.

151 **Cestode and ocanthocephalan infections in captive bustards:**
   new host and location records, with data on pathology, control,
   and preventive medicine.
   A. Jones (et al.). *Journal of Zoo and Wildlife Medicine*, vol. 27, no. 2
   (1996), p. 201-8.

A study of the helminth parasites in 78 captive houbara bustards, ten rufous-crested bustards and three kori bustards in the United Arab Emirates, with a detailed medical report on the effects. Amongst the findings was the success of proziquental in treating kori bustards infected by the parasite.

152 **Parasites of wild houbara bustards in the United Arab Emirates.**
   A. Jones (et al.). *Journal of Helminthology*, vol. 70, no. 1 (1996),
   p. 21-25.

Reports on an examination for helminth parasites of seven free-living wild houbara bustards caught in the United Arab Emirates. Fewer species of parasite were discovered in comparison with the incidence in imported captive birds. Also, the wild birds revealed no significant pathological changes attributable to the parasites but only localized responses at the site of parasitical attachment. This is the first report on the parasites of free-living bustards in the UAE as opposed to captive birds.

153 **New records of the flora of the United Arab Emirates (Part 3).**
   F. M. Karim. *Arab Gulf Journal of Scientific Research*, vol. 11, no. 3
   (1993), p. 391-401.

A report on ten new taxa of the flora of the United Arab Emirates collected from the Al-Ain, Dhaid and Hatta districts in the east of the country.

154 **New records of the flora of the United Arab Emirates (Part 4).**
F. M. Karim. *Arab Gulf Journal of Scientific Research*, vol. 12, no. 1 (1994), p. 109-18.
An account of new flora recorded in the United Arab Emirates from the Masafi, Khor Fakhan and Hatta districts in the north-east of the federation. These are listed in the article.

155 **Scolopendromorph and geophilomorph centipedes from Oman and the United Arab Emirates.**
J. G. E. Lewis, M. D. Gallagher. In: *Fauna of Saudi Arabia, vol. 13*, edited by W. Buttiker, F. Krupp. Basle, Switzerland: Pro Entomologica Naturhistorisches Museum, 1993, p. 55-62.
A record of five species of centipedes recorded in Oman and the United Arab Emirates, two of which were new to Oman.

156 **Arabia: sand, sea, sky.**
Michael McKinnon. London: BBC Books, 1990. 224p. map. bibliog.
A study of the complete flora and fauna of the Arabian Peninsula, the present ecological transformation, and its effects on the future of the inhabitants and wildlife. There are references to the United Arab Emirates scattered throughout the text which is well illustrated with a number of coloured photographs.

157 **Flora of the Arabian Peninsula and Socotra, vol. 1.**
A. G. Miller, T. A. Cope. Edinburgh: Edinburgh University Press, 1996. 586p. maps. bibliog.
This illustrated work aims to provide a regional framework for the flora of the countries of the Arabian Peninsula, including the United Arab Emirates. The introduction to the work details the geology and topography of the area, climate, vegetation, conservation, and includes a brief note on botanical exploration of the region. The bulk of the work comprises a listing of the various flora, together with botanical descriptions of the plants, and distribution maps. References to the UAE are scattered throughout the text.

158 **Parasitic infection in a flock of rufous-crested bustards (*Eupodotis ruficresta*) in the United Arab Emirates.**
P. K. Nicholls (et al.). *Journal of Zoo and Wildlife Medicine*, vol. 26, no. 4 (1995), p. 590-96.
The authors examined of a flock of rufous-crested bustards which died in the United Arab Emirates following importation from Somalia. They give details of the various parasites found in the birds, and the effects on the internal organs which were found in post-mortem examinations.

159 **Comparisons of camelpox viruses isolated in Dubai.**
M. Pfeffer (et al.). *Veterinary Microbiology*, vol. 49, nos. 1-2 (1996),
p. 135-46.

Describes an outbreak of pox-like exanthemate between October 1993 and March
1994 in several camel-raising farms in Dubai, and provides the findings resulting from
the examination of twenty camels with local or generalized lesions.

160 **Diterpene glycosides from *Iphioni aucheri*.**
E. Roeder (et al.). *Phytochemistry*, vol. 32, no. 2 (1994), p. 353-55.

Iphioni aucheri was responsible for poisoning racing camels in the United Arab
Emirates and this is a report on the toxic nature of the plant.

161 ***Babesia shortii* infection in a Saker falcon (*Falco cherrug*).**
J. H. Samour, M. A. Pierce. *Veterinary Record*, vol. 139, no. 7
(1996), p. 167-68.

A veterinary report on a Saker falcon which was imported into the United Arab
Emirates and which died from a grossly enlarged liver, spleen, and pale friable kidneys.

162 **Dragonfly records from Saudi Arabia, with an annotated checklist
of the species from the Arabian Peninsula (Insecta: Odonata).**
W. Schneider, F. Krupp. In: *Fauna of Saudi Arabia, vol. 13*, edited
by W. Buttiker, F. Krupp. Basle, Switzerland: Pro Entomologica,
Naturhistoriches Museum, 1993, p. 63-78.

Details the appearance of three types of dragonfly which were reported for the first
time in the Arabian Peninsula. Also provides a checklist of the 56 species so far
recorded in this area, which includes the United Arab Emirates.

163 **New species and records of terrestrial isopods (Crustacea) from
the Arabian Peninsula.**
S. Taiti, F. Ferrara. In: *Fauna of Saudi Arabia, vol. 12,* edited by
W. Buttiker, F. Krupp. Basle, Switzerland: Pro Entomologica,
Naturhistorisches Museum, 1991, p. 209-24.

Records twenty species of terrestrial Crustacea in various countries of the Middle
East, including the United Arab Emirates. Two species are identified as totally new
and a further seven newly recorded in the Arabian Peninsula. The total number of
species recorded in the region is 32.

164 **Equine intestinal clostridiosis in a group of polo ponies in Dubai,
United Arab Emirates.**
T. Wernery (et al.). *Berliner und Münchener Tierärztliche
Wochenschrift*, vol. 109, no. 1 (1996), p. 10-13.

An examination of an outbreak of enterotoxaemia amongst horses in a Dubai polo
club that was suspected as having been caused by hay with a fungal contamination. In
all, eight horses died as a result of the outbreak.

Dissertation

165   **Miocene geology and palaeontology of the United Arab Emirates
      and the State of Qatar (Arabian Gulf): the closure of Tethys and
      mammal 'migrations' between Afroarabia and Eurasia.**
      P. J. Whybrow.   MPhil thesis, Reading University, England, 1987.
      [n.p.]. (Available from the British Library, Boston Spa, Wetherby,
      West Yorkshire).

A review of the structure and Neogene geology of Arabia as they relate to theories
concerning mammal migrations between Asia and Africa. The first known fauna of
late Miocene age is described at Jabal Barakah in the United Arab Emirates. The specimens were found in rocks (which indicated a fluvial environment), and consisted of
freshwater molluscs, catfish, crocodiles, ostrich eggshell fragments, and animals such
as elephant and hippopotamus. The fossil-bearing rocks indicate a swamp environment subject to seasonal drying out and flooding and would also seem to indicate the
probability of a land connection between Arabia and south-western Asia.

Prehistory and Archaeology

166 **Occupation humaine et environnement au 5e et au 4e millénaire sur le côte Sharjah–Umm al-Qaiwain (UAE).** (The natural environment and human occupation on the Sharjah–Umm al-Qaiwain coastline (UAE).)
R. Boucharlot (et al.). *Arabian Archaeology and Epigraphy*, vol. 2, no. 2 (1991), p. 93-106.

This French-language article examines archaeological sites along the west coast of the United Arab Emirates, and views these pre-Bronze Age sites in a broader geographical context. The excavated material resulted from a series of French digs undertaken between 1985 and 1990.

167 **A possible link between the Jemdet Nasr and the Umm an-Nar graves of Oman.**
Karen Frifelt. *Journal of Oman Studies,* vol. 1 (1975), p. 58-80. maps.

This illustrated report of a 1972-73 Danish archaeological survey considers the possible relationship between Bronze Age settlements found on the island of Umm an-Nar off the Abu Dhabi coastline and mainland settlements in the Sultanate of Oman.

168 **A third millennium kiln from the Oman Peninsula.**
K. Frifelt. *Arabian Archaeology and Epigraphy*, vol. 1, no. 1 (1990), p. 4-15.

The discovery of a pottery kiln in 1970 by a Danish expedition at Hili in Al-Ain was dated to the second half of the third millennium BC and provided important information on prehistoric ceramic production in the Oman Peninsula.

169 **Excavations at ed-Dur (Umm al-Qaiwain, UAE) – preliminary report on the second Belgian season (1988).**
E. Haerinck (et al.). *Arabian Archaeology and Epigraphy*, vol. 2, no. 1 (1991), p. 31-60.
These are the results of a seven-week excavation at ed-Dur in Umm al-Qaiwain during 1988 in the southern part of the site. Close to the temple were found a well, three altars, and a stone basin with a long Aramaic inscription. It is suggested that the temple was dedicated to the sun god Shamash. The graveyard north of the temple provided important information on burial rites and a large grave contained many incised bone/ivory plaques with smaller unplundered graves yielding glass vessels, bronze objects and a large variety of beads.

170 **Excavations at ed-Dur (Umm al-Qaiwain, UAE) – preliminary report on the third Belgium season (1989).**
E. Haernick (et al.). *Arabian Archaeology and Epigraphy*, vol. 3, no. 1 (1992), p. 44-60.
The results of a seven-week excavation programme in 1989, which revealed a fourth altar, graves and a semi-subterranean tomb with a barrel vault.

171 **Excavations at ed-Dur (Umm al-Qaiwain, UAE) – preliminary report on the fourth Belgian season (1990).**
E. Haernick. *Arabian Archaeology and Epigraphy*, vol. 3, no. 3 (1992), p. 190-208.
Describes the excavations at ed-Dur in the Emirate of Umm al-Qaiwain during a six-week period in 1990. The research concentrated on the central part of the site and a previously undisturbed semi-subterranean tomb with a barrel vault and enclosure was excavated. The tomb contained glass and bronze vessels, bone plaques and iron weapons. A nicely built circular stone-lined well together with graves and other structures were also discovered.

172 **Les pointes de flèches en fer des sites préislamiques de Mleiha et ed-Dur.** (The iron arrowheads of pre-Islamic sites at Mleiha and ed-Dur, UAE.)
M. Mouton. *Arabian Archaeology and Epigraphy*, vol. 1, nos. 2-3 (1990), p. 88-103.
This French-language article, with English summary, describes excavations at Mleiha in Sharjah and ed-Dur in Umm al-Qaiwain which yielded a large collections of arrowheads dating from the last centuries BC and the first centuries AD. Mouton provides a typological and chronological analysis of the finds.

173 **The diffusion of light by translucent media in antiquity: apropos two alabaster windowpane fragments for ed-Dur (United Arab Emirates).**
D. T. Potts. *Antiquity*, vol. 70, no. 267 (1996), p. 182-88. map.
Reports on the discovery of two fragments of sheet alabaster recovered from the remains of a large private house dated to the first century AD and used as a

light-diffusing medium. Ethnohistorical observation, literary sources, and ancient epigraphic evidence substantiate the conclusions. This use for alabaster has been observed and documented from the first century AD up to the 20th century.

174 **Rethinking some aspects of trade in the Arabian Gulf.**
D. T. Potts. *World Archaeology*, vol. 24, no. 3 (1993), p. 423-40.
Excavations at Tell Abraq in the United Arab Emirates have brought to light material dating from the third, second, and first millennium BC which calls into question long-held views on the archaeology of the Gulf region. Trade between the Oman Peninsula (Magan) and her neighbours is discussed, with the evidence showing that there had been greater continuity in Magan's external relations than had previously been thought.

175 **The archaeology of the Arabian Gulf c5000-323BC.**
Michael Rice. London and New York: Routledge, 1994. 369p. maps. bibliog.
This illustrated work on the archaeology of the Arabian Gulf is centred largely on Bahrain where the author worked for a number of years. He was responsible for opening a museum there, and this led to further commissions in Qatar, Oman and Saudi Arabia. The United Arab Emirates is dealt with as part of the chapter 'Dilmun's neighbouring lands' which is regarded as the site of the earliest developed culture in the Gulf, with settlements located near copper mines and the offshore islands, which were transhipment points to Dilmun (Bahrain) and Mesopotamia. The section discusses early settlement, society, culture, trade, pottery, and architecture, together with an assessment of the interests of the various states in their archaeological past. This work has an excellent bibliography on the archaeology and early history of the Gulf region.

History

Pre-20th century

176 **A collection of treaties, engagements and sanads relating to India and the neighbouring countries: revised and continued up to the 1st June 1906.**
Compiled by Charles Umpherston Aitchinson. Calcutta, India: Government Printing Office, 1909. 13 vols. maps.
Part 2 of volume 12 cites material relating to Trucial Oman and the Persian Gulf in general, and deals with the official documentation relating to British interest in the area, including agreements with rulers, subsidies, the slave trade, smuggling, etc. The affairs of the area were at the time looked after by the India Office.

177 **The pirate coast.**
Charles Dalrymple Belgrave. London: Bell, 1966; Beirut: Librairie du Liban, 1972. 200p. maps. bibliog.
An extremely good illustrated introduction to the history of the area, particularly the lower Gulf States which now comprise the UAE. The work deals with the arrival of the Portuguese in the area, and increasing European influence especially from Great Britain, in response to the needs of trade and the East India Company. The work is largely based on the diary of Francis Lock, commander of HMS *Eden*, and discusses naval peace-keeping operations in the area during the years 1818-21. The military operations against Ras al-Khaimah and the threats from Arab 'piracy' are largely dealt with in Chapters XII and XIII.

178 **The blood-red Arab flag: an investigation into Qasimi piracy 1797-1820.**
Charles E. Davies. Exeter, England: University of Exeter Press, 1997. xxi+453p. maps. bibliog.

This work represents a further challenge to the hitherto accepted view that Qawasim maritime activity in the Gulf, the Red Sea, and off north-west India between the years in question were acts of piracy. The Qawasim acquired a reputation as ruthless pirates and their main territory, Ras al-Khaimah and Sharjah, became known as the Pirate Coast. The work begins with an introductory section which sets the period in its historical context. It deals with the importance of the pearling industry to traditional society and the economy, inter-tribal relations and rivalries, and the long-standing feud between the Qawasim and the Sultanate of Oman, with the former threatening the integrity of the northern part of the Sultanate and challenging Oman's maritime aspirations, particularly with regard to control over the entrance to the Gulf. In 1798 treaty relations were established between Britain and Oman and, as a consequence of this treaty, the East India Company stationed a European Resident at Muscat in order to look after its interests in the region. The Qawasim was a term employed by the British to describe the inhabitants of present-day Ras al-Khaimah and Sharjah who dominated the other ports, peoples and settlements in the vicinity though, in fact, the Qawasim proper were an Arab family, or small tribe, who made up the ruling families of the two city-states and, at the start of the twentieth century, numbered only some sixty individuals. The family also controlled Linga on the Persian coast and, with their allies and dependants, straddled the entrance to the Gulf and were the major maritime power in the region, trading widely within the Gulf, western India and the Red Sea. The work then begins to examine the charges of piracy by studying specific cases based on eyewitness accounts which exist as photocopies of British or East India Company records held in the Bombay Archives or the India Office Library in London. The writer concludes that some of the acts of the Qawasim could be constituted as piracy but that they were motivated by a variety of concerns: restrictions on commercial trade with India due to the activities of the East India Company; bitter rivalry with Oman in the region; and the influence of Wahhabism from present-day Saudi Arabia. It is also clear that some of the acts were more akin to the plundering of wrecks brought about by natural hazards rather than armed aggression at sea. The British and East India Company expeditions mounted against the Qawasim in 1809-10 and 1819-20 were not solely an attempt to end what were regarded as acts of piracy but, is has been argued, were the result of a covert desire to destroy the Qawasim as rival carriers for the Gulf trade. Davies concludes that this was not the primary reason, though the piracy issue was a good moral issue on which to focus. He argues that the prime motive was Britain's concern for the Gulf as a channel of communication, fear of French activity in Turkish Arabia, Muscat and Iran and, 'for the first-time a haunting spectre of a European invasion of India from the north-west, a potential scenario in which Russia was soon to assume the leading role'. Muscat was initially seen as the key to the Gulf and the British Residents worked assiduously to keep French influence out but they also provided much of the evidence on Qawasim activity and intentions, some of which must have been coloured by Muscat's deep mistrust and animosity towards the Qawasim. It is this cocktail of concerns and motives which led to the expeditions against Ras al-Khaimah, the second of which resulted in a treaty of perpetual maritime peace with the Gulf Arabs and so opened the door to 150 years of British involvement in the region. The work is based almost exclusively on contemporary primary sources consisting of: photocopies of 20,000 pages of documents relating to the Gulf and Arabia from the Bombay Archive and largely consisting of transcripts of letters sent and received by the Bombay Council of the East India Company; material in the India

Office Library, especially the Bushire Residency Files; the diaries of Captain Loch RN in the Scottish Record Office; notes by Captain Brucks of the Bombay Marine in the British Library; and Arabic source material which is limited in nature. The extensive appendices deal with: Qawasim seizures off the coast of India; Qawasim voyages to South Arabia; Ras al-Khaimah's war with Muscat, and the political fortunes of Za'ab and the Tanajj 1808-1809; and hostilities between Muscat and the Wahhabis in the aftermath of the first Ras al-Khaimah expedition of 1809-10. This work needs to be balanced by a consideration of *The pirates of Trucial Oman* by H. Moyse-Bartlett and the *The myth of Arab piracy in the Gulf* by Sultan Muhammad Al-Qasini, both of which are represented in this bibliography (see items 183, 185).

179   **Precis on the slave trade in the Gulf of Oman and the Persian Gulf,**
       1873-1905, with a retrospect into previous history from 1852.
       Indian Government. Foreign and Political Department.   Calcutta:
       Government of India, 1906.
An important source of material relating to this trade, the efforts of British naval vessels to prevent it and the various agreements with the sheikhdoms to ensure suppression of the trade.

180   **Report on the administration of the Persian Gulf Political**
       Residency and Muscat Political Agency for the years 1873-4 to
       1903-4.
       Indian Government. Foreign and Political Department.   Calcutta:
       Superintendent of Government Printing, 1823/4-1903/4. annual.
Accounts of relations between Great Britain and the Trucial States and relations between the states themselves during the years in question. British affairs in the area were handled from India and the Political Resident for the Trucial States was based in Dubai.

181   **Paper relative to the measures adopted by the British government,**
       1820-1844, for effecting the suppression of the slave trade in the
       Persian Gulf. To which are appended copies of the engagements
       entered into with the British government, 1822-1851, by His
       Highness the Imam of Muskat, the Arab chiefs of the Persian Gulf,
       and the government of Persia, for the attainment of the above
       object.
       Arnold Burrowes Kemball.   *Selections from the Records of the*
       Bombay Government, no. 24 (1856), p. 635-87.
A valuable source of basic data on the suppression of the slave trade, with a copy of each of the agreements between the British and the various sheikhs. These agreements formed the basis for further agreements and a growing British involvement in the area.

182   **India and the Persian Gulf region 1858-1907: a study in British**
       imperial policy.
       Ravinder Kumar.   Bombay, India: Asian Publishing House, 1965. 259p.
Wider in coverage than the Trucial States, but of relevance to a study of British involvement in the Gulf, particularly in relation to the East India Company's trading

activities and attempts to suppress the slave trade. At the time, policy in the Gulf was the concern of the Indian Government.

183   **The pirates of Trucial Oman.**
Hubert Moyse-Bartlett.   London: MacDonald, 1956. 256p. maps. bibliog.

Deals mainly with 'pirate' activity along the coasts of the Trucial States and Oman, although the definition of such activity was a British one and has been challenged by Arab sources (see Al-Qasini, *The myth of Arab piracy in the Gulf*, item no. 185). The work deals with British military activity against the Qawasin traders in Ras al-Khaimah with a description of the campaign, the outcomes, and the subsequent establishment of friendly relations with the Sheikh, and with British efforts to suppress the slave trade. Various agreements relating to the slave trade and with the various Trucial States are also listed.

184   **British policy towards the Arabian tribes on the shores of the Persian Gulf (1864-1868).**
Dharm Pal.   *Journal of Indian History*, vol. 24 (1945), p. 60-76.

Pal examines British policy which was determined by trade interests in the area and the protection of the sea route to India. He also deals with the inter-tribal disputes, including attacks by Abu Dhabi on Qatar, and the differences between the present-day UAE and the Sultanate of Oman.

185   **The myth of Arab piracy in the Gulf.**
Sultan Muhammad Al-Qasini.   London: Croom Helm, 1986. 344p. bibliog.

The British were the dominant power in the Arabian Gulf in the late eighteenth and early nineteenth centuries and the conventional view was that British imperialist expansion was justified because of the need to suppress Arab piracy. This book is significant in that it challenges the myth of Arab piracy, and argues that the threat was created by the East India Company's orders to take over the trade with India at the expense of the Arab traders. As the East India Company did not have the warships to defeat the Qawasin traders it was necessary to create a threat in order to persuade the British government to send warships to the area. The defeat of the Qawasin and the storming of Ras al-Khaimah opened the door to British expansion in the remainder of the Trucial States and Oman. Based on extensive use of the Bombay Archives (which had not been used before), this book provides a re-interpretation of a crucial period in Gulf history.

186   **A sketch of the historical geography of the Trucial Oman down to the beginning of the sixteenth century.**
C. Wilkinson.   *Geographical Journal*, vol. 130, no. 3 (1964), p. 337-49.

Deals with the present area of the United Arab Emirates in some detail, though the bulk of the article is concerned with the Sultanate of Oman. The article highlights the paucity of material available on the early history of the area together with the fact that, at that time, archaeological work on the area was only just beginning.

20th century

General

187 **Britain's withdrawal from the Middle East 1947-1971:**
the economic and strategic imperatives.
Jacob Abadi.   Princeton, New Jersey: Kingston Press, 1982.
xvii+283p. map. bibliog.
A detailed study of Britain's withdrawal from the Middle East which was largely
motivated by the financial near-collapse of the economy following the Second World
War. This resulted in a major rethink of imperial and strategic commitments.
However, because of concern about the Far East, links continued to be maintained in
the Arabian Gulf States and Aden despite the domestic financial constraints. This
aspect is covered in Chapter VII, 'Imperial remnants: Aden and the Persian Gulf',
which deals with the lead up to British withdrawal in 1971, and the policy objective of
creating a federation of states in the Gulf for which Britain would provide military
assistance and maintain a naval presence in the area. The British government also proposed that the Trucial Scouts be maintained to form the basis of a federal defence
force. The work concludes with the announcement of British withdrawal made on
1 March 1970 following the resolution of border disputes between Saudi Arabia,
Oman and Abu Dhabi.

188 **The development of the Gulf States.**
Ahmad Mustafa Abu Hakima.   In: *The Arabian Peninsula: society*
and politics, edited by Derek Hopwood.   London: Allen & Unwin,
1972, p. 31-53. bibliog.
This contribution discusses the Gulf States in general and then examines each of the
states in turn. In the case of the United Arab Emirates the historical aspect of the association with Britain is dealt with, as are the security reasons behind the creation of the
federation. The author also considers the administrative infrastructure of the area.

189 **Yesterday's Abu Dhabi.**
Annette Bingham.   *History Today*, vol. 39, no. 10 (1989), p. 3-4.
A brief illustrated review of the historical heritage of Abu Dhabi and of the remains of
the various buildings still extant in the city

190 **The winds of morning.**
Hugh Boustead.   London: Chatto & Windus, 1971. 240p. maps.
The autobiography of the former Political Agent in Dubai. It provides an insight into
British involvement in the Trucial States and the pattern of the traditional tribal infra-
structure.

191 **Britain, Iran and the Persian Gulf: some aspects of the situation in the 1920s and 1930s.**
M. Burrell. In: *The Arabian Peninsula: society and politics*, edited by Derek Hopwood. London: Allen & Unwin, 1972, p. 160-88.
The chapter is primarily concerned with British policies in the area towards Iran. These had implications for the rest of the Gulf, particularly in relation to the territorial claims by Iran to various islands in the Gulf, and her aspirations to be the dominant power in the region. The situation, especially for the Arab states, was complicated by the conflicting policies pursued towards Iran by the Foreign Office and towards the Gulf States by the India Office.

192 **Footsteps in the sand: the Gulf in transition, 1953-1958.**
Bernard Burrows. Salisbury, England: Michael Russell Publishing, 1990. 175p. maps.
The author was British Political Resident in the Gulf during the period in question and this account is based on personal recollections and access to official records in the Public Record Office. In terms of the Trucial States the author deals with early history, boundaries between the various states, social customs, the limits of authority of the rulers and relations with Great Britain and Saudi Arabia. Abu Dhabi is dealt with separately in connection with the tripartite dispute between that state, Oman and Saudi Arabia over the ownership of the Buraimi Oasis with Britain representing the interests of Abu Dhabi and Oman.

193 **Britain and the Persian Gulf, 1894-1914.**
Briton C. Busch. Berkeley, California: University of California Press, 1967. 432p. maps. bibliog.
An important work which provides the background to British interests in the region. Busch discusses the policies pursued, policies which were influenced by the perceived needs of the Indian Empire. He also deals with the growth of trade in the area through the East India Company, the strategic concerns of Britain and the various treaties and understandings reached with the rulers in the area.

194 **Departmental Records: Political and Secret Memoranda, Section B.**
London: India Office, Political Department, 1902-31.
The collection includes the Persian Gulf and contains details of a number of secret political documents and memoranda of relevance. Amongst topics covered are the subsidies to rulers, various treaties and agreements, political control, slavery, smuggling, and the infrastructure.

195 **Departmental Records: Political (External) Files and Collections.**
London: India Office, Political Department, 1931-50.
The External Department of the India Office was responsible for the foreign policy of the Government of India, and in the series L/P and S/12 records are to be found those documents relating to the Gulf States. The collection is divided into fifty-nine subject divisions of which the following are the most relevant: Arabia, vols. 2064-2158; establishment and secretariat procedure, vols. 2773, 2782-4, 2790-1, 2800; Persian Gulf, vols. 3709-3967; slavery and slave trade, vols. 4088-4099.

196   **Empire by treaty: Britain and the Middle East in the twentieth century.**
Mathew A. Fitzsimons.   London: Benn; Notre Dame, Indiana:
University of Notre Dame Press, 1964. 235p. map.

An examination of the way in which Britain secured the land route to India through a series of treaties and agreements in the region, including the aptly named Trucial States. This was an alternative to colonization of the region and was just as effective in terms of securing British trading and strategic interests.

197   **The Gulf States and Oman in transition.**
Frauke Heard-Bey.   *Asian Affairs*, vol. 59 (1972), p. 14-22.

An examination of the political transition in the area following the British withdrawal after 1971, including the creation of the new federation of the United Arab Emirates. The author also considers the need for changes in the existing jurisdiction to cover dealings with foreigners and the new codes which economic improvement and Western influences may necessitate, though a move from the Islamic tenets is not considered necessary. The article also deals with the structure of the administration and traditional forms of government, with particular relevance to the state of Abu Dhabi which is seen as the key state in the federation.

198   **The legal and historical basis of the British position in the Persian Gulf.**
John Barrett Kelly.   London: Chatto & Windus, 1958, p. 118-40.
(St. Antony's Papers, no. 4).

An extremely useful survey by an authority on the subject. The treaties and understandings between Britain and the various Gulf States are presented, providing an essential background to British influence in the area.

199   **The invasions of the Gulf: radicalism, ritualism, and the Sheikhs.**
Paul Rich.   Cambridge, England: Allborough Press, 1991. 313p.
bibliog.

This is an in-depth study of the history of the Gulf which is primarily concerned with the significance of Britain's influence on Gulf politics, the historical roots of Britain's Indian Empire, and the profound influence of the Indian Political Service Officers between 1858 and 1947. The states of the United Arab Emirates are not dealt with specifically, but against this colonial backcloth. There are references to the character of the federation, geography, military expenditure, and a list of the Political Agents based in Abu Dhabi and Dubai, the latter serving all of the other Emirates.

Border disputes

200 **Arbitration for the settlement of the territorial dispute between Muscat and Abu Dhabi on one side and Saudi Arabia on the other: memorial of the Government of Saudi Arabia.**
Cairo: al-Maaref Press, 1955. 3 vols. map.

The official Saudi case for the Buraimi Oasis territory, presented at the arbitration hearing. It ended in failure. This item should be used in conjunction with *United Kingdom memorial: arbitration concerning Buraimi and the common frontier between Abu Dhabi and Saudi Arabia* (see item no. 203), issued by the British Foreign Office.

201 **Buraimi: a study in diplomacy by default.**
Howard Bushrod, Jr. *Reporter* (23 Jan. 1958), p. 13-16.

A consideration of the tripartite dispute over the Buraimi Oasis, concentrating on the Saudi Arabian support for the Imam in Oman and the dimension of the problem seen in relation to American and British oil interests. The writer produces evidence to substantiate claims that the dispute was being fostered by the Aramco oil company to increase its concession area.

202 **Arbitration agreement between the government of the United Kingdom acting on behalf of the ruler of Abu Dhabi and His Highness the Sultan Said bin Taimur, and the government of Saudi Arabia. Jedda: 30 July 1954.**
Great Britain. Foreign and Commonwealth Office. London: HM Stationery Office, 1954. 9p. (Cmnd 9272).

The text of the official agreement with Saudi Arabia to the settling of the Buraimi Oasis dispute by arbitration.

203 **United Kingdom memorial: arbitration concerning Buraimi and the common frontier between Abu Dhabi and Saudi Arabia.**
Great Britain. Foreign and Commonwealth Office. London: HM Stationery Office, 1955. 2 vols.

The arbitration proceedings of 1955 were abortive, and this account assesses the difficulties that prevented settlement of the territorial dispute among the three interested parties. See also item 200.

204 **The Middle East states and the law of the sea.**
Ali A. El-Hakim. Manchester, England: Manchester University Press, 1979. 293p. maps. bibliog.

Deals with the settlement of offshore boundary disputes between Abu Dhabi and Qatar and the various agreements in the period 1970-75 between Iran, the UAE, Qatar and Oman over continental shelf boundaries. These were crucially important because of the offshore presence of oil and gas and the strategic position of the tanker routes through the Gulf.

205 **The Persian Gulf States and their boundary problems.**
Rupert Hay. *Geographical Journal*, vol. 120, no. 4 (1954), p. 433-54.
map.
Hay considers the tripartite border dispute between Abu Dhabi, Oman and Saudi
Arabia over the Buraimi Oasis and also the dispute between the Trucial States and
Oman over the Musandam Peninsula.

206 **The Buraimi Oasis dispute.**
John Barrett Kelly. *International Affairs* (London), vol. 32, no. 3
(1956), p. 318-26.
A detailed examination of the problem of the disputed oasis involving Saudi Arabia,
Abu Dhabi and Oman. The article presents the Saudi Arabian case in some depth, on
the basis that it is the Saudi Arabian government which had laid claim to the oasis and
it is therefore on them that the burden of proof had to rest.

207 **Eastern Arabian frontiers.**
John Barrett Kelly. London: Faber; New York: Praeger, 1964. 319p.
map. bibliog.
This important book provides a detailed study of the conflicting claims between Saudi
Arabia, Abu Dhabi and the Sultanate of Oman to the area around Buraimi Oasis in
particular, and also the general problem of the delimitation of frontiers in the area.

208 **Sovereignty and jurisdiction in eastern Arabia.**
John Barrett Kelly. *International Affairs* (London), vol. 34, no. 1
(1958), p. 16-24.
A consideration of the problems and complications resulting from the absence of
agreed frontiers between the various states, including those between Saudi Arabia and
the Trucial States.

209 **Security in the Persian Gulf: 2. Sources on inter-state conflict.**
Robert Liwak. London: Gower, for the International Institute for
Strategic Studies, 1981. 105p. maps.
Liwak's work deals with the complex problem of the inter-relationship between the
various states in the area. Chapter 3, 'The lower Gulf States' (p. 41-72), is of the
greatest relevance here, dealing with border disputes and settlements between
the UAE and her neighbours and also within the federation itself. Also covered are the
various disputes and settlements over the continental shelf boundaries; these are of
great importance because of offshore exploration for oil and gas.

210 **Iran, Saudi Arabia and the law of the sea: political interaction and
legal developments in the Persian Gulf.**
Charles G. MacDonald. Westport, Connecticut; London: Greenwood
Press, 1980. 226p. maps. bibliog.
Discusses regional problems and developments, and considers, in detail, the inter-state
agreements on the continental shelf boundaries between Saudi Arabia and Abu Dhabi.
These agreements were of crucial importance because of the exploration of the off-
shore area for oil and gas.

211   **The Persian Gulf in the twentieth century.**
      John Marlowe.   London: Cresset Press, 1962. 278p. maps. bibliog.
This work is concerned with a study of the Gulf as a whole, with the Trucial States
being mentioned throughout the book. A considerable portion of the text is concerned
with oil concessions, exploration and development, but the work also deals with the
various border disputes, including that over the Buraimi Oasis, the traditional claims
of Iran to offshore islands in the Gulf, and the rise of nationalism in the area.

212   **The Buraimi Oasis dispute.**
      Alexander Melamid.   *Middle Eastern Affairs*, vol. 7. no. 2 (1956),
      p. 56-63.
An explanatory background to the dispute between Abu Dhabi, Saudi Arabia and the
Sultanate of Oman which was unsuccessfully subjected to arbitration in 1955. The situation had arisen out of grazing rights and water supplies but was soon complicated
by the possible presence of oil in the area, and it was suspected that Aramco was fer-
menting the dispute on the behalf of the Saudi Arabian government to increase its
concession area.

Dissertations

213   **Saudi Arabia's territorial limits: a study in law and politics.**
      Abdulkarim Mohamed Hamadi.   PhD thesis, Indiana University,
      Bloomington, Indiana, 1981. 145p. (Available from University
      Microfilms International, Ann Arbor, Michigan, order
      no. AAD81-12463).
A study of the processes through which Saudi Arabia established boundaries with its
neighbours, including those with the United Arab Emirates. The author shows that war
has been relatively unimportant in this process which has largely centred on diplomacy. He concludes that there is an absence of general principles of international law
governing the delimitation of territorial authority among states.

214   **Britain and the United Arab Emirates 1820-1956: a documentary
      study.**
      S. H. Al-Sagri.   PhD thesis, Kent University, Canterbury, England,
      1988. [n.p.]. (Available from the British Library, Boston Spa,
      Wetherby, West Yorkshire).
An examination of the relationship between Great Britain and the United Arab
Emirates during the period in question, beginning with the series of treaties aimed at
consolidating British interests in the area which became known as the Trucial States.
This period of the relationship lasted from 1820 to 1945 and during this time Britain
refrained from interfering in the internal affairs of the Sheikhdoms. The second period
from 1945 to 1956 saw a change in the relationship as Britain adopted a policy of
developing the social, economic and political conditions in the Emirates and operated

through a Trucial States Council which unified the Sheikhs for the first time in the history of the area. The main results of this policy were the establishment of an education system, a legal system, an administrative infrastructure, and a stable economy. This was the first move of the Sheikhdoms from a tribal society into a nation-state, although this development was only to come to fruition after British withdrawal from the Gulf.

Population and Social Structure

215 **Adolescents' perceptions of family functioning in the United Arab Emirates.**
Ahmed A. Alnajjar. *Adolescence*, vol. 31, no. 122 (1996), p. 433-42.
Describes the use of the Family Functioning Questionnaire to assess family psychological health among 710 adolescents aged 14-19 in the United Arab Emirates. The questionnaire was used to measure seven dimensions relating to the family: family structure; emotional fulfilment; internal relations; behavioural control; value transmission; basic requirements; and external relations.

216 **Children's game and toy preferences: a cross-cultural comparison.**
Marie E. Bathiche, Jeffrey L. Derevensky. *International Play Journal*, vol. 3, no. 1 (1995), p. 52-62.
The authors discuss the results from a questionnaire which was used to compare the game/toy preferences of 336 children living in the United Arab Emirates and the equivalent number living in Canada. The results suggested that both sets of children share similar game/toy preferences.

217 **The demographic challenge in the Arab Gulf.**
John Stace Birks. In: *The Arab Gulf and the Arab World*, edited by B. R. Pridham. London: Croom Helm, 1988, p. 131-52.
This contribution attempts to assess the significance of demographic change in the Gulf States, including the United Arab Emirates, and the relative shares of nationals and non-nationals which are seen as a critical issue of concern to planners. The decline of oil prices and revenues gave rise to questions as to the levels of migrant workers' remittances home, and the future role and size of the non-national population. Accurate demographic information is needed in order to plan for future development. In the case of the United Arab Emirates, the national population constitutes 30 per cent of the population of the Arab Gulf; 22.7 per cent of its population in 1983 was non-national, and the indigenous population amounted to only 18.9 per cent of the active labour force.

218 **The geographical mobility of a rural Arab population: some implications of changing patterns.**
John Stace Birks. *Journal of Tropical Agriculture*, vol. 48 (June 1979), p. 9-18. maps.
This study of the effects of mobility on a small community in Oman is of relevance here because Abu Dhabi accounts for employment of 46.5 per cent of the migrants and Dubai 2.3 per cent. Although the article is largely concerned with the effects on the home community, such a migration also has an effect on the host countries.

219 **Medunaradna migracya u arapsho, regiji.** (International migrations in the Arab region.)
Ruzica Cicak-Chand. *Migraciijske tera*, vol. 6, no. 4 (1990), p. 481-95.
The 1973 oil price rises brought about a large-scale immigration of labour to the Gulf States, including the United Arab Emirates, such that by 1985 expatriate workers there numbered more than five million. The article gives a socio-economic profile for the major immigrant groups in the region. The article is in Serbo-Croat with Roman alphabet, and is amplified with tables and references.

220 **Research facilities in the Arabian Gulf: Kuwait, Bahrain, Oman, Qatar and the United Arab Emirates.**
Jill Crystal. *Middle East Studies Association Bulletin*, vol. 18, no. 2 (1994), p. 175-81.
Crystal's survey of research opportunities in the social sciences in the named states includes the regulatory framework and comments on various aspects of daily life.

221 **Development anomalies in the bedouin oases of al-Liwa.**
Frauke Heard-Bey. *Asian Affairs*, vol. 61, no. 3 (1974), p. 272-86.
A study of the area around the oases which, because of its water resources, has always had potential for agriculture and agricultural development. However, the article points out that this was a seasonable and unreliable economic activity and the income had to be supplemented by migration to the pearling grounds. The article deals in some detail with the tribal and social structure of the area, the effects of the seasonal migration on the society, and the impact of new economic wealth on agriculture in terms of finance, education and technical assistance. Also considered are flora and fauna, climate, domestic architecture, and culture and customs.

222 **Some social aspects of the Trucial States.**
A. Lienhardt. In: *The Arabian Peninsula: society and politics*, edited by Derek Hopwood. London: Allen & Unwin, 1972, p. 219-30.
An examination of the status and role of women in the society of the Trucial States which seeks 'to give an account of the traditional position of women in Trucial Coast society. One cannot, after all, notice change, let alone assess or analyse it, without first considering its point, or points, of departure.'

223 **Immigrants in the Arab Gulf countries: 'sojourners' or 'settlers'.**
George Sabagh. In: *The Arab State*, edited by Giacomo Luciani.
London: Routledge, 1990, p. 349-72.

This contribution is a study of international migration from one Arab State to another and the relationship that may exist between the pattern of migration and integration. In the mid-1970s, at the peak of the demand for migrant labour, the United Arab Emirates had the highest percentage (75.4 per cent), with the vast majority being temporary settlers. The move from Arab to Asian workers is an indication that the UAE, and other Gulf States, did not wish to encourage settlement by migrant workers.

224 **The status and ontology of Arab intellectuals: the academic group.**
Mohammed Sabour. *International Journal of Contemporary Sociology*, vol. 28, nos. 3-4 (1991), p. 221-32.

Discusses the aspirations of Arab academics in the context of developing societies, including the United Arab Emirates. Problems faced by academics include socio-economic conditions and political uncertainty, and a sense of personal crisis stemming from cultural, societal, and existential circumstances.

225 **Sozialgeographische Aspekte der Siedlingsentwicklung im Emirat Dubai, Vereinigte Arabische Emirate, oder Siedlingsentwicklung einzig ein bauliches Phänomen?** (Socio-geographical aspects of settlement development in the Emirate of Dubai, United Arab Emirates, or is settlement development solely a building phenomenon?)
F. Scholz. *Erde*, vol. 122, no. 2 (1991), p. 97-115.

This German-language article studies the expansion of the oil market in the United Arab Emirates, something which had many political, economic, social, and settlement effects. The latter were important, and not purely architectural. Dubai is used as a case-study to examine architectural and socio-geographical effects, segregation, differentiation into quarters, and consciousness of property and status. The implications of Dubai's population growth from 0.6 million in 1975 to 1.8 million in 1990 are also discussed.

Dissertation

226 **The impact of the foreign migrants on national integration of the United Arab Emirates.**
Ahmad Jaser Mahmoud. PhD thesis, University of Missouri, Warrenberg, 1985. 241p. (Available from University Microfilms, Ann Arbor, Michigan, order no. AAD86-07924).

This study concentrates on the effects of foreign workers on the political, economic and social aspects of the United Arab Emirates, in an attempt to clarify the relationship between foreign workers and national integration. The author concludes that the presence of foreign workers is a disruptive factor working against the national integration of the federation and recommends measures to reduce dependence on migrant workers.

Social Change

227 **Bedouins, wealth and change: a study of rural development in the United Arab Emirates and the Sultanate of Oman.**
Rainer Cordes, Fred Scholz. Tokyo: United Nations University, 1980. (NRTS-7-UNUP-14).
A consideration of the changes in traditional bedouin society brought about by the influence of the oil economy, such as the attraction of the oil industry as an employer and the rural development made possible by oil revenues.

228 **Social changes in the Gulf States and Oman.**
Frauke Heard-Bey. *Asian Affairs* (London), vol. 59, no. 3 (1972), p. 309-16.
Examines social change in the context of each state but also as a comparison between the Gulf States and Oman, two places which have experienced different rates of development. The author assesses the changes brought about by the new affluence, which has as a fundamental basis its uneven distribution, resulting in the splitting up of society and the adoption of new ways of life. An additional problem is the lack of trained manpower, resulting in the need for large amounts of migrant labour. This is also seen as having an impact on the political scene, but 'in the Union of Arab Emirates the process of levelling out this unevenness is well under way now, through a sharing of wealth, manpower and responsibility'.

229 **The Persian Gulf after the storm.**
Phebe Marr. In: *Riding the tiger: the Middle East challenge after the Cold War,* edited by Phebe Marr, William Lewis. London; Boulder, Colorado: Westview Press, 1993, p. 109-35.
This contribution examines the impact on the Gulf States of the 1991 Gulf War which is not regarded as a decisive event but a contribution to future instability. In terms of the GCC states, including the United Arab Emirates, the contribution examines pressures on society and the social structure largely resulting from modernization,

including; demand for open accountable government; the need to accommodate the new generation of educated citizens; a reassessment of links with the West due to the rise of political Islam; and the further development of secular democratic forces. Also considered is the cohesion of the Gulf Co-operation Council, the significance of oil, and relations with the United States.

230 Factors influencing the consumer process in UAE society.
M. A. J. Al-Mutawa. *International Sociology*, vol. 11, no. 3 (1996), p. 337-57.

Reports on the results of an inquiry into consumer behaviour patterns in the United Arab Emirates using a random-sample questionnaire. Amongst the topics examined were the effect of expatriate–national relationships on shopping; attitudes towards spending and consumption in general; and the processes of decision-making within the family and the effects on purchasing patterns.

231 Problems of oasis development.
John C. Wilkinson. Oxford, England: University of Oxford, School of Geography, 1978. 40p. bibliog. (Research Paper, no. 20).

The thesis of this paper is that there has been a general decline in oasis life, with a breakdown of the old ways and the rural economy due to sedentarization. Suggestions are advanced for reversing this trend by a process of dynamic planning, with a view to reintegrating pastoral and cultivator societies. The paper examines the traditional patterns of nomadic bases, agriculture, crafts, and the problem of social change and modernization. This is a general study based on a number of oases, of which al-Liwa in Abu Dhabi was one.

Nomadismus im Niedergang: 'desert farming' mit Perspektiven? Wendel im ländlichen Raum des Emirates Dubai, Vereinigte Arabische Emirate.
(Nomadism in decline: 'desert farming' with prospects? Change in the rural area of the Emirate of Dubai, United Arab Emirates.)
See item no. 529.

Women

232 Women and the law in the United Arab Emirates.
Doreen Hinchcliffe.   In: *Arabia and the Gulf: from traditional society to modern states*, edited by Ian Richard Netton.   London: Croom Helm, 1984. 235-44.

An examination of the law relating to women in the United Arab Emirates which has not changed as a result of development. The law of personal status is still *shari'a* law which governs marriage, divorce, guardianship of children, and succession on death. As a result, women in the United Arab Emirates enjoy one of the highest standards of living in the world, whilst at the same time being subject to a law which was developed over a thousand years ago, making their legal status often inferior to that of their servants. The various branches of *shari'a* law are described, and discussed in relation to women and the various legal situations that can arise within the family structure. However, it is pointed out that women in the United Arab Emirates own a large amount of property, though purchased through agents, and a growing number are employed in nursing, teaching, commerce and the banking sector. This development is seen as critical given the size of the indigenous population.

233 The political status of women in the Arab Gulf States.
J. E. Peterson.   *Middle East Journal*, vol. 43, no. 1 (1989), p. 34-50.

An examination of the status of women in the Gulf Co-operation Council member states with a view to assessing their potential for playing a political role. The changing economic and social climate is considered in order to analyse the effects of these changes on the traditional woman's domain. A positive evaluation shows the likely progress in the field of women's advancement through three phrases: increasing steady government employment for women; the emergence of a growing sector of women in senior positions when present male government employees retire; a possible socio-political change leading to constitutional monarchies incorporating representative democratic institutions. These prospects are balanced by an examination of the trends towards neo-conservatism among Gulf women, which are seen as a threat to development in those states. The United Arab Emirates forms part of this consideration.

Women

234 The role of women in the economy of the United Arab Emirates.
Linda U. Soffan. *Labour and Society*, vol. 5, no. 1 (1980), p. 3-17.

Arab women have traditionally played a small role in the economy of the United Arab Emirates, but work opportunities have grown steadily in the twentieth century, largely as a result of access to education and a realization that work opportunities were guaranteed by Islam. The oil-based economy also brought rapid development and increasing professional openings for women in education, health and social work. These were primarily in the public sector, however, for the private sector still had strictures against female employment and posts were largely filled by expatriate workers. Soffan concludes that there will be an increase in the numbers of working women in both sections of the economy as migrant labour declines.

235 The women of the United Arab Emirates.
Linda Ursa Soffan. London: Croom Helm; New York: Barnes & Noble, 1980. 127p. bibliog.

Deals with the problem of reconciling the family-oriented role of women in Islamic society with the efforts being made to provide education for females. The work begins with a consideration of Islamic law in relation to women and the problems of reconciling the law with tribal traditions and modern practice, and then goes on to consider the marriage contract and the structure of family life in the United Arab Emirates (UAE). The success of the education policy and the female commitment to study and course completion is measured against the prejudice which largely prevents women from taking jobs which bring them into open contact with the public. The study concludes with an examination of the role of governmental and non-governmental organizations in improving the status of women in the UAE. Their commitment is seen as relatively high in terms of family role, education and economic activity, with possibilities for further strengthening due to the support from local leaders within the federation.

236 Women in the United Arab Emirates.
Women's International Network News, vol. 22 (Winter 1996), p. 39-40.

Examines a report prepared by the United Arab Emirates Women's Federation covering a growing role for women in society, legal guarantees for women, female education, the role of women in the labour market, and the expansion of health and welfare services for women and children. The UAE Women's Federation is funded by the government, granted autonomy by law, and empowered to represent the female community with Ministries and Government Departments.

62

Dissertation

237 **Role conflict among working women in the United Arab Emirates and its relationship with personality traits and socio-economic factors: a study of female preparatory and secondary school teachers.**
A. A. A. Al-Hammadi.   PhD thesis, Hull University, England, 1995. [n.p.]. (Available from the British Library, Boston Spa, Wetherby, West Yorkshire).

A study of role conflict amongst working women in the United Arab Emirates based on a sample of 372 women teachers all of whom were married to UAE nationals with at least one child and educated to first degree level or above. Various inventories were used to test the sample and amongst the findings were the following: a positive correlation between role conflict and neuroticism; significant correlations between role-conflict dimensions and trait anxiety; and more role conflict between wives and husbands with daughters, rather than sons. Overall, it was determined that working women involved in multiple roles faced no real threat to their psychological well-being.

Urbanization

238 **Urbanisation in the Middle East.**
F. Costello. London and New York: Cambridge University Press, 1977. 121p. map. bibliog.

Urbanization is considered in relation to the region as a whole, and the factors involved in modern urban development, social adjustment, occupation and social strata and rural–urban migration are examined. The question of urbanization in the UAE is considered in these terms and also in terms of the differing effects of urbanization between Abu Dhabi and Dubai.

239 **Desert yields to cities of the future.**
Liz Kirkwood. *Middle East Economic Digest*, vol. 37, no. 48 (1993), p. 42-43.

An examination of urban growth and change in the United Arab Emirates, assessing changes in each of the Emirates and prospects for the new millennium. The projects for civil improvements, public works and city planning in relation to space constraints are also assessed.

240 **The impact of planning new cities on development in the Gulf States.**
Walid Al-Menayes. *Journal of the Gulf and Arabian Peninsula Studies*, vol. 13, no. 50 (1987), p. 75-117.

Discusses the reasons for new city planning in the Gulf States including Jebal Ali in the United Arab Emirates. Planning objectives are deemed to be: absorption of high population density of main urban areas; direct urban development into isolated areas; establishment of political boundaries in areas of dispute.

241 **Urbanization and labor migration in the Arab countries of the Gulf.**
Galal Abdulla Moawad. *Journal of the Gulf and Arabian Studies*, vol. 13, no. 51 (1987), p. 189-214.
An Arab-language article which examines the emergence of nation-city states in the Arabian Gulf, including the United Arab Emirates, where the capital cities comprise over 70 per cent of the total populations. This has been largely brought about by momentum from immigrant labour which, having been tempted by work opportunities and economic benefits, now accounts for over 80 per cent of the population. The cultural and socio-economic impact of this migration and the resultant problems are examined. Amongst the problems considered are: pressure on urban services, particularly housing; conflicts between the migrant and the indigenous population and between different ethnic migrant communities; limitations on the productivity of indigenous workers; and social and political threats to native Arab culture and identity. Suggestions are offered for developing strategies to deal with these problems, particularly with reference to Asian workers.

242 **An urban profile of the Middle East.**
Hugh Roberts. London: Croom Helm, 1979. 239p. maps. bibliog.
The UAE is dealt with throughout this work, but particular reference is made to the problem of population growth in relation to housing needs and provision. The Jebal Ali new town near Dubai is considered in great detail (p. 128-47) as one of the case-studies, covering all aspects from planning and design to the industrial and social environment.

Dissertation

243 **Sharjah, UAE: the urban conservation dilemma.**
G. Anderson. MA thesis, University of Durham, England, 1991.
[n.p.]. (Available from the British Library, Boston Spa, Wetherby, West Yorkshire).
Anderson outlines and analyses the urban development of the city of Sharjah which contributed to the expansion of the settlement. The second part of the work aims to create a series of conservation areas in the city based upon the historical, architectural and cultural significance of groups of buildings, together with an assessment of their suitability for preservation in terms of their physical condition.

Religion

244 The Shii Imami community and politics in the Arab East.
Abbas Kalidar. *Middle Eastern Studies*, vol. 19, no. 1 (1983), p. 3-16.
Examines the importance of the three distinct features of the Shii Imami in the history
of Islam: the community's rebellion; suppression and alienation; and its sense of right-
eousness. These aspects are considered of value to a perception of the community's
role in the politics of the countries where they are represented, which includes the
United Arab Emirates, and this is of significance because of relations with Iran.

245 Religion and nationalism in the Arab world.
Elie Kedourie. In: *Islam in the modern world.* London: Mansell,
1980, p. 53-74.
A consideration of the influence of Islam on Arab politics and society and its role as a
unifying factor in the development of Arabism. This aspect is seen as particularly true
of the Gulf area where the rulers take for granted the equation of Islam and Arabism.
This view has become more important because of the shift in the political centre of the
Arab world brought about by the income derived from oil.

246 The Islamisation of the Arab Gulf.
F. Omar. In: *The Arab Gulf and the Arab World*, edited by B. R.
Pridham. London: Croom Helm, 1988, p. 29-40.
A study of the conditions of the Arab Gulf region at the advent of Islam and the
acceptance of the new religion by the Arabs. Omar concludes that a prime reason for
the ready adoption of Islam was that it was seen as a power capable of throwing off
the Persian yoke. It was also regarded as an opportunity to open up maritime trade
with the rest of the world, and contacts with their Arab brothers elsewhere in the
region.

247   **This world is political! The Islamic revival of the seventies.**
      Daniel Pipes.   *Orbis*, vol. 24, no. 1 (1980), p. 35-36.
Examines the political implications of the Islamic fundamentalist movements which
began to make their presence felt in the 1970s. These movements have implications
for the West but also for the traditional monarchical rulers of the Gulf States and
Saudi Arabia.

248   **American missionaries in the UAE region in the twentieth century.**
      Fatma Al-Sayegh.   *Middle Eastern Studies*, vol. 32, no. 1 (1996),
      p. 120-39.
The Arabian mission was an American Protestant mission organized to convert the
Arabs to Christianity. The first mission in the United Arab Emirates was established in
1891 and lasted until the 1960s. The missions were largely unsuccessful in making
converts, but they had a major impact on the area through the introduction of new
ideas on health, education and employment. The reports of the missions were also
more accurate and factual than other contemporary reports from the area.

Health

249 **Nutrition mission to the Gulf Area (UAE, Bahrain, Qatar and Oman), 25 February 1979 to 31 March 1979. A. The General Report.**
M. Autret, S. Miladi.   Abu Dhabi: UNICEF Gulf Area Office, 1979. 43p.

The report is an assessment of the food and nutrition situation with particular reference to children, and aimed at advising government on the future orientation of policies and programmes in the field of nutrition. It was found that marasmus and malnutrition were frequent problems, and anaemia was present in 60 per cent of the children. Malnutrition and marasmus were often the result of underfeeding, mainly due to the over-dilution of processed milk. In the case of marasmus, the main factors were underfeeding and infections, bottle-feeding and lack of hygienic knowledge. The report recommends that breast-feeding should be encouraged and that environmental sanitation and general hygiene should be improved, in an effort to eradicate the intestinal infections associated with malnutrition and marasmus.

250 **Emergency room scheduling: a simulation model.**
M. A. Badri, J. A. Hillingworth.   In: *Proceedings of the 24th Annual Computer Simulation Conference*, held in Reno, Nevada, 27-30 July 1992. Edited by P. Kuher.   San Diego, California: Summer Computer Simulation Conference, 1992, p. 194-98.

A need had been identified for different scheduling strategies in the emergency room of a hospital, and a simulation model was developed and applied to the 600-bed Rashid Hospital in the United Arab Emirates. The model was designed to assess the effectiveness of the initial service system and to improve management's ability to anticipate the impact of patient throughput flow changes. The simulation determined the effects of changes in scheduling practices, allocation of resources, patient demand patterns, and priority rules for servicing patients. The model was used to enable managers at Rashid to select an operational strategy to maintain a high level of care.

251   **Alkaloids with antimicrobial activity from the root of *Rhazya stricta* Decn. growing in the United Arab Emirates.**
        A. K. Bashir.   *Arab Gulf Journal of Scientific Research*, vol. 12, no. 1 (1994), p. 119-31.

Rhazya stricta is used in traditional medicine for the treatment of diabetes mellitus, skin infections and stomach disorders. A study of chloroform and methanol extracts from plants growing wild in the United Arab Emirates revealed antimicrobial activity against a number of bacteria, and these are listed in the article.

252   **Flavonoids of *Limonium axillare*.**
        A. K. Bashir (et al.).   *International Journal of Pharmacognosy*, vol. 32, no. 4 (1994), p. 366-72.

Describes the use of chromatographic techniques to test the methanol extract from *Limonium axillare* which is used to treat wounds or inflammation in traditional medicine practised in the United Arab Emirates. The methanol extract was found to be more effective than the chloroform extract in antibacterial and antifungal activities of the plant.

253   **Methylated flavones of *Teucruim stocksianum*.**
        A. K. Bashir.   *Journal of Herbs, Spices and Medicinal Plants*, vol. 3, no. 1 (1995), p. 17-24.

Teucruim stocksianum is used in traditional medicine for the treatment of diabetes mellitus and stomach problems and five methylated flavones were isolated from this plant. The plants were collected from the Khor Fakkan area and their structures elucidated from spectral data.

254   **Phytochemical and antimicrobial studies on the leaves of *Rhazya stricta* growing in United Arab Emirates.**
        A. K. Bashir (et al.).   *Fitoterapia*, vol. 65, no. 1 (1994), p. 84-85.

A study of the antimicrobial activity and inhibitory concentrations of the leaf properties in the preparation of chloroform, butanol and water-soluble solutions taken from the *Rhazya stricta*. Details the chemical composition of the leaves and tests the activity against a number of pathogens.

255   **Triterpene saponins from *Xeromphis nilotica*.**
        A. K. Bashir.   *International Journal of Pharmacognosy*, vol. 34, no. 3 (1996), p. 202-6.

Xeromphis nilotica is used to treat jaundice and as a fish poison. Three triterpene saponins were collected from *Xeromphis nilotica* trees in the United Arab Emirates and subjected to spectral and chemical analyses to determine their structures.

Health

256   The Dubai Community Psychiatric Survey II: development of the
       Socio-cultural Change questionnaire.
       P. Bebbington (et al.).   *Social Psychiatry and Psychiatric
       Epidemiology*, vol. 28, no. 2 (1993), p. 60-65.
This survey was carried out to assess the impact of rapid social change on the mental
health of women in Dubai. The Socio-cultural Change questionnaire was used to measure social change at an individual level in a wide range of behaviour and in attitudes
to a set of varied situations. The article gives an account of the considerations behind
the form of the questionnaire, its structural characteristics, and validity.

257   Smoking among health professionals.
       A. Bener (et al.).   *Medical Education*, vol. 28, no. 2 (1994), p. 151-57.
A study was conducted between December 1991 and November 1992 to determine the
extent of smoking amongst doctors and other health-care professionals in Al-Ain hospitals and clinics. Responses came from 268 health professionals of whom 197 were
male and 71 female. Amongst the men, 43.7 per cent were smokers, 12.2 per cent
were ex-smokers, and 44.2 per cent were non-smokers; amongst the women, 5.6 per
cent were smokers, 1.4 per cent were ex-smokers and 93 per cent were non-smokers.
All of the staff were aware of the detrimental effects of smoking, and so provided with
the motivation for stopping or working to stop; the links with bladder cancer, soft
tissue lesion and neonatal death were not well known. The counselling of patients
about the danger of smoking was less prevalent amongst doctors who smoked.

258   Predictors of employment status of treated patients with
       DSM-III-R diagnosis. Can a logistic regression model find a
       solution?
       T. K. Daradkeh, L. Karim.   *International Journal of Social
       Psychiatry*, vol. 40, no. 2 (1994), p. 141-49.
A study of psychiatric patients and their employment outcomes using a logistic regression model. The study revealed that the most significant predictors were marital status;
absence of schizoid personality; freedom from illness or with only minimal symptoms
of it; later age of onset; and higher educational attainment. The article includes illustrations, tables and references.

259   Faculty evaluation of educational strategies in medical schools.
       Mondiras Das (et al.).   *Medical Teacher*, vol. 16, no. 4 (1994),
       p. 355-61.
The authors used the medical curricula of two medical schools in the United Arab
Emirates and Malaysia to evaluate faculty opinion in terms of six educational strategies. Significant differences between the educational plans of the two institutions
were identified.

260   Paracetamol prescribing – an epidemic?
       K. P. Dawson (et al.).   *Family Practice*, vol. 13, no. 2 (1996),
       p. 179-81.
Examines the prescribing patterns of paracetamol on a national basis in the United
Arab Emirates and the detailed pattern for one primary health-care centre. The

70

authors found that the drug was included in 35.5 per cent of all prescriptions, of which 58.5 per cent were for children under 12 and 13.5 per cent for infants under 1 year. This pattern is reflected in the national figures, which are considered to be nearing epidemic proportions. The danger of hepatotoxicity, and the inhibition of the immune response in children, are both highlighted. The article is illustrated, and includes tables and references.

261   **Systemic reactions to the Samsum ant: an IgE-mediated hypersensitivity.**
G. Dib (et al.).   *Journal of Allergy and Clinical Immunology*, vol. 96, no. 4 (1995), p. 465-72.
Describes the use of an allergenic extract of the Samsum ant to carry out skin tests to prepare a reagent for specific IgeE titration. Results of tests on 31 patients with anaphylactic reactions to stings from the ant showed that the diagnosis could be confirmed by skin tests.

262   **Arab perceptions of gender as mirrored in the search for a kidney donor.**
E. B. Gallagher.   *Sociologicae Focus*, vol. 24, no. 4 (1992), p. 311-19.
Examines gender stereotyping as an influencing factor concerning who among the patient's relatives is most likely to donate a kidney. The subjects were female medical students in the United Arab Emirates and the findings are interpreted in relation to Arab culture, patriarchalism, family structure, and pronatalism.

263   **Handbook of Arabian medicinal plants.**
S. A. Ghazanfor.   Boca Raton, Florida: CRC Press, 1994. 265p. map.
Deals with the botany, morphology and uses of 260 traditional medicinal plants in the countries of the Arabian Peninsula, including the United Arab Emirates. The plants are listed alphabetically by family with vernacular and Latin names, accompanied by line-drawings and notes on geographical distribution, flowering and fruiting. The medicinal use of each plant is detailed, together with any other uses such as for food, fodder or dyes. The appendix lists the various diseases and aliments and the plants used in their treatment.

264   **The Dubai Community Psychiatric Survey: acculturation and the prevalence of psychiatric disorder.**
R. Ghubash, E. Hamdi, Paul Bebbington.   *Psychological Medicine*, vol. 24, no. 1 (1994), p. 121-31.
A report on the results of interviews of 300 women in Dubai to study the effects of radical social change on the mental health of female nationals. At an individual level, the association between psychiatric morbidity and social change as reflected in the subject's behaviour was not significant. However, at the community level the relationship was significant, and it was found that there was more psychiatric morbidity in areas at the extremes of social change.

265 **The Dubai Community Psychiatric Survey I. prevalence and socio-demographic correlates.**
R. Ghubash. *Social Psychiatry and Psychiatric Epidemiology*, vol. 22, no. 2 (1992), p. 53-61.

Describes the methods and socio-demographic findings of this psychiatric survey of 300 women in Dubai using the Present State Examination Index of Definition-CATEGO system. The overall prevalence of psychiatric disorder was 22.7 per cent. There was little association with socio-demographic variables, however, though prevalence was found to be high in divorced, widowed and separated married women, and in polygamously married women and single parents. It is considered that this high prevalence may be attributed to rapid socio-cultural change.

266 **Doing randomized controlled trials in a developing country: some practical realities.**
M. J. Glasgow (et al.). *Family Practice*, vol. 13, no. 1 (1996), p. 98-103.

An account of the problems encountered in conducting a randomized, double-blind, parallel drugs study in the United Arab Emirates. It took longer to complete than expected, and recruitment and participation levels fell short of expectations. Amongst the reasons advanced are the demography of the UAE, cultural factors, and the existence of an established doctor–patient relationship.

267 **Growth and survival of *Listeria monocytogenes* in two traditional foods from the United Arab Emirates.**
V. S. Gohil (et al.). *Food Microbiology*, vol. 13, no. 2 (1996), p. 159-64.

A study of the growth and survival of *Listeria monocytogenes* in concentrated yoghurt and hummus, using tests for storage at varying temperatures and for different periods of time. The authors conclude that concentrated yoghurt could be regarded as safe from *Listeria*, but that high numbers of *Listeria monocytogenes* could survive in hummus for up to three days, the limit of its expected shelf-life.

268 **Incidence of *Listeria* spp. in retail foods in the United Arab Emirates.**
V. S. Gohil (et al.). *Journal of Food Production*, vol. 58, no. 1 (1995), p. 102-4.

Reports on a survey of 1,101 samples of retail food items in the United Arab Emirates, covering dairy products, fresh vegetables, fresh/frozen meat, poultry and a range of ready-to-eat meals. It indicated that the incidence of *Listeria* was extremely low. *Listeria* was detected only in imported frozen chicken. Some local meat was also contaminated, but the risks to consumers would be minimal.

269 **The role of the Skills Laboratory in the integrated curriculum of the Faculty of Medicine and Health Sciences at the United Arab Emirates University.**
Ishrak Hamo. *Medical Teacher*, vol. 16 (1994), p. 167-78.

The Skills Laboratory is used to simulate medical situations in a clinical setting before the students apply their skills on real patients. The role is primarily to consolidate the students' knowledge, to provide motivation, and to integrate various aspects of the curriculum. Hamo concludes that the Skills Laboratory is a useful clinical setting, particularly when clinical teaching is introduced early in the curriculum. In the case of the United Arab Emirates University clinical skills are introduced in the first medical year which follows two preparatory years.

270 **Patients' evaluations of their consultations with primary health care doctors in the United Arab Emirates.**
A. Harrison. *Family Practice*, vol. 13, no. 1 (1996), p. 59-66.

Reports on the results of a questionnaire issued to 152 patients to evaluate their consultations with primary health clinic doctors. The results showed that less than one-tenth were completely satisfied. Harrison discusses whether doctors should be routinely involved in addressing social, family and affective issues, and suggests that patients in the Emirates would value the inclusion of such components.

271 **Does sharing a mother-tongue affect how closely patients and nurses agree when rating the patient's pain, worry and knowledge?**
A. Harrison, H. K. Al-Awadi, A. A. Busabir. *Journal of Advanced Nursing*, vol. 24, no. 2 (1996), p. 229-35.

A study of 50 hospital patients who had experienced nursing care from two nurses, one of whom shared their mother-tongue of Arabic and the other who did not, to assess the level of agreement regarding pain, worry and knowledge. The main significant difference was in relation to the pain ratings, where the mother-tongue nurse's ratings correlated with those of the patients.

272 **The reactions of patients and doctors in the United Arab Emirates towards smoking.**
Ann Harrison (et al.). *Journal of Addictive Diseases*, vol. 15, no. 1 (1966), p. 75-92.

A survey of 50 smokers and 50 non-smokers who rated their own risks of developing heart disease, arthritis, and having a car accident. Smokers were optimistic about their risks, whereas non-smokers were pessimistic about their chances of having heart disease or a car accident. A study was also undertaken with 41 male smoking doctors and 41 male non-smoking doctors over two hypothetical patients, one obese and the other having contracted lung cancer. Compared with smokers, the non-smoking doctors expected to be more uncomfortable in dealing with the smoking patient who was considered more responsible for his condition than the obese patient.

273 **The prevalence and correlates of anaemia among young children and women of childbearing age in Al Ain, United Arab Emirates.**
M. M. Hossain (et al.). *Annals of Tropical Paediatrics: International Child Health*, vol. 15, no. 3 (1995), p. 227-35.

During 1992 and 1993, 309 children aged 1-22 months who visited an immunization facility in Al-Ain City, Abu Dhabi, were studied along with their mothers to: define blood haemoglobin levels; estimate the prevalence of anaemia; examine the role of iron deficiency in causing anaemia; identify the correlates of anaemia prevalence; assess the acceptability to parents of an anaemia screening test for young children. The results of the study revealed that iron deficiency is probably the predominant cause of anaemia in young children and women of reproductive age in Al-Ain. The authors conclude that the widespread prevalence of anaemia needs constructive action.

274 **Implementation of the global strategy for health for all by the year 2000, Second evaluation: Eighth report on the world health situation: vol. 6, Eastern Mediterranean region.**
Alexandria, Egypt: World Health Organization, 1996. ix+261p.

Deals with the second evaluation of national health strategies in the Eastern Mediterranean region, including the United Arab Emirates, and shows that there are good prospects for achieving 'health for all by the year 2000'. The report examines the following issues: socio-economic development trends; health care and trends in health-care coverage; health resources; patterns and trends in health status; health and development; and assessment of achievement.

275 **Hospital airborne microbial pollution in a desert country.**
A. A. Jaffal (et al.). *Environment International*, vol. 23, no. 2 (1997), p. 167-72.

A report on a study of indoor airborne microbial pollution in Al-Ain hospital using a bacterial air sampler. The research team found that the largest quantity of isolated micro-organisms were unidentified bacteria, though the number of potentially pathogenic organisms was low. The highest counts were obtained in the paediatric ward and in the female medical wards.

276 **Neonatal sepsis in Dubai, United Arab Emirates.**
A. Koutouby, J. Habibullah. *Journal of Tropical Paediatrics*, vol. 41, no. 3 (1995), p. 177-80.

Reports on the results of an examination of the case records of all neonates admitted to Al Wasl hospital in Dubai from May 1987 to April 1992. It was revealed that 106 of the children admitted had sepsis. Prematurity, low birthweight and nosocomial sepsis were high-risk factors associated with fatal outcomes.

277 **Contribution of body fat and fat pattern to blood pressure level in school children.**
M. A. A. Moussa (et al.). *European Journal of Clinical Nutrition*, vol. 48, no. 8 (1994), p. 579-90.

The data in this article were based on a survey of 220 obese and 220 non-obese schoolchildren aged 7-18 years from Al-Ain in the United Arab Emirates. The survey was conducted over the period September 1992 to May 1993. Each group consisted of 120 males and 120 females from two schools which were randomly selected from primary, junior and secondary levels. The detailed clinical results of the survey are presented.

278 Factors associated with obesity in school children.
M. A. A. Moussa (et al.). *International Journal of Obesity*, vol. 18, no. 7 (1994), p. 513-15.

Describes a controlled case-study of 220 obese and 220 non-obese children from the ages of 6 to 18. The survey took place in Al-Ain, between September 1992 and May 1993. The criteria used in the study are listed, together with the questions covered by the questionnaire. Analysis of the data showed that family history of obesity, diet, physical activity and maternal education were all significant factors for development of obesity, and that smoking and socio-economic status were not related to obesity.

279 Anaemia among 6 year old children in the United Arab Emirates.
A. O. Musaiger. *European Journal of Clinical Nutrition*, vol. 50, no. 9 (1996), p. 636-37.

A report on tests conducted amongst 11,880 children aged from 6 to 6.9 years old in the school year 1994-95. It showed that the total prevalence of anaemia was 31 per cent. Boys were found to be more susceptible than girls and nationals were more likely to have anaemia than non-nationals. Results suggested that anaemia had declined between 1981 and 1995 and that programmes to prevent and control anaemia were to be recommended.

280 Breastfeeding patterns in the Arabian Gulf countries.
A. O. Musaiger. *World Review of Nutrition and Dietetics*, vol. 78, no. 1 (1995), p. 164-90.

A study of breastfeeding in the Arab Gulf countries, including the United Arab Emirates. Amongst other topics, it deals with breastfeeding practices; weaning practices; factors affecting breastfeeding age and education of mother, geography, employment, role of housemaids and health workers, and sex of child; activities to encourage and support breastfeeding; and marketing of baby foods.

281 Aetiology of onychomycosis in Al Ain, United Arab Emirates.
H. Nsanze. *Mycoses*, vol. 38, nos. 9-10 (1995), p. 421-24.

A study was conducted over a period of a year on 151 patients with toenail or finger diseases who were attending a dermatology clinic in Al-Ain. Nail scrapings or chippings were collected and investigated for direct microscopy and fungi. This article presents the detailed results.

282 Learning preferences of medical students.
Sarla Paul (et al.). *Medical Education*, vol. 28, no. 3 (1994), p. 180-86.

An investigation into the learning preferences of 58 first-, second- and fourth-year medical students in the United Arab Emirates, and the difference in learning preferences between first- and second-year students, and first- and fourth-year students. The results from using the Learning Preferences Inventory showed no differences in learning preferences amongst the three groups. They also revealed that students preferred teacher-structured experiences dealing with concrete examples rather than abstract tasks. Female students preferred more teacher-oriented programmes and practical learning, whilst male students preferred to work with other students, or in groups. The fourth-year students indicated a preference for teacher-oriented learning but they also liked abstract and individual learning, indicating a more mature approach to the learning process.

283   **The role of medicinal plants in the health-care system of the United Arab Emirates: past, present and future.**
S. Paul (et al.).   *Acta Horticulturae*, no. 332 (1993), p. 145-51.

Discusses the historical background leading to the current state of herbal therapy in the United Arab Emirates. The authors also considers the structure of the health-care system, the direction of future strategies, and the possible uses of medicinal plants or their active constituents.

284   **Acute schizophrenic episode: is it a culture-related syndrome?**
Omar E. El-Rufaie.   *Acta Psychiatrica Scandinavica*, vol. 73, no. 3 (1986), p. 263-65.

A study of 25 labourers aged 20-45 years in Abu Dhabi. They all had psychiatric problems, with symptoms of sleeplessness, disordered or violent behaviour, and thought disorders. The subjects were Pakistani, Iranian or Indian and, although other nationalities work under stressful conditions, it is suggested that cultural factors play a role in the development of this syndrome.

285   **Minor psychiatric morbidity in primary health care: prevalence, nature and severity.**
Omar E. El-Rufaie, Gamel H. Absood.   *International Journal of Social Psychiatry*, vol. 39, no. 3 (1993), p. 159-66.

Reports on the usage of the Clinical Interview Schedule to investigate the prevalence, rate, nature and severity of minor psychiatric disorders amongst 217 United Emirates nationals attending a primary health-care centre in Al-Ain. Amongst the findings was that the morbidity rate was higher among females than males and among the 35 to 54-year-old age group. The overall severity level amongst the 37.6 per cent identified patients was mild to moderate.

286   **Retesting the validity of the Arabic version of the Hospital Anxiety and Depression (HAD) Scale in primary health care.**
Omar E. El-Rufaie, G. H. Absood.   *Social Psychiatry and Psychiatric Epidemiology*, vol. 30, no. 1 (1995), p. 26-31.

Describes a testing of the validity of the Arabic version of the Hospital Anxiety and Depression Scale on 217 patients aged 16-80 years attending a primary health-care centre in the United Arab Emirates. A single consultant psychiatrist screened the patients and the results were assessed against the same psychiatrist's clinical judgements. The findings were that the Arabic version was a valid instrument and that the depression scale was more accurate and predictive than the anxiety scale.

287 **Validity study of the Self-Reporting Questionnaire (SRQ-20) in primary health care in the United Arab Emirates.**
Omar E. F. El-Rufaie, Gamel H. Absood. *International Journal of Methods in Psychiatric Research*, vol. 4, no. 1 (1994), p. 45-53.

A study to determine the validity of the 20-item Arabic version of the Self-Reporting Questionnaire as a screening instrument for non-psychotic mental disorders in primary care. The Arabic version of the Hospital Anxiety and Depression Scale was used during the screening process, which involved 217 patients aged between 16 and 80 years. Interviews were conducted by a psychiatrist and it was determined that the Self-Reporting Questionnaire was a valid instrument for the detection of minor psychiatric morbidity in primary health-care settings. However, there were variations of sensitivity, specifically between men and women and between literate and illiterate subjects.

288 **High mortality among recipients of bought living-unrelated donor kidneys.**
A. K. Salahudeen. *Lancet*, vol. 336 (Sept. 1990), p. 725-28.

Describes a follow-up study made of patients from the United Arab Emirates and Oman who purchased kidneys from donors in Bombay. Salahudeen discusses clinical findings, the high mortality rate, and a classification of living donor transplantation.

289 **Polymerase chain reaction for diagnosis and identification of distinct variants of Crimean–Congo hemorrhagic fever virus in the United Arab Emirates.**
T. F. Schwaz (et al.). *American Journal of Tropical Medicine and Hygiene*, vol. 55, no. 2 (1996), p. 190-96.

This analysis of the re-emergence of viral haemorrhagic fever in the United Arab Emirates after 1993 also provides the results of tests on infected humans. The disease could have been carried by ticks on imported host animals.

290 **Iron deficiency in children in Um Al-Quwain, United Arab Emirates.**
R. M. Shawky, S. S. El Din. *Journal of the Egyptian Society of Parasitology*, vol. 12, no. 1 (1982), p. 217-24.

Reports on a study of 500 children under 6 years old, 46.6 per cent of them with anaemia. A number of other identified parasites are listed but not implicated in the anaemia.

291 **Antimicrobial and phytochemical screening of medicinal plants of the United Arab Emirates.**
M. O. Tanira. *Journal of Ethnopharmacology*, vol. 41, no. 3 (1994), p. 201-5.

Tanira analyses the use of 21 medicinal plant species for their antifungal and antibacterial activities against a number of diseases and ailments. These are listed, as are the names of the plants.

Health

292 **Evaluation of the relaxant activity of some United Arab Emirates plants on intestinal smooth muscle.**
M. O. Tanira. *Journal of Pharmacy and Pharmacology*, vol. 48, no. 5 (1996), p. 545-50.
This study of the effects on intestinal smooth muscle activity of extracts from 23 plants includes an analysis of their chemical composition and use their in traditional medicine in the United Arab Emirates. When tested on animals, the plants were found to have potential as sources of antispasmodic agents.

293 **Antiinflammatory activity of some medicinal plants of the United Arab Emirates.**
B. A. Wasfi. *International Journal of Pharmacognosy*, vol. 33, no. 2 (1995), p. 124-28.
Using rats as models, extracts from 22 plants used in folk medicine were tested for anti-inflammatory properties.

294 **World malaria situation in 1993. Part III. La situation du paludisme dans le monde en 1993. Part III.**
Weekly Epidemological Record, vol. 71, no. 5 (1996), p. 37-39.
This article, in English and French, is a review of the malaria situation in the part of Asia west of India. This region covers nine countries, including the United Arab Emirates.

295 **A profile of alcohol and drug misusers in an Arab community.**
Y. O. Younis, A. G. Saad. *Addiction*, vol. 90, no. 12 (1995), p. 1683-84.
This examination of the problem of alcohol and drug use in the United Arab Emirates is based on a survey of 747 male patients, aged 18-35 years, who were admitted as inpatients to a psychiatric ward over a two-year period. The survey revealed that 71 were found to have alcohol and drug disorders, and of these 33.6 per cent were repeated admissions and 93.4 per cent came as voluntary patients. The authors conclude that, in a society which is intolerant to alcohol drinking and drug misuse, motivation is essential for abstinence and spiritual force can be a major factor.

Student and faculty perceptions of the characteristics of an ideal teacher in a classroom setting.
See item no. 607.

Attitudes towards counselling in the Middle East.
See item no. 608.

Politics

296 Transformation amidst tradition: the UAE in transition.
John Duke Anthony. In: *Security in the Persian Gulf: 1. Domestic political factors*, edited by Shahram Chubin. London: Gower, for the International Institute for Strategic Studies, 1981, p. 19-37. map.

Anthony considers that the UAE has done well to survive for a decade, given the pessimism of observers at its birth. However, the author identifies a number of problems yet to be solved, the most important of which is the need for the federation to play a dominant role, particularly with regard to development.

297 Arabia without Sultans.
Fred Halliday. London: Penguin Books, 1974; New York: Random House, 1975. 527p. map.

This work gives a left-wing view of the political unrest in Arabia. The author aims to show the state of the working class under the authoritarian regimes of Arabia, the divisions in Arabian society, and the capitalist influences in the economies and politics of the Arabian Peninsula. The United Arab Emirates is considered with regard to British imperialism, the question of the oil economy, and the activities and significance of the Popular Front for the Liberation of the Arabian Gulf.

298 Arab politics: the search for legitimacy.
Michael C. Hudson. New Haven, Connecticut; London: Yale University Press, 1977. 434p. map.

A detailed analysis of political behaviour in the Arab world which asserts that the current problems in Arab politics are due to the insufficient legitimacy accorded by their people to their ruling structures, ideologies and leaders. In the first part of the book the Arab world is discussed as an entity, dealing with the Islamic identity, ethnic and religious minorities, the crisis of authority and the effects of Western imperialism and modernism. The second part of the study is a series of case-studies, with the United Arab Emirates considered as one of the modernizing monarchies.

Politics

299 Concepts of sovereignty in the Gulf region.
George Joffe.   In: *Territorial foundations of the Gulf States*, edited by
Richard Schofield.   London: UCL Press, 1994, p. 78-93.

An assessment of the concepts of sovereignty in the Gulf States. These are based primarily on British imperial policy which was determined by commercial control of the area and the need to access oil deposits. The status of the United Arab Emirates existed in an embryonic form by the end of the nineteenth century, but only as coastal trading and pearling posts. The present concepts of the states began to develop along with British interest in the area, primarily through treaty relationships and supervision from the local British Residency which began in 1763. The domestic affairs of the Trucial States were largely left to the tribal rulers, though Britain did adjudicate in disputes between the states and maintained strict control over foreign affairs. The crucial factor which changed this policy was the presence of oil, and Britain exerted pressure on all of the states to grant oil exploration concessions only to parties nominated by itself, with exploration beginning in Abu Dhabi in 1934. This meant that the hinterlands of the various states acquired a new significance in terms of their borders and the potential oil discoveries. The UAE's establishment in 1971 was undertaken with some territorial disputes still in being but territorial sovereignty has, instead, become the essential source of legitimacy for statehood in the Gulf.

300 The United Arab Emirates: its political system and politics.
Enver M. Koury.   Hyattsville, Maryland: Institute of Middle Eastern
and North African Affairs, 1980. 147p.

Koury's analysis of the complex relationships within the United Arab Emirates discusses the variables that could lead to greater integration or disintegration. He considers that the UAE will continue to develop with alternating periods of integration and stagnation, or even regression. The work is divided into five main sections: leadership and formation of the United Arab Emirates; problems of federation; the governing circle and decision-making body; the functional capabilities of the decision-making body; 'the captain and the ship'. The final section is an assessment of the role of President Zayed who, at all times, has sought to preserve the union and has succeeded in keeping the level of mass discontent and political dissidence to a bare minimum.

301 Arab nationalism and the Gulf.
Riad N. El-Rayyes.   In: *The Arab Gulf and the Arab World*, edited by
B. R. Pridham.   London: Croom Helm, 1988, p. 67-94.

This contribution deals with the implications of British withdrawal from the Arabian Gulf and the negotiations between the Gulf States which led to the formation of the United Arab Emirates, the question of regional security, and the formation of the Gulf Co-operation Council. The contribution concludes with a consideration of reform and democracy in the Gulf States which points out that liberalization will not mean democracy in the Western sense, but participation of the educated class who will wish to share in the decision-making and in responsibility for the development of the state.

302 **Politisches Lexikon Nahost/Nordafrika.** (Political lexicon of the
Middle East/North Africa.)
U. Steinbach, R. Hofmeier, M. Schonborn. Munich, Germany:
C. H. Beck, 1994. 3rd ed. 377p.

This German-language publication studies the present political system of all the countries in the region, including the United Arab Emirates, and covers historical development, social structures and economics. It also examines regional groupings such as the Organization of Petroleum Exporting Countries (OPEC).

Dissertations

303 **Political dependency: the case of the United Arab Emirates.**
Abdulkhalaq Abdulla. PhD thesis, Georgetown University,
Washington, DC, 1985. 370p. (Available from University Microfilms,
Ann Arbor, Michigan, order no. AAD86-06898).

An assessment of the internal political consequences resulting from the integration of the United Arab Emirates into the world capitalist system, and its emergence as a dependent and peripheral capitalist social formation. Abdulla argues that the dependency of the UAE is a product of a long history of colonialism, shaped by the prevailing authoritarian system, and by policies initiated and implemented by some distinct social classes and groups.

304 **International politics of the Persian Gulf States from a subsystemic core perspective.**
William Leroy Dowdy. PhD thesis, Tulane University, New Orleans,
1982. 571p. (Available from University Microfilms, Ann Arbor,
Michigan, order no. AAD82-26691).

An in-depth study of the underlying characteristics of the Gulf States, including the United Arab Emirates, dealing specifically with the relations between and among them during the 1970s.

305 **The United Arab Emirates: an assessment of federalism in a developing polity.**
Muhammad Salih Al-Musfir. PhD thesis, State University of New
York at Binghampton, 1985. 243p. (Available from University
Microfilms, Ann Arbor, Michigan, order no. AAD85-08851).

This study is an attempt to assess the development of federalism and the effectiveness of the federal government and its institutions from 1971 to 1984. In addition to the historical background to the United Arab Emirates and the implications of British withdrawal from the Gulf, the roles of the regional and global actors are discussed in relation to the UAE. A study is also made of the contrast between the UAE's constitutional provisions and the actual achievements of federalism in the areas of health provision, education and defence. The inter-relationships among the seven Emirates, and the extent to which they are participating in federalism, are also discussed.

Law and Constitution

306   Business laws of the United Arab Emirates, vols. 1-4.
Edited by Dawoud El-Alami.   London: Graham & Trotman, 1996.
2,300p. loose-leaf.

This work is now in its sixteenth edition and is produced in loose-leaf form and
updated by six-monthly supplements. The work provides a complete translation from
Arabic to English of the business laws, regulations, resolutions and decrees of the
United Arab Emirates. An indispensable work for anyone doing business in the UAE.

307   Islamic marriage and divorce laws of the Arab World.
Dawoud El-Alami, Doreen Hinchcliffe.   London and The Hague:
Kluwer, 1996. 298p.

El-Alami provides details of the provisions, both codified and uncodified, that apply to
marriage and divorce in Arab countries. In the case of the United Arab Emirates no
codes have been enacted and the doctrines of the locally applicable schools of Islamic
law are used in this area of personal status laws. This aspect is covered in Part 1 of the
work which deals with the uncodified law of Saudi Arabia and the Arab Gulf States,
and includes an introduction to the provisions with sections on marriage and divorce.

308   The laws of commercial procedure of the United Arab Emirates.
Edited by Dawoud El-Alami.   London: Graham & Trotman, 1994.
214p.

This work provides a translation and explanation of Federal Law no. 18 of 1993 which
was the culmination of a project aimed at producing comprehensive unification of all
areas of commercial activity. This major piece of legislation covers the following
topics: commerce in general terms; commercial obligations and contracts; and banking
operations.

309 **Bahrain–Iran, Iraq–Kuwait–Oman–Qatar–Saudi Arabia–United Arab Emirates: agreements from the Kuwait regional conference on the protection and development of the marine environment and the coastal areas.**
International Legal Materials, vol. 17, no. 3 (1978), p. 501-40.
The agreements, dealing with conservation, planning and prevention of pollution of the coasts and seas, were concluded at a conference held in Kuwait, 15-23 April 1978.

310 **Register of laws of the Arabian Gulf.**
William M. Ballantyne. London: Graham & Trotman, 1996. 1,500p.
This loose-leaf work provides a complete database of all laws and regulations originating in each country of the Arabian Gulf, including the United Arab Emirates. The register covers all laws and regulations from the commencement of legislative promulgation to date, and a subject-heading list is provided for each country. The work is updated by quarterly supplements.

311 **The law of business contracts in the Arab Middle East.**
Nayla Comair-Obeid. London and The Hague: Kluwer, 1996. 255p.
Although wider in coverage than the United Arab Emirates, this work is of relevance as it provides a detailed examination of the influence of Islamic law on modern legislation relating to trade, contracting, banking and financial operations. The work is divided into two parts: 'The Classical Contractual Islamic System'; and 'The Moral Code of Islamic Law in the Procedure of Legal Business Matters'.

312 **Federal code of procedure of the United Arab Emirates.**
Arab Law Quarterly, vol. 7, no. 4 (1992), p. 290-91.
A description of the new Code of Civil Procedure which is intended to govern the procedure of civil cases in all of the courts of the United Arab Emirates. It includes detailed rules covering all civil legal matters, but is particularly significant to the business community because of the code's comprehensive new rules on arbitration, conciliation, and amicable settlement of disputes.

313 **The arrest and trial of Malayali Indians in the United Arab Emirates: when performance, (inter)culture, and human rights collide.**
Jose George. *TDR* (Cambridge, Mass.), vol. 32, no. 2 (1994), p. 138-49.
Reports on the case of eleven Indian immigrants in Sharjah who were arrested and sent to prison for six years for performing a play called *The Corpse Eating Ants*. The main charge was that the play was blasphemous and an insult to the Muslim community. The article considers the human rights issues raised by the case, questions of freedom of expression, and multicultural issues. The article also has an interview with the playwright and provides information on the cultural context and history of Malay one-act plays.

314 **The civil code of the United Arab Emirates.**
Edited by Marjorie Hall, James Whelan. London: Graham &
Trotman, 1987. 404p.
An English translation, with explanatory notes, of the Civil Code in the United Arab
Emirates that came into effect in March 1986.

315 **Commercial and civil companies in UAE law.**
Sayed M. Hosni. *Arab Law Quarterly*, vol. 7, no. 3 (1992), p. 159-74.
This article begins by defining civil companies under the United Arab Emirates law
before examining the principles governing civil and commercial companies and dealing with the following aspects: formalities; capital; profits; relations between partners;
administration of the companies; responsibilities of partners; and liquidation. The article concludes by examining specific types of civil companies, namely: the Work
Company; the Prestige Company; and the Speculation Company.

316 **Changes to expedite business.**
Babul Parekh. *Middle East Economic Digest*, vol. 38, no. 18 (1994),
p. 53-54.
Legal development in the United Arab Emirates is having to respond to the development of the federation into an international business centre. Parekh examines changes
to the commercial code, companies law, intellectual property in relation to patents,
banking laws and the environment, together with a number of changes in other areas.

317 **The theory of contracts in Islamic law: a comparative analysis with
particular reference to modern legislation in Kuwait, Bahrain and
the UAE.**
Susan Rayner. London: Graham & Trotman, 1987. 304p. bibliog.
This volume examines the complex nature of contract law within Islam and provides
an analysis of these principles against the legislation enacted in the United Arab
Emirates to enable the economy to function in international markets.

318 **Commercial agency and distributorship in the Arab Middle East.**
Samir Saleh. London: Graham & Trotman, 1996. rev. ed. 580p.
This loose-leaf production covers the laws affecting agency and distributorship in the
Middle East, including the United Arab Emirates, and provides translations into
English of all the relevant key laws and regulations. The administrative practice relating to implementation is also covered, as is the absence of uniformity of legal principles, the lack of effective legal remedies upon termination of an agency, the
ministerial regulatory framework, and the influence of the *shari'a* on the laws of
agency and distributorship.

319 **Protecting intellectual property.**
Khaled El-Shahakany. *Middle East Economic Digest*, vol. 40, no. 20
(May 1996), p. 42-43.
The growth of the entrepôt trade in the United Arab Emirates, and Dubai in particular,
had led to the federation becoming a base for the distribution of counterfeit goods or

pirated copies. The federal government has recognized this problem and laid the legal bases to counter the activity and it intends to enforce the legislation. The relevant legislation is the Trade Mark Law no. 37 of 1992, and the Protection of Intellectual Works and the Rights of the Author Law no. 40 of 1992, both of which came into force in 1993. The article reviews the two laws and comments on practical implementation and enforcement issues. Under Law no. 37, trade marks are initially protected for ten years, renewable for ten-year periods, with control vested in the Ministry of Economy and Trade, and enforcement through local administrative action. Law no. 40 is administered by the Ministry of Information and Culture, which is responsible for the deposit of protected works and maintenance of the register. Enforcement measures include the power to search and confiscate goods and the means of copying, but subsequent proceedings are left to the general principles of law.

Dissertations

320 **The system of arbitration in the UAE: problems and prospects.**
O. S. Busit. PhD thesis, Durham University, England, 1991. [n.p.]. (Available from the British Library, Boston Spa, Wetherby, West Yorkshire).
Discusses the growth of business disputes resulting from rapid economic growth and the problems of the legal system which could not provide reliable and expeditious resolution of the legal actions. Busit recognizes the need for a system of arbitration which must be capable of being enforced by the courts in a straightforward and reliable manner.

321 **The role of the Supreme Court in the constitutional system of the United Arab Emirates – a comparative study.**
H. R. Al-Owais. PhD thesis, University of Durham, England, 1989. [n.p.]. (Available from the British Library, Boston Spa, Wetherby, West Yorkshire).
A study aimed at determining the importance of the Supreme Court in the constitutional system of the United Arab Emirates, by discovering its possible contributions to constitutional development and then making recommendations to improve the effectiveness of the Court. The author provides an analysis of the modern history of the UAE and the characteristics of the individual societies. He also reviews the role of the constitutional court within each federal system and draws on the examples of other similar systems to determine how its effectiveness could be improved.

Women and the law in the United Arab Emirates.
See item no. 232.

Administration and
Local Government

322 **A cross-national perspective on managerial problems in a
     non-Western country.**
     Abbas J. Ali, Ahmed Azim.   *Journal of Social Psychology*, vol. 136,
     no. 2 (1996), p. 165-72.

An examination of managerial problems in the United Arab Emirates, comparing the
perceptions of expatriate managers with the indigenous managers. The survey used a
questionnaire completed by 201 managers from seven private, state and government
service organizations. It posed questions on both subjective and objective managerial
problems. The results showed that foreign expatriates scored higher on both subjective
and objective problems and that they took more notice of subjective problems such as
personal loyalty at work, bad timekeeping, primacy of personal over work relationships, and weakness in research and theory. The major objective problems identified
were the centralization of authority, and inadequate planning and information systems.

323 **Arab bureaucracies: expanding size, changing roles.**
     Nazih Ayubi.   In: *The Arab state*, edited by Giacomo Luciani.
     London: Routledge, 1990, p. 129-49.

As part of this contribution, Ayubi examines bureaucratic growth in the Gulf States,
including the United Arab Emirates. The main concentration is on Abu Dhabi and
illustrates the growth in the administration – 2,000 were employed in 1968, rising to
24,078 by 1993, of which 83.6 per cent were non-nationals. Ayubi also considers the
bureaucracy of the federal government which had quadrupled between 1972 and
1982. However, budgetary constraints in the 1980s resulted in a halt to the growth of
this sector.

324 **Development and development administration in the UAE: a case study.**
Abel Kale Nassau. *Journal of the Gulf and Arabian Peninsula Studies*, vol. 15, no. 57 (1989), p. 97-146.

An Arabic-language study of development administration in the United Arab Emirates as part of a project evaluating administrative reform agencies in the member states of the federation. Data were collected using field visits and interviews, conducted between January and February 1988. Public administration officials, informed individuals and official documents were all involved. The focus of the study was on: development challenges in the UAE; the UAE administrative system; problems facing the administration and possible solutions; and the contribution of agencies to the resolution of problems. Nassau concludes that development suffers as a result of the poor definition of objectives and policies, and from the inadequacy of the goals, organization, functions and resources of administrative development agencies. He recommends a review of planning strategies to formulate a new plan for administrative development. This lengthy article is accompanied by tables.

325 **Government and administration in the United Arab Emirates.**
A. Rashid. *Bulletin of Arab Research and Studies*, vol. 6 (June 1975), p. 71-85.

An assessment of the administrative infrastructure of the federation that also examines the relationship between the federal and the state structure.

Foreign Relations

326 **Oil power and politics: conflict in Arabia, the Red Sea and the Gulf.**
Mordechai Abir. London: Cass, 1974. 221p. maps.

Deals with relations between the Arab states and the degree of intervention by outside powers which has resulted from the presence of oil. The United Arab Emirates is dealt with in relation to the birth of the federation and the decisions of the states of Bahrain and Qatar to remain outside the new union. Abir also considers the question of stability in the Gulf and the possible consequences if the federation should not succeed.

327 **The foreign policy of the United Arab Emirates.**
Hassan Hamdam Al-Alkim. London: Saqi Books, 1989. 306p. maps. bibliog.

An extremely detailed study of the foreign policy of the United Arab Emirates since its birth in 1971. The work considers the establishment of the UAE, and provides a history of the Gulf States from the sixteenth century to 1971, with particular emphasis on Britain's withdrawal from the Gulf providing the impetus for the establishment of the federation. The elements of foreign-policy making are dealt with through a consideration of: the domestic political and social factors, including strengthening of the federal structure; the significance of the migrant population; the social structure of the federation; internal factors affecting unity; and the dynamics of political aggregation. The work continues by examining external factors affecting foreign policy in terms of the regional context and the role of the superpowers in the region, and this is followed by an examination of the process and apparatus for determining foreign policy. Part III presents three significant case-studies: UAE–Saudi Arabian relations 1971-83, with particular reference to border disputes and regional security which directly influenced the evolution of relations; UAE–Iran relations 1971-83, with particular reference to Iran's perceived role as policeman of the Gulf, disputes over the ownership of islands in the Gulf, the impact of the Iranian revolution, and the impact of the Iraq–Iran war; and the UAE's commitment to the Palestine question 1971-83, which considers the determining factors behind the policy, the relationship to Arab policy on Palestine, attempts to influence other governments, and relations with Palestinian liberation

movements. The appendices reproduce: the Federation of Arab Emirates; Agreement
of 27 February 1968; and Steps towards Co-operation between the conservative Gulf
States, 1973-81. This study has a comprehensive bibliography and numerous notes,
and was based on extensive interviews with personalities involved in the determination of the foreign policy of the UAE.

328　**The GCC States in an unstable world: foreign-policy dilemmas of
small states.**
Hassan Hamden al-Akim.　London: Saqi Books, 1994. 234p. maps.
bibliog.

An examination of the strategic importance of the member states of the Gulf Co-operation Council, which is solely due to their ownership of 60 per cent of the world's
proven oil reserves. The author traces the theme that in the 'new world order' the
GCC has become heavily dependent upon foreign powers, particularly the United
States, for its survival. Amongst the topics considered are: the framework for foreign
policy issues; the historical legacy; political and social dynamics; strengths and weaknesses within the GCC; inter-state relations; the turbulence of the region; the implications of the new world order; and the decision-makers of foreign policy. There are
numerous references to the United Arab Emirates throughout the text, particularly in
relation to the oil industry, the Abu Dhabi Fund for Arab Economic Development,
inter-state border disputes within the GCC, Iran's claim to Abu Musa Island, and the
strengths and weaknesses of the economy. Specific appendices of relevance are: the
UAE–Saudi Agreement on Security Co-operation; the Unified Economic Agreement
between the countries of the GCC; and the Oil Concession Agreement between Ras
Al-Khaimah, the Union Oil Exploration and Production Company and the Southern
Natural Gas Company.

329　**Small islands, big politics: the Tunbs and Abu Musa in the Gulf.**
Edited by Hooshang Amirahmadi.　London: Macmillan, 1996. 262p.
maps. bibliog.

A study of the dispute between the United Arab Emirates – in particular Sharjah and
Ras al-Khaimah – and Iran over ownership of these islands in the Arabian Gulf. The
islands have a strategic significance but Abu Musa is also contested because of its
hydrocarbon reserves from which Iran currently receives a share of revenues, despite
the century-old dispute that surfaced again in 1992.

330　**Shared zones as a solution to problems of territorial sovereignty in
the Gulf States.**
Gerald Blake.　In: *Territorial foundations of the Gulf States*, edited by
Richard Schofield.　London: UCL Press, 1994, p. 200-10. maps.
bibliog.

An examination of the phenomenon of shared zones in the Arabian Gulf, which were
often introduced as a means of temporarily resolving territorial disputes, but which
have been in place for a number of years and seem to be working well. In terms of the
United Arab Emirates this contribution considers the Abu Dhabi–Dubai neutral zone
established in 1961 and the Abu Dhabi–Qatar maritime boundary established in 1969.
Other arrangements are also listed, covering shared zones between: Sharjah–Oman;
Fujairah–Sharjah; Ajman–Oman; and Iran–Sharjah; and seabed agreements covering:
Abu Dhabi–Qatar; and Iran–Sharjah.

331　**Body-building Iran (aggressive international stance).**
The Economist, vol. 324, no. 7777 (1992), p. 75-77.
Discusses the involvement of Iran in international disputes, including one with the
United Arab Emirates, over the Abu Musa strait in the Arabian Gulf.

332　**Maritime delimitation in the Gulf.**
Rodman R. Bundy.　In: *Territorial foundations of the Gulf States*,
edited by Richard Schofield.　London: UCL Press, 1994, p. 176-86.
map.
A study of the maritime boundary situation in the Arabian Gulf which is complicated
by the fact that coasts are separated by less than 400 nautical miles and by the presence of islands, preventing any state from enjoying its full complement of continental
shelf or exclusive economic zone, as determined by the yet-to-be adopted UN
Convention on the Law of the Sea. Bundy deals with individual settlements including
those between Abu Dhabi and Dubai of 1968; Abu Dhabi and Qatar of 1969; Iran and
Abu Dhabi (no date); and Iran and Dubai – this is complicated by the claim to Abu
Musa and the Tunbs islands by Iran and Sharjah. The work concludes with a review of
outstanding disputes primarily in the northern Gulf and the previously cited disputed
islands. The whole subject has achieved greater significance because of the question of
ownership over mineral rights in offshore areas and across boundaries.

333　**Hostages of fortune: the future of Western interests in the Arabian
Gulf.**
Michael Cunningham.　London: Brassey's Defence Publications,
1988. 138p. maps.
Cunningham's study of the problems faced by the Western powers in guaranteeing
access to the oil reserves of the Arabian Gulf, highlights the economic, political and
strategic difficulties. The United Arab Emirates is dealt with as part of the region and
as a member of the Gulf Co-operation Council. Amongst topics covered are: Arabian
Gulf hydrocarbon reserves; the Gulf States as a market-place for Western goods;
superpower interests in the region, the economic impact of oil and regional stability;
the perspective of the Gulf States in the Iraq–Iran war; the threats to Gulf security and
options for the West. A chronology of the Iraq–Iran war is provided as an appendix.

334　**Kuwait and the Gulf: small states and the international system.**
Hassan Ali Al-Ebraheem.　London: Croom Helm; Washington, DC:
Centre for Contemporary Arab Studies, 1984. 117p. bibliog.
An analysis of the foreign policy and economic factors governing the activities of
small states, particularly Kuwait and the other Gulf States, including the United Arab
Emirates. There are references to the UAE throughout the text, covering the oil market
and the economy, and in Chapter Six in particular which deals with the Gulf Co-oper-
ation Council.

335　**Desert Shield to Desert Storm: the second Gulf War.**
Dilip Hiro.　London: HarperCollins, 1992. 591p. maps. bibliog.
This analysis of the Gulf War begins with the premiss that it was a direct descendant
of the Iraq–Iran war, caused by the build-up of Iraqi military forces from 242,250 in
1980 to 1,200,000 by 1988, and by indebtedness to the Kuwaiti government for about

£14 billion. In terms of the United Arab Emirates consideration is given to Iraq's view that the federation was partially responsible for the decline in the price of oil due to overproduction. Iraq was also in debt to the UAE as a result of interest-free loans made during the Iraq–Iran war. In terms of the Gulf War the work discusses the presence of French ground forces and United States air forces in the United Arab Emirates, loans to the Soviet Union, and the possibility of internal destabilization caused by oil revenues being concentrated in the hands of the ruling families.

336   **The New Arab Cold War.**
Hilal Khashan.   *Journal of Social, Political and Economic Studies*,
vol. 21, no. 4 (1996), p. 431-53.
An examination of what Khashan describes as the 'New Arab Cold War' which includes rifts within the Gulf Co-operation Council and the struggles within Iraq, as well as relations between Egypt and Sudan. He considers that the two major factors affecting these fronts are economic problems and the rise of Islamic Fundamentalism.

337   **Hydrocarbons and Iranian policies towards the Arab Gulf States: confrontation and co-operation in island and continental shelf affairs.**
Keith McLachlan.   In: *Territorial foundations of the Gulf States*,
edited by Richard Schofield.   London: UCL Press, 1994, p. 223-38.
A study of the territorial aspirations of Iran and the Gulf States which centres on the hydrocarbon reserves in the offshore areas and around the various islands in the Arabian Gulf. It is also contended that competition for hydrocarbon reserves has been the main factor behind intra-Gulf and border arrangements following Britain's withdrawal from the Gulf in 1971. The main consideration of relevance to the United Arab Emirates deals with the problem of Iranian claims to Abu Musa and the Tunbs, claims which had surfaced again in 1992 and heightened the suspicion of the Arabian states regarding Iranian attentions in the Gulf.

338   **Britain's moment in the Middle East.**
Elizabeth Monroe.   London: Chatto and Windus; Toronto, Canada:
Clark Irwin, 1981. 2nd ed. 254p. maps. bibliog.
This is an important work for the study of Britain's position in the Middle East from 1914 to 1971. The section of relevance to the United Arab Emirates is the chapter entitled 'Nightfall' (p. 207-19) which deals with Britain's withdrawal from the Gulf and the establishment of the federation of the United Arab Emirates following negotiations which began in 1968 and ending with Bahrain and Qatar deciding to become independent.

339   **The Gulf Cooperation Council: policies, problems and prospects.**
Emile A. Nakhleh.   New York: Praeger, 1986. 128p.
An introductory study of the Gulf Co-operation Council (GCC) which attempts to assess the impact of the organization on the security and stability of the Gulf region. The work begins with a background description of the member states, including the United Arab Emirates, and provides a brief description of the GCC charter and by-laws. The study continues with an examination of the regional role of the organization through the perceptions of the six leaders, though the emphasis leans heavily towards

the views of Bahrain. The volume also contains a summary of five studies covering development issues relating to publicly owned projects, bureaucracy, industry, education, and demographic questions.

340 **Political stability in the Gulf Cooperation States.**
Emile A. Nakhleh. *Middle East Insight*, vol. 6 (Winter 1989), p. 40-46.
Nakhleh examines the sources of legitimacy of the ruling families of the member states of the Gulf Co-operation Council which includes all of the member states of the United Arab Emirates. He also covers the concept of regional co-operation as represented by the GCC and the challenges faced by the organization, and includes a list of the ruling families in each of the GCC states.

341 **Regional military involvement: a case study of Iran under the Shah.**
Maqsud Ul Hasan Nuri. *Pakistan Horizon*, vol. 37, no. 4 (1984), p. 32-45.
Following British withdrawal from the Arabian Gulf, Iran undertook the task of policeman of the Gulf and demonstrated its intentions by two military interventions. The first was in the Dhofar Province of Oman at the request of the Sultan, and the second the seizure of Abu Musa Island which belonged to Sharjah and the Greater and Lesser Tunbs which belonged to Ras al-Khaimah.

342 **The Gulf Cooperation Council: search for unity in a dynamic region.**
Erik R. Peterson. Boulder, Colorado; London: Westview Press, 1988. 346p.
A comprehensive and systematic account of the Gulf Co-operation Council's development and its progress towards political and economic integration. The first part of the work considers the historical links and rivalries between the member states, common links in terms of political structures and common institutions, as well as the role of regional instability in the formation of the GCC. Part two examines the ideological reasons for co-operation amongst the member states, including the role of Arabism and the tendency of the Gulf States to support pan-Arab interests. In addition to general coverage of the United Arab Emirates, the work deals briefly with the economy, finance, educational developments, health, the infrastructure, the development of the oil industry, and relations with Egypt, the Soviet Union, and the United States.

343 **The foreign policy of the United Arab Emirates.**
William A. Rugh. *Middle East Journal*, vol. 50, no. 1 (1996), p. 57-70.
The United Arab Emirates regards Iran as the biggest threat to its security as a result of traditional rivalries in the Gulf, the arms build-up in Iran, and the regime's support for terrorism. Disputes over the Gulf islands of Abu Musa, and the Greater and Lesser Tunbs islands are symbols of this distrust as they have little intrinsic value other than their strategic location, with only Abu Musa having a limited amount of oil. The UAE is still part of the international coalition against Saddam Hussein and supports the Arab–Israeli peace process, though without taking an active role in it. The Gulf Co-operation Council is regarded by the UAE as a cornerstone of its foreign policy and support is also given to the Arab League. At the same time, the UAE maintains

good relations with the United States and other Western powers as a means of securing assistance to protect its security, particularly in case of a conflict with Iran, though
foreign bases are not allowed and sovereignty is not compromised.

344 **Iraqi invasion of Kuwait and UAE's political orientations.**
     Jamal S. Sanad. *Journal of South Asian and Middle Eastern Studies*,
     vol. 18, no. 2 (1994), p. 51-64.
Based on a survey of 399 students after the Iraqi invasion of Kuwait in 1991 which
showed that most felt Iraq's claim was unfounded and that Saddam Hussein was
clearly the aggressor. However, the students also aligned themselves with Islam rather
than pan-Arabism or the Emirates.

345 **Borders and territoriality in the Gulf and the Arabian Peninsula
     during the twentieth century.**
     Richard Schofield. In: *Territorial foundations of the Gulf States,*
     edited by Richard Schofield. London: UCL Press, 1994, p. 1-77.
     maps.
A study of the territorial framework of the Gulf States and its evolution during the
period of Britain's treaty relations with the sheikhdoms from the nineteenth century to
withdrawal from the Gulf in 1971. In terms of the United Arab Emirates this contribution deals with the complex boundaries in the area which were largely set in the late
1950s by British authorities in the Gulf. The Political Agents attempted to delimit the
respective tribal territories of the various sheikhdoms in an attempt to bring greater
stability to the area and to prevent future war between the various ruling families.
Agreement was reached between all of the states except for boundaries between
Sharjah and Ras al-Khaimah with the Sultanate of Oman, but resolution was to come
in the late 1960s with the defining of neutral zones between the two Emirates and
Oman. Agreements were also reached between Saudi Arabia and Abu Dhabi over
access to the Gulf and, in 1993, all UAE territorial disputes with Oman were deemed
to have been resolved. In terms of Iran, consideration is also given to the continuing
long-standing claims by Iran to the islands of Abu Musa and the Greater and Lesser
Tunbs which had been ongoing for over a century but had arisen again in 1992.

346 **Territorial foundations of the Gulf States.**
     Edited by Richard Schofield. London: UCL Press, 1994. 256p. maps.
This work covers all aspects of boundary formations in the Arab Gulf States, including the problem of offshore boundaries and the significance of hydrocarbon reserves.
Disputed areas, shared zones, and problems with Iran are considered at length. Each of
the relevant contributions from the volume is separately annotated in the appropriate
section (see, for example, items 332, 337, 345).

347 **The Arab Gulf States and Japan: prospects for co-operation.**
     Edited by Walid Sharif. London: Croom Helm, 1986. 216p.
This series of contributions examines the growing relationship between the Arab Gulf
States, as represented by the Petroleum Information Committee, and Japan. About 65
per cent of Japan's oil imports come from the Arabian Gulf; Japanese exports to the
Gulf are also rising and by the mid-1980s accounted for 8 per cent of exports. The
work deals with the Arabian Gulf on a regional basis and covers: security of oil

supplies; oil prices and marketing; research and development, training; the economics of petrochemical industries and co-operation between the Gulf States and Japan. In terms of the United Arab Emirates specific mention is made of the Abu Dhabi aid programmes, dependence on the oil economy, and Japanese petrochemical projects in the federation.

Dissertation

348 **The impact of arms and oil politics on United States relations with the Arabian Gulf States, 1968-78.**
Abdul-Reda Ali Assiri.   PhD thesis, University of California at Riverside, 1981. 324p. (Available from University Microfilms International, Ann Arbor Michigan, order no. AAD81-22892).

An assessment of the increased role adopted by the United States following Britain's withdrawal from the Arabian Gulf. The basis of the interdependence is on arms and oil, with oil revenues enabling the Gulf States, including the United Arab Emirates, to engage in extensive arms purchases and to play the role of United States surrogate in the region. In domestic terms interdependence operates on a dual pattern with oil revenues being utilized to provide a sedative for social, economic and political problems.

Oil, the Persian Gulf States, and the United States.
See item no. 444.

Regional Security

349 **Military security and political stability in the Gulf.**
Gawdat Bahgat. *Arab Studies Quarterly*, vol. 17, no. 4 (1995), p. 55-70.

An analysis of the military security challenges faced by the member states of the Gulf Co-operation Council in the early 1990s. These included financial pressures caused by reduction in oil revenues, and an overall rise in military expenditure due to political uncertainty in the region. Further problems were caused by the policies of the Western powers in the region aimed at preserving access to oil supplies, and political unrest resulting both from Iraqi policies and from suspicion over Iranian activities in the Gulf.

350 **The Gulf Cooperation Council's security role.**
Ursula Braun. In: *The Arab Gulf and the Arab World*, edited by B. R. Pridham. London: Croom Helm, 1988, p. 252-67.

This contribution analyses the potential and limitations of the Gulf Co-operation Council states with regard to the creation of an effective defence force, their concept of security, and internal and external security efforts since its establishment in 1981.

351 **Bahrain, Oman, Qatar and the UAE: challenges of security.**
Anthony H. Cordesman. Boulder, Colorado: Westview Press, 1997. 423p.

This work is an examination of the changing economic and internal security challenges faced by the Arab Gulf States and, in particular, the problems they face in their relations with Iraq and Iran. The United Arab Emirates is initially covered in the opening chapter entitled 'The Southern Gulf States', dealing mainly with problems of the economy, demography and social development, strategic needs and vulnerability, differences and similarities. This section is backed by a series of relevant charts and tables. The United Arab Emirates is also dealt with specifically in Chapter 5 (p. 290-383) with a wide-ranging survey of issues which were dealt with collectively in Chapter 1. In terms of the federation the work deals with its establishment, the federal structure, the leadership, the role of the Consultative Council and individual Emirates, and power movements within the UAE. Security is examined from both the internal and external viewpoint, covering rivalries within the ruling families, divisions within the federation, relations with the other Gulf States, problems to be confronted with Iraq and Iran, and relations with the West, Russia and the former states of the Soviet Union. In the case of Iran, the crisis over the ownership of Abu Musa and the Tunbs islands is treated as a specific case-study. The economy is considered in relation to oil and gas production and reserves, downstream and petrochemical industries, trade, moves towards economic diversification, agriculture and the problems of water constraints, and the reliance on migrant labour which has attendant security implications. The financial status of the federation is also considered in relation to cash reserves, budget deficits, and the cost of sustaining the welfare state. The last section of this chapter deals solely with military aspects and covers the military forces in general and levels of expenditure and inputs, prior to dealing with the Army, the Air Force and the Navy. Finally, the question of paramilitary and security forces is considered, together with the strategic interests of the federation, the need for greater co-operation and military cohesion, and the long-term need to sustain economic development and indigenous labour.

352   The military implications of the Gulf Cooperation Council.

Brian E. Fredericks.   *Military Review*, vol. 67, no. 1 (1987), p. 70-77.

Assesses the joint defence plan of the Gulf Co-operation Council which addresses arms procurement policy, joint military co-operation, and quick-reaction facilities. The author considers that implementation of the plan would increase the capabilities of the member states to resist incursions from hostile neighbours.

353   Gulf Cooperation Council: the security policies.

Laura Guazzone.   *Survival*, vol. 30, no. 2 (1988), p. 134-48.

Discusses the establishment and policies of the Gulf Co-operation Council and considers threats to its continued existence, both internal and external.

354   Arabia imperilled: the security imperatives of the Arab Gulf States.

Mazhar A. Hameed.   Washington, DC: Middle East Assessments Group; London: Croom Helm, 1986. 188p. bibliog.

This important volume provides a very detailed examination of the security implications of the area, and considers amongst other topics: the geopolitics of Gulf security; the security environment; the security resources of the Gulf States; problems of security and gaps in provision; and United States interests in the Gulf. In terms of the United Arab Emirates consideration is given to the air strength of the federation, land forces, military resources and infrastructure, oil revenues, inter-state rivalry, relations with the Soviet Union, and general background information. The Gulf is seen as one of three critical areas affecting Western strategic interests because it is threatened by radical pressures, internal tensions and Soviet interests, and possesses fifty per cent of proven oil reserves.

355   The Gulf Cooperation Council: containing the Iranian revolution.

Joseph A. Kechichian.   *Journal of South Asian and Middle Eastern Studies*, vol. 13, nos. 1-2 (1989), p. 146-65.

An examination of the collective and individual responses of the Gulf Co-operation Council States, including the United Arab Emirates, to the revolutionary threats from

Iran. The threat was particularly worrying for those states with significant Shi'ite minorities.

356 The Persian Gulf and the West: the dilemmas of security.
Charles A. Kupchan.   London; Boston, Massachusetts: Allen & Unwin, 1987. 254p. bibliog.

The Persian Gulf is used as a case-study to examine the post-war debate about regional security because of growing Western dependence upon its oil reserves, and as a centre of United States–Soviet competition for regional influence. The objective of the work is to examine how the Western community, in particular the United States, has defined and dealt with security interests in the Gulf. In terms of the United Arab Emirates there are relevant sections dealing with the attempts to create a Gulf-wide defence network, with military capability, and with the UAE as a member of the Gulf Co-operation Council.

357 Defending Arabia.
J. E. Petersen.   London: Croom Helm, 1986. 275p. bibliog.

This work is an examination of the defence of the Arabian Gulf as a vital strategic concern from the time of the earliest British involvement to the Iraq–Iran war. British interest in the Gulf was initially concerned with the protection of the sea routes to India and reinforced by its use as a staging-post with the development of air routes. The implications of British withdrawal from the Gulf in 1971 are also considered, as is the replacement of these interests by American interests, set against a backcloth of regional concerns and intra-regional conflicts. In terms of the United Arab Emirates the work deals with its formation, threats to its continuing existence, the military capabilities of the federation, and the composition of the Union Defence Force.

358 The Gulf Cooperation Council – oil and survival.
Ian Skeet.   In: *The politics of Middle East oil: the deliberations of the Royaumont Group*, edited by Paul Tempest.   London: Graham & Trotman, 1993, p. 34-38.

A study of the security problems of the Gulf Co-operation Council states set in the context of the significance of their hydrocarbon reserves and strategic location. The political situation is also examined in relation to external support, primarily from the United States, based on the question of security of oil supplies and the internal problems of education, maintenance of social services, trade, and industrial diversification. Skeet concludes that, from all aspects whether economic, social or strategic, the GCC requires that oil remains vital to international development in order to survive as an entity.

359 Close-out sale at Commerce.
Kenneth Timmerman.   *American Spectator*, vol. 28 (Aug. 1995), p. 36-41.

A report on the moves by Republicans in the US Congress to have the Department of Commerce abolished, the major reason advanced being that it had engaged in illegal practices through the sale of sensitive technology to hostile countries. The United Arab Emirates is cited as being a base for front companies established by Iran whose sole purpose was to provide false end-user documentation to enable high-tech goods to be purchased from the United States. Various cases of orders that had 'gone missing' once imported into the UAE are cited in support of these allegations.

Dissertations

360   **The Gulf Cooperation Council: Arabia's model of integration.**
Ghalib Tulhab Etaibi.   PhD thesis, Boston College, Chestnut Hill,
Massachusetts, 1984. 269p. (Available from University Microfilms,
Ann Arbor, Michigan, order no. AAD 85-10684).
An analysis of the foundation and emergence, in 1981, of the Gulf Co-operation
Council which is regarded as unique amongst contemporary integrative schemes. The
thesis identifies the relevant local, regional and international factors that helped to
shape the GCC. The United Arab Emirates is a key member of the GCC and in terms
of the local forces related to the GCC the traditional religio-political systems of the
Gulf States are examined, together with the implications of dependence on hydrocarbons, and the presence of large migrant populations who were in the majority within
the UAE. Amongst the regional factors considered are the Arab League, Arab nationalism, and the Islamic revolutionary movement in Iran, and its impact on the Shi'i
populations within the Arab Gulf States.

361   **The Gulf Cooperation Council: search for security in the Persian
Gulf.**
Joseph Albert Kechichian.   PhD thesis, University of Virginia,
Charlottesville, Virginia, 1985. 596p. (Available from University
Microfilms, Ann Arbor, Michigan, order no. AAD86-15597).
This study examines the conservative governments of the Gulf Co-operation Council's
(GCC) search for regional security in the Persian Gulf. The threats to the member
states are analysed in relation to the policies being pursued by Iran, Israel, the Soviet
Union and its proxies, and Iraq, and the author considers that they represent a real
challenge to the security and stability of the GCC. The capabilities of the GCC to
respond to these threats in military and non-military terms are examined, as are relations with external powers who could contribute to their defence, though there may be
domestic problems to be faced as a result of the development of special relationships.
Finally, the reactions of the GCC to perceived regional threats are also examined, in
particular, the Iraq–Iran war, the Arab–Israeli conflict, the threat from the Soviet
Union, and the potential sources of political dissidence within member states.
Although the GCC had adopted a number of joint policies the states did not respond,
or initiate action, on the Iranian revolution, the Palestine conflict, the Soviet occupation of Afghanistan, the Gulf War, or the Israeli invasion of Lebanon.

Economy

362 Abu Dhabi, United Arab Emirates.
Financial Times (16 April 1989), p. 39-42. maps.
Primarily, this survey centres on the economy following the easing of regional tensions, increased safety of the Gulf sea lanes and stability in oil prices, all of which had created a mood of confidence amongst business people. A major consideration within business is the diversification of the oil-dependent economy.

363 Annual Report.
Abu Dhabi Fund for Arab Economic Development, 1972- . annual.
The annual report of the fund provides background information on the structure of the fund, government projects administered by the fund, and projects under consideration. Financial statistics relating to the year in question are also provided.

364 Dubai.
Robin Allen, Nicholas Hills. *Financial Times*, no. 32208 (3 Nov. 1993), Special Section p. 1-4.
An assessment of the economic growth of the Emirate of Dubai, which has a comprehensive infrastructure, funded by oil revenues. The government had established a strong position within the federation, but was concerned with maintaining the strength of the economy, both through investment in the road network and through promotion of investment by its Economic Department. At the same time the ruling family has maintained political stability and freedom from the pressures of Islamic conflicts.

365 The Gulf Cooperation Council.
John Duke Anthony. *International Journal* (Canada), vol. 41, no. 2 (1986), p. 383-401.
Assesses the Gulf Co-operation Council, which was initially founded as an economic union modelled on the European Community with the objective of promoting economic and political co-operation in the region. Anthony examines the perception of

individual political vulnerability and concludes that the modern states are quite stable, particularly in terms of longevity of leadership and absence of civil unrest. The GCC can ensure oil supplies to the West only with external military and technical support.

366 From tents to high rise: economic development of the United Arab Emirates.
S. N. Asad-Rizvi. *Middle Eastern Studies*, vol. 29, no. 4 (1993), p. 664-78.

An examination of the economy of the United Arab Emirates which stresses dependence upon the oil industry, expatriate labour, and the world oil market. However, considerable investment has been made in the financial, industrial and transport sectors, with a view to utilizing oil revenues to diversify the economy.

367 The Arab Gulf economy in a turbulent age.
Hazem Beblawi. New York: St Martin's Press, 1984. 241p.

Argues that the existence of the Gulf Co-operation Council had at this time (ca. 1984) a long way to go before it could be considered to be a political and economic reality. The author argues that a long history of fragmentation, political disputes, internal feuds, and boundary problems cannot be eliminated at the stroke of a pen. Amongst the topics dealt with in detail are: the economy of Abu Dhabi; lack of development caused by dependence on oil; the size of the indigenous populations; and growing opposition to significant immigration to assist with nation building.

368 Debt difficulty is a thing of the past.
Middle East Economic Digest, vol. 40, no. 49 (1996), p. 47-48.

A report on the revival of the fortunes of Sharjah which had gone heavily into debt following the oil price reductions of 1985 and an inability to service loans taken out for infrastructure projects. The turning point was reached in 1992 with a rescheduling of loans with local banks and settlement of the gas payment dispute with the federal government over supplies to the northern Emirates. The economic situation was further improved with significant gas finds in the offshore Kahaif field, resulting in record production within the Emirate. Activity has risen since 1995, with a steady stream of public tenders, but conscious efforts are being made to ensure that the mistakes of the past are not repeated.

369 Arab development funds in the Middle East.
Soliman Demir. Oxford, England: Pergamon Press, for UNITAR, 1979. xvii+130p. bibliog.

A detailed study of Arab development funds such as the Abu Dhabi Fund for Arab Economic Development and the Arab Fund for Economic and Social Development in which the UAE is a major shareholder. The study looks at the recipients and projects for which funds have been used in relation to the policies of the funds. Demir also examines the administration of each fund, the control mechanisms and the charters under which they operate. Finally, consideration is given to the role of the funds, including that of Kuwait, in regional development.

370 **Economic problems of Arabian Peninsula oil states.**
Michael Field.   In: *Security in the Persian Gulf: 1. Domestic political factors*, edited by Shahram Chubin.   London: Gower, for the International Institute for Strategic Studies, 1981, p. 38-57.

Economic policies have been determined by the fact that oil is a non-renewable resource and that reserves must be conserved and the highest price exacted for production. At the same time the oil states, including the UAE, have been investing the revenue from oil and gas in industrial and economic diversification. At some stage the rate of progress will have to slow down and the state may become an institution which has to be supported through taxation rather than being an undemanding benefactor.

371 **Busy agenda covers all the Emirates.**
Angus Hindley.   *Middle East Economic Digest*, vol. 40, no. 20 (May 1996), p. 34-38.

A survey of the major current activity and forthcoming projects across all of the Emirates. It includes consideration of the major five-year investment programme of the Abu Dhabi National Oil Company at Ruwais in the oil and gas sectors, and major investment in generating and distillation projects. Also covered are telecommunications projects, civil construction, tourist infrastructure, airport expansion, and road construction.

372 **The cooperative movement in the United Arab Emirates: objectives and obstacles.**
M. Al-Jassin.   *Journal of Interdisciplinary Economics*, vol. 3, no. 2 (1990), p. 131-43. maps.

The co-operative movement in the United Arab Emirates is still in its infancy and faces obstacles to its development, primarily because its socio-economic role has not been fully understood by either the government or its members. The movement emerged as a result of the oil boom and has achieved a measure of success.

373 **Reach for the sky.**
Isamdar Karti.   *The Banker*, vol. 146, no. 839 (1996), p. 62-63.

The non-oil sector of the economy of the United Arab Emirates has continued to grow. It is dominated by construction, trade and the property market. In 1994 the non-oil sector accounted for 67 per cent of gross domestic product. The banking sector also increased business and in 1995 the value of bank shares rose and domestic loans grew by 10 per cent in the first half of the year, most of the increase going to the private sector.

374 **Edging away from oil dependency.**
Peter Kemp.   *Middle East Economic Digest*, vol. 38, no. 18 (1994), p. 33-35.

Examines the United Arab Emirates' plans to diversify the economy and to reduce dependence upon oil by channelling funds into new infrastructure projects providing power, water, roads, and public amenities. The fastest-growing sectors of the economy were in the construction sectors, real estate, transport and communications. Tight federal budgets were causing problems for the smaller Emirates, which depended upon federal investment, and it is clear that the private sector and not the state must meet the high expectations of young people. The elders were also concerned at values being imported from the West and the effects of rapid modernization on traditional culture.

375 **Frenzy of growth is easing up.**
Peter Kemp. *Middle East Economic Digest*, vol. 38, no. 18 (1994), p. 36-38.

Development of the United Arab Emirates economy had slowed down after a boom period up to 1993 and the economic windfall following the invasion of Kuwait had faded. The reduction in spending on major projects and a decline in the oil sector illustrate the slowdown, but the underlying soundness of the economy should mean a growth in the demand for goods and services. The article includes details of the 1993/94 Federal Budget and economic statistics from 1990 to 1993.

376 **Eye-catching economy slows down.**
Liz Kirkwood. *Middle East Economic Digest*, vol. 37, no. 48 (1993), p. 25-27.

From 1990 the United Arab Emirates had been riding a wave of prosperity, with a trade and construction boom providing a boost to the economy and attracting business from around the world. By the end of 1993, the federation was one of the region's leading markets with high living standards and a range of facilities not found elsewhere in the area. However, the prospects for 1994 were gloomier, and there was a perception that economic activity would slow down with, for example, Dubai's imports slipping back by 8 per cent. The article includes statistical data from the Emirates Industrial Bank.

377 **The profits of peace and prosperity.**
Liz Kirkwood. *Middle East Economic Digest*, vol. 37, no. 18 (1993), p. 29-31.

The period after Iraq was ousted from Kuwait was prosperous for the region and, in particular, the United Arab Emirates: Abu Dhabi's oil and gas sector was subject to major expansion, and trade in Dubai was booming. However, defence was still seen as a major concern as evidenced by the Gulf Co-operation Council's summit discussions in December 1993 and purchases of defence equipment increased because of on-going security concerns. In domestic policies, the UAE was increasing popular consultation through the revival of the Federal National Council which had last met in 1991 and had more teeth than other consultative assemblies.

378 **Oil revenues in the Gulf emirates: patterns of allocation and impact on economic development.**
Ali Khalifa Al-Kuwari. Boulder, Colorado: Westview Press; London: Bowker, 1978. xxiv+218p. bibliog.

Covers the four countries of Bahrain, Kuwait, Qatar and the United Arab Emirates, ending with the situation as of 1970. The work covers pre-oil history, the development and growth of oil revenues, factors determining the allocation of oil revenues, the impact of oil revenues on economic development, and the need for alternative approaches.

379 **Arab institutionalized development aid: an evaluation.**
Ragaei El Mallakh, Mihssen Kadhim. *Middle East Journal*, vol. 30, no. 4 (1976), p. 471-84.

An examination of the various organizations set up to provide aid from surplus oil revenues, including a consideration of the fund administered by Abu Dhabi. The article provides an overall survey, analyses the objectives of the various funds, assesses the quality of aid, and discusses the various problems.

380 **The economic development of the UAE.**
Ragaei El Mallakh. London: Croom Helm, 1981. 215p. maps.

A useful introduction to the economic policies and problems of the UAE, offering a comprehensive review of past, present and future economic facts and issues. In addition to discussing the policies for social and economic development and the strategy for public investment, the work provides a number of useful statistical tables.

381 **The Jebel Ali Free Zone in the Emirate of Dubai: a commercial alternative after the Gulf crisis.**
Rolf Meyer-Reumann. *Arab Law Quarterly*, vol. 6, no. 1 (1991), p. 68-78.

Dubai had, at the outset of the Gulf crisis, concentrated on its economy adopting a policy of 'business as usual' and looking to the future. However, UAE company law requires companies to have a local majority and the Jebel Ali Free Zone is seen as a perfect alternative, with companies enjoying far greater liberty. The article describes the commercial activities of the zone and details the Competent Authority and the available licences, the process of registration within the zone, and the methods of staffing for foreign companies operating within the zone.

382 **Mission to promote the post-oil vision.**
Middle East Economic Digest, vol. 40, no. 49 (1996), p. 42-45.

An examination of Dubai's development in the post-oil era with the World Trade Centre and the Jebel Ali free-trade zone and port seen as tangible signs of economic development. The Emirate has produced a five-year strategic plan based on achieving growth without the cushion of oil reserves. The basis for the plan has already been laid as Dubai has attained the status of regional centre for business, industry and a growing tourist industry. There is a more than adequate infrastructure in place and a very strong private sector, which will reduce the need for significant investment from the public sector to sustain development.

383 **Economic development and industrialisation in the United Arab Emirates.**
Abdul Rasaf Al-Murarek. *American Arab Affairs*, no. 32 (1990), p. 12-17.

This article examines the need for the economy to diversify in order to reduce dependence upon oil and to achieve a more stable and balanced growth. In addition to oil being a finite resource, it is also dependent upon the international oil market which, because of price fluctuations, makes orderly planning difficult. The contribution provides a brief historical introduction, before going on to consider the economic development of the 1980s and the moves towards industrialization. It covers: the

Economy

manufacturing sector; the non-metallic minerals production sector; the metal products
sector; construction industries; chemical industries; the food and beverage industry;
and other manufacturing. The author concludes that progress is being made, but that it
is essential for government and the private sector to work together if diversification is
to be successful.

384 **The welfare effects of oil booms in a prototypical small Gulf state.**
A. Al-Mutawa, J. T. Cuddington. *OPEC Review*, vol. 18, no. 3
(1994), p. 245-63.
Uses the United Arab Emirates as a case-study to examine the effects of 'booms and
busts' in the world oil market on the economy of a small Gulf state. The productive
structure of the economy, including the public sector, is also described. The authors
assess the role of OPEC and provide an analysis of the impacts of price changes and
oil quotas. They go on to query whether a small state is better off seeking price rises
or relaxed quotas, and also examine the effects of price fluctuations on goods and the
labour market, together with the welfare effects of government policy changes.

385 **Dilemmas of non-oil economic development in the Arab Gulf.**
Tim Niblock. London: Arab Research Centre, 1980. 36p.
The author has identified five dilemmas facing the Gulf States in devising coherent
development strategies: the distribution of national resources, which is unbalanced;
the size of the indigenous labour force; socio-economic change resulting from development; the size of the states as entities for forming cohesive planning units; and the
international implications of surplus oil revenues. The article appears in both English
and Arabic.

386 **The experience of the Abu Dhabi Fund in the aid process.**
Nasser Al Nowais. *Arab Gulf Journal*, vol. 4, no. 1 (1984), p. 7-17.
Considers the nature, size, and effectiveness of aid provided by the Abu Dhabi Fund
for Arab Economic Development to Arab, African, Asian and other developing countries. Statistical tables are included, showing the destination and size of aid packages.

387 **The United Arab Emirates: a lucrative oasis for business.**
S. S. Y. O'Grady. *Business Quarterly*, vol. 60 (Summer 1996),
p. 85-90.
This article focuses on the opportunities available to Canadian business in the United
Arab Emirates which, at the time of writing, had been under-exploited. The author
provides a brief survey of the federation – with a political, economic and social profile
– and an insight into culture and language. In terms of business, the article focuses on
the benefits of investing in the United Arab Emirates, problems of accessing the
market, and the attendant financial and management costs.

388 **Gulf economies still glitter.**
Edmund O'Sullivan, Angus Hindley, Charlotte Blum. *Middle East
Economic Digest*, vol. 38, no. 27 (1994), p. 2-4.
An examination of the economies of the Gulf Co-operation Council states, including
the United Arab Emirates, which were still vigorous despite the 1993 drop in oil
prices. The economy of the federation was expected to continue to grow despite cutbacks

in federal expenditure, thus reflecting the development of a trend towards a balanced economy between oil, trade and services. In terms of government investment in the construction sector, the balance was expected to shift to infrastructure development with more emphasis on power, power distribution, water desalination and sewage.

389 **The philosophy of aid – a question of priorities.**
South, no. 15 (Jan. 1982), p. 71-73.
A report on the workings of the Abu Dhabi Fund for Arab Economic Development (ADFAED) in assisting developing countries with soft loans over a fifteen- to twenty-five-year repayment period. The philosophy behind the establishment of the ADFAED was that of helping the poor, both Muslim and non-Muslim, with priority being given to projects involving industrial undertakings and infrastructure development.

390 **Gulf aid and investment in the Arab World.**
R. S. Porter. In: *The Arab Gulf and the Arab World*, edited by B. R. Pridham. London: Croom Helm, 1988, p. 189-213.
A study of Gulf aid to the Arab World which includes a consideration of the work of the Abu Dhabi Fund for Arab Economic Development established in 1971. The contribution concentrates on aid provided in the form of general support assistance or finance for development projects. Statistical data are included. The geographical areas to which aid was distributed are examined, largely in relation to foreign-policy objectives, including aid to the front-line states in the struggle against Israel.

391 **The United Arab Emirates through the 1990s: fitful recovery ahead.**
Sarah Searight. London: Economist Intelligence Unit, 1990. 104p. map. (Special Report, no. 2020).
This special report examines the economy and development process within the United Arab Emirates and attempts to predict future prospects. Searight begins by considering the federation, its dependence for finance on Abu Dhabi, and the role of the federal government. Amongst the subjects considered are: society and politics; planning and the welfare state; federal finances; energy; industrial diversification; trade; construction and infrastructure; the economic outlook; and the evolution of the business environment.

392 **Gulf's dream.**
Patrick Smith. *International Management*, vol. 49, no. 6 (1994), p. 32-33.
A survey of all the major economies of the Middle East which had been suffering from declining oil revenues and two decades of uncontrolled expenditure. Dubai is seen as an exception on account of the diversification of its revenue base and its expanding role as the new entrepôt of the region.

393 **Smooth ride on the road to success.**
Middle East Economic Digest, vol. 39, no. 48 (1995), p. 32-35.
A review of the economy of the United Arab Emirates which continued to show no signs of slowdown and looked set to accelerate to a five-year high in 1996. The

growth was largely based on an increase in oil prices, and the buoyancy of the non-oil sector. Continued economic development and stability had been largely determined by the ability of Abu Dhabi and Dubai to maintain a high level of public expenditure, especially in the area of capital projects.

394 Trying ways of spreading wealth.
Middle East Economic Digest, vol. 40, no. 49 (1996), p. 39-40.

The economy of Abu Dhabi has made it one of the richest states in the world. It contributes 90 per cent of the federal budget and supplies external assistance through the Abu Dhabi Fund for Arab Economic Development. However, beneath the surface it is still a conservative, traditional society, and oil riches have tended to reinforce this. The Emirate is considering a policy of privatization, which is not driven by cash flow problems but as a means of spreading wealth in the community. A further argument in favour of the programme is that it could provide much-needed investment opportunities to satisfy the aspirations of the growing population.

395 UAE: falling oil revenues will hit aid.
Middle East Economic Digest, vol. 27, no. 10 (March 1983), p. 60-63.

The Abu Dhabi Fund for Arab Economic Development (ADFAED) was still able in 1983 to meet existing commitments, but declining oil revenues had meant a reduction in new loans, with a possible halving of the revenue available. During the period 1971-81 the ADFAED lent 950 million dollars and gave a further 470 million dollars for Third World projects. By 1979 aid had reached twenty per cent of the gross domestic product of the United Arab Emirates.

396 Major companies of the Arab World.
Edited by J. Wassall. London: Graham and Whiteside, 1992. 21st ed. 1,470p. (Also available on CD-ROM).

This work covers 7,000 of the largest companies in the Arab World, including the United Arab Emirates. It is organized alphabetically by country. The data provided for each company gives: company name; address, phone, fax, e-mail and telex numbers; names of major executives; business activities; branches and agencies; subsidiaries and associated companies; brand names and trademarks; number of employees; financial data; principal shareholders; and date of establishment. The work is accessible alphabetically by country, by company name and by business activity, including Standard Industrial Classification.

Dissertations

397 **The theory of foreign direct investment in capital-rich, labour-short economies: the case for Saudi Arabia, Kuwait and United Arab Emirates.**
Mohammad A. Ghanayem.   PhD thesis, Southern Methodist University, Dallas, Texas, 1981. 104p. (Available from University Microfilms, Ann Arbor, Michigan, order no. AAD81-28586).

Ghanayem's analysis of foreign direct investment in capital-rich, labour-short countries, including the United Arab Emirates, used three models. The first model examined the emergence of the multinational corporations and showed that the overall capital utilization and the national income of the host country increased. The second was expanded to include training agreements between the host country and the multinationals that proved beneficial as the increased productivity of the national trainees reduced the harmful effect on the country's national income. The final model concentrated on the migrating labour force from neighbouring countries and showed that such an emergence would reduce the host countries' utilized capital but increase the size of the migratory labour force.

398 **The east coast of the United Arab Emirates: an evaluation of economic activities and future prospects.**
S. S. H. Saif.   PhD thesis, University of Durham, England, 1992. [n.p.]. (Available from the British Library, Boston Spa, Wetherby, West Yorkshire).

A study of the economy of the eastern coastal area of the United Arab Emirates up to the border with Oman, an area which has no oil deposits. During the pre-oil period, fishing and farming were the main activities, whilst in the oil era there was also significant migration for employment to the oil states of Abu Dhabi and Dubai. The eastern coast has received considerable investment in new facilities, seaports, airports and other infrastructure facilities, and there were plans to exploit the natural resources of the Jajar mountains.

399 **The applicability of the theory of customs unions to the case of the Cooperation Council for the Arab States of the Gulf.**
Abdulaziz Ali Suleiman As-Sudais.   PhD thesis, University of Colorado at Boulder, 1985. 343p. (Available from University Microfilms, Ann Arbor, Michigan, order no. AAD85-22640).

One of the major objectives of the Gulf Co-operation Council (GCC) is regional economic integration, which the organization has chosen to approach in a gradual manner. This study investigates the applicability of the theory of customs union to the GCC at the time of writing. The economies of the member states have similar characteristics, with reliance on oil, petrochemicals, and little diversity in industrial production. However, it is pointed out that genuine integration will be achieved only if strict co-ordination of industrial plans, policies and regulations is achieved, as that is more urgently required than customs union.

Economy. Dissertations

The impact of arms and oil politics on United States relations with the Arabian Gulf States, 1968-78.
See item no. 348.

Oil, the Persian Gulf States, and the United States.
See item no. 444.

Policies for development: attitudes towards industry and services.
See item no. 491.

Finance and Banking

400 Loan boom puts system to the test.
Edmund Blair. *Middle East Economic Digest*, vol. 39, no. 31 (1995), p. 5-9.
The banking sector in the United Arab Emirates had been showing vigorous growth, but in the domestic sector competition had been fierce in the development of a lucrative personal loan sector. However, concerns were being expressed at the abandonment of prudent financial ratios and the lack of market depth. A further major concern is the growth of a credit culture in the 1990s, and the possibility that banks could leave themselves overexposed. This led the Central Bank to encourage banks to spread their risks.

401 Burying BCCI.
The Economist (London), vol. 321 (30 Nov. 1991), p. 76.
Discusses the reconvening of the High Court in London to dissolve the Bank of Credit and Commerce International (BCCI) and to approve an agreement whereby the depositors would obtain more compensation from the Sheikh of Abu Dhabi than from the sale of BCCI assets. This is one article of several which appeared in the international press and economics/news magazines.

402 Banking in the Middle East: structures of finance.
Andrew Cunningham. London: Financial Times, 1996. 2nd ed.
This updated edition provides a comprehensive coverage of banking in the Middle East and the rapid change in the banking system, including the new regulatory regimes developed to control the sector. The work begins with an introductory chapter, which covers the Middle East in general, and the development of the financial markets, the role of the banking system, the regulatory framework, and leading banks in the Middle East. The United Arab Emirates is dealt with in Chapter 22, where we find: an introduction; structure and size of the banking system; the role of the Central Bank and the regulatory framework; financial markets in the United Arab Emirates; and profitability and performance of the banking sector. Also of relevance is Chapter 2 which provides

a market overview of the Gulf Co-operation Council, and Chapter 10 on the subject of Islamic banking.

403 **Middle East market (Banking).**
A. Dixon. *Banking Technology*, vol. 5, no. 1 (1988), p. 46-48.
Discusses the automation of the banking sector in the United Arab Emirates and the use of high-tech products as an aggressive marketing tool. This is not in response to public demand, but because banks are chasing retail customers. The ATM (automatic teller machine) is the most popular product.

404 **An end in sight.**
Economist (London), vol. 330 (3 Dec. 1994), p. 87.
Deals with the announcement by the Bank of Credit and Commerce International's liquidators, Touche Ross, that the Abu Dhabi government was prepared to waive claims against the bank and to pay over to the assets $1.8 billion. The resultant settlement, if approved by the courts, would give creditors about 20 per cent of their claims. This is included as a sample of the extensive press coverage of this matter.

405 **Importance of foreign investment for the long-run economic development of the United Arab Emirates.**
Y. H. Farzin. *World Development*, vol. 21, no. 4 (1993), p. 509-21.
Assesses the economic needs of the United Arab Emirates after oil has run out and concludes that, if living standards are to be maintained, investments must be made that yield high rates of return. Domestic investments are severely limited by structural bottle-necks, thus increasing reliance upon an active programme of foreign investments. However, foreign investment had followed a risk-free strategy leading to a portfolio with highly liquid assets offering negligible rates of return.

406 **The relationship between bank managers' beliefs and perceptions towards automation of services: a comparative study of the UAE national vs foreign banks.**
K. E. Ghorab. *International Journal of Information Management*, vol. 15, no. 6 (1995), p. 437-50.
Presents the results of a survey of 38 bank managers in the United Arab Emirates, 16 national and 22 foreign, to investigate their perceptions towards automation. Ghorab found that national bankers adopted automation in the expectation of enhancing their assets utilization, whereas foreign bankers were striving to improve their equity multiplying effect. Both sets of bankers perceived improved quality of services, improved operations accuracy and reduced customer complaints as the most important benefits of automation. The most significant problems were identified as systems security, staff training and customer awareness.

407 **Giving credit where it is due.**
Economist, vol. 334 (2 April 1995), p. 68-69.
A report on the approval by a Luxembourg court of a $1.8 billion compensation scheme from the government of Abu Dhabi in connection with the liquidation of the Bank of Credit and Commerce International (BCCI). The proposal would enable

some 250,000 creditors to obtain payments covering about 20 per cent of their losses. This article is included as a representative sample of the numerous articles on the demise of BCCI.

408 Taken for a royal ride.
J. Greenwald, J. Beaty (et al.). *Time*, vol. 138 (22 July 1997), p. 46-48.

Examines the role of Sheikh Zayed in purchasing the Bank of Credit and Commerce International (BCCI) in 1990 and the impact of the closure by liquidators in the following year. The institution had suffered from two decades of fraud by its Pakistani managers and neglect by the regulatory authorities world-wide. The Sheikh had invested $1 billion in an attempt to shore up the bank but was facing the humiliation of losing control of the institution and ending up with a moral obligation to compensate depositors who were victims of the fraud.

409 An analytical study of the balance of payments of the GCC countries, 1970-1983.
F. I. al-Habib, M. M Metwally. *Asian Profile* (Hong Kong), vol. 14, no. 1 (1986), p. 61-72.

Presents an analysis of the balance of payments and other economic factors of the Gulf Co-operation Council states during the years of oil price rises and declines. The authors show the effects of such fluctuations and outline the need for greater co-operation and controls.

410 High returns from a haven of trade.
Middle East Economic Digest, vol. 40, no. 31 (1996), p. 5-6.

A report on the buoyant banking sector in the United Arab Emirates responding to a growing economy fuelled by Abu Dhabi's oil revenues and Dubai's trade flows. The economy is still primarily oil-based, but the commercial activities of Dubai have done a great deal to reduce reliance on oil revenues. The marketing approaches of the various banks are also discussed.

411 Boom year will be hard to better.
Angus Hindley. *Middle East Economic Digest*, vol. 39, no. 20 (1995), p. 40-42.

A review of the performance of the banking sector in the United Arab Emirates in 1994 which, although fiercely competitive, was a year of bumper profits. Banks elsewhere were affected by soft oil prices and turmoil in the bond and equity markets, but the UAE sector was cushioned by the buoyancy of the local construction industry, services and trade. Total assets grew by almost 5 per cent. Tables are included.

412 Sailing on as others slow down.
Angus Hindley. *Middle East Economic Digest*, vol. 39, no. 20 (1995), p. 25-27.

Dubai Investments was floated to promote investment in local companies within the federation and achieved a positive response with the issue of 71.5 million shares.

413 **Central Bank sets a stricter regime.**

Peter Kemp. *Middle East Economic Digest*, vol. 38, no. 18 (1994), p. 40-41.

The banking sector in the United Arab Emirates has grown rapidly and become essential to the country's success as a major trading centre, accounting for about 50 per cent of gross domestic product. The Central Bank has begun to play a more assertive role by setting rules and standards in order to allay international concerns about the credibility of the sector.

414 **Offshore banking – competition hots up.**

Josh Martin. *Middle East*, no. 259 (Sept. 1996), p. 19-21.

Concerns over stability in Bahrain and Lebanon had led many banks to question whether they should remain in those countries. Dubai was being considered as a potential offshore banking centre.

415 **Most banks move ahead steadily.**

Middle East Economic Digest, vol. 40, no. 31 (Aug. 1996), p. 7-10.

A special report on banking in the United Arab Emirates which shows that the sector as a whole produced good results in 1995, though the factors behind performance levels vary slightly in each Emirate. In Abu Dhabi, banking business has long depended upon oil and infrastructure projects and this sector continues to be active; major investment is planned by the Abu Dhabi National Oil Company, and there are plans to create a free zone on the island of Saadiyat near Abu Dhabi city. In Dubai the four major banks saw net profits rise by twenty-five per cent largely through Dubai's trading activities in overseas markets, including the former Soviet Union. Activity in Sharjah was modest because of the restructuring of the government debt, but medium-sized industrial growth was aiding the sector. The remaining Emirates showed smaller levels of activity and produced mixed performances.

416 **Looking east: a new style in retail banking.**

Patricia Oris. *Bank Marketing*, vol. 36 (Nov. 1994), p. 39-45.

An assessment of the effect of the Mashreq Bank's (formerly the Bank of Oman) introduction of retail principles into its marketing in Dubai. The marketing techniques included personal interactions with customers, co-ordinated market research programmes, development of lifestyle products targeted at specific groups, and a heavy investment in new technology.

417 **Banking beehive builds a honeypot.**

Edmund O'Sullivan. *Middle East Economic Digest*, vol. 38, no. 31 (1994), p. 7-10.

An examination of the banking sector in the United Arab Emirates. It is largely centred on Dubai where the banks are more attuned to the fluctuations of the market, whereas in Abu Dhabi the response is to the wishes of the government. The combined assets of the UAE banking sector are greater than the gross domestic product of the UAE and, in the Arab World, are exceeded only by Saudi Arabia. However, it is recognized that there are too many banks and that mergers are desirable.

418 **Keep the ball rolling (United Arab Emirates developing into an important financial center in the Middle East).**
Mark Selway. *The Banker*, vol. 147, no. 851 (1997), p. 62-64.
Describes the emergence of the United Arab Emirates as a financial centre in the Middle East, with the Central Bank implementing measures to boost banking activity, including revision of the banking law. The growing emergence is being fuelled by its trading history, expansion of neighbouring markets, and investment in infrastructure projects. However, at the time of writing the contribution of the banking industry to the economy was not significant.

419 **The Gulf capital markets at a crossroads.**
Jean-François Seznec. *Columbia Journal of World Business*, vol. 30 (Fall 1995), p. 6-14.
A survey of capital markets and financial organizations in the Gulf States, except in the case of the United Arab Emirates where only the latter are considered. The market is gradually being liberalized by governments anxious to utilize private savings to finance economic growth, in order to maintain standards of living and offset declines in cash reserves.

420 **Finance and international trade in the Gulf.**
Ahmed Al-Suwaidi.   London: Graham & Trotman, 1994. 480p.
This work is wider in coverage than the United Arab Emirates as it covers the whole of the Arab Gulf region. It examines the Islamic banking system in the area, which includes the UAE, and addresses the methods of financing and investing in international trade within both the Islamic and the conventional banking systems. The work also examines existing *shari'a* principles and the current empirical practices of the Islamic banks.

Dissertation

421 **Banking in the United Arab Emirates.**
D. McGratton.   MSc thesis, Heriot-Watt University, Edinburgh, 1993.
[n.p.]. (Available from the British Library, Boston Spa, Wetherby, West Yorkshire).
At the time of writing (1993) banking was still a relatively new activity in the United Arab Emirates. This review of the sector was based largely on personal interviews with bankers and academics in the UAE to assess the pace of, and prospects for, development.

Trade and Development

422 Expatriates' and national employees' perception of the role of MNCs in development.
A. J. Ali, A. Azim. *Journal of Transnational Management Development*, vol. 1, no. 2 (1994), p. 57-71.

An analysis of the views of expatriates and United Arab Emirates indigenous managers of the role of multinational corporations (MNCs) in national development in the areas of politics, culture, economy and technology. The research showed that expatriates have a negative attitude towards the role of MNCs whilst the indigenous managers value their role in development.

423 Dubai: an oasis of modern commerce.
Patricia M. Chandler. *Transportation and Distribution*, vol. 37, no. 2 (1996), p. 88-93.

An assessment of the significance of Dubai as a trade centre, built on centuries of tradition, but now reinforced by the modernization and development of its infrastructure. The Emirate has now assumed a regional significance which has been strengthened by the Jebel Ali free-trade zone, excellent port facilities, and the Dubai Cargo Village designed for the handling of air freight.

424 Customs tariffs rise.
Middle East Economic Digest, vol. 38, no. 32 (1994), p. 33-34.

Details the 4 per cent customs duty levied across the seven Emirates by the Federal Government over a range of imported goods. This was seen as a move to harmonize the countries' tariff rates with the rest of the Gulf Co-operation Council in preparation for a possible Gulf common market. The increase would also boost customs revenues at a time when oil revenues were low – the prediction was of a rise from $135 to $405 million in customs revenues.

425   Dubai: United Arab Emirates.

Financial Times (29 March 1989), p. 19-21. maps.

Examines the prospects for Dubai's trade following the cease-fire in the Gulf War between Iraq and Iran. It was seen as a test of skill in matching products with markets.

426   Gulf gateway expands its customer base.

Middle East Economic Digest, vol. 39, no. 7 (1995), p. 10-11.

A report on the increasing economic role played by Fujairah following the opening of an international airport in 1987 and a modern container port that opened for business in 1986. Growth in traffic was motivated by the Iraq–Iran war and the fears of shippers in relation to journeys to the upper Gulf States, along with a subsequent realization that there were economic benefits. It was considered cheaper to offload containers at Fujairah for onward transhipment by truck or feeder vessels to other destinations in Arabia, the Indian subcontinent and the Red Sea, and this greatly increased the attraction of the facility.

427   Horticultural products make a splash in Gulf countries.

J. Harman.   *AgExporter*, vol. 5, no. 7 (1993), p. 4-8.

Assesses the potential of the Gulf Co-operation Council member states as a market for horticultural products from the United States, though there was competition from Jordan and Iran which had lower transport costs. The United Arab Emirates is identified as a market concerned with both quality and price.

428   Jebel Ali.

Kings Lynn, England: Charter International, 1987- . annual.

This annual publication is produced in association with the Jebel Ali Free Zone Authority and Port Authority of Jebel Ali, and provides information on the activities of the zone and the port, including a wealth of statistical material.

429   Jebel Ali makes its mark.

Middle East Economic Digest, vol. 39, no. 14 (1995), p. S14-S17.

A report on the success of the port at Jebel Ali which had become the fourteenth most active port in the world; container traffic had expanded by 12 per cent between 1993 and 1994. The facilities offered are seen as central to the growth of the Emirate's economy and to helping to reduce the non-oil sector deficit.

430   UAE: hot contest as rivals vie for trade.

Liz Kirkwood.   *Middle East Economic Digest*, vol. 37, no. 12 (1993), p. 10-13.

Examines the intensifying competition between the east and west coast ports of the United Arab Emirates. The west coast ports of Port Rashid and Jebel Ali were still in the ascendancy, but the east coast ports of Khorfakkan in Sharjah and the port of Fujairah were rapidly closing the gap. The main bulk of the business handled was in the transhipment sector, with 50 per cent of handled goods being destined for the Indian subcontinent or the upper Gulf area.

431 **Oil, industrialization and development in the Arab Gulf States.**
Atif A. Kubursi. London: Croom Helm, 1984. 144p.
An examination of the problems faced by the Gulf States in trying to diversify away from oil and to plan for sustainable development when hydrocarbon reserves are exhausted. The United Arab Emirates is mentioned briefly as an entity but also within the context of the Gulf Co-operation Council, and is detailed in each of the statistical tables.

432 **Patterns of Arab Gulf exports: implications for industrial diversification of increased inter-Arab trade.**
R. E. Looney, D. Winterford. *Orient*, vol. 33, no. 4 (1992), p. 579-97.
Examines the contribution of industrial exports to the economic diversification of the states of the Gulf Co-operation Council, all of which have invested heavily in the creation of an individual infrastructure. However, success will need to be measured in the export market and the states face a number of problems, namely: lack of an integrated manufacturing base; parallel development of industries in mutual competition; growing diversity of income between oil producers and non-oil producers; and differential customs tariffs and quota systems. Inter-Arab trade has also declined and the author provides a series of recommendations for improving this trade as a basis for sustained industrial development.

433 **Cargoes of the East: the ports, trade and culture of the Arabian Seas and western Indian Ocean.**
Esmond Bradley Martin, Chrysee Perry Martin. London: Elm Tree Books, 1978. 244p.
An essential work on the dhow trade of the Middle East, with numerous references to Dubai in particular. It is extremely readable and highly informative, being especially of great value to the study of trade patterns with India and East Africa, the slave and spice trades, and smuggling activities. The book also contains a great deal on the traditions and cultures of the sailors and merchants and on the construction of their ships.

434 **Potential markets in the UAE.**
Nation's Business, vol. 80 (Oct. 1992), p. 52-53. map.
Aimed at encouraging US business to invest in the United Arab Emirates and to consider the federation as a good trading partner. Highlights the access that the UAE provides to markets elsewhere in the region, East Africa, and the Indian subcontinent. The aftermath of the Gulf War is also identified as having created a favourable environment for US business.

435 **Sharjah ports handbook.**
Downham Market, England: Charter International, 1985- . annual.
This annual publication is produced on behalf of the Sharjah Ports Authority and provides information on the activities of the port, including a wealth of statistical data.

436   **Shopping spree: liberated post-Soviet citizens flock to Dubai for bargains.**
      Yaroslav Trofimov.   *Far Eastern Economic Review,* vol. 58, no. 2 (1995), p. 50-51.

Reports on the flood of citzens from the Commonwealth of Independent States to Dubai. It began in 1993 and now averages about 50,000 visits a year to purchase consumer goods. The income from this trade currently represents 10 per cent of local GNP (gross national product) and has helped to offset declining oil revenues.

Dubai's wealth and the greening of the Emirates.

See item no. 34.

Oil

General

437 **Petroleum hydrocarbons in the nearshore marine sediments of the United Arab Emirates.**
Ahmad H. Abu-Hilal, Hosny K. Khordagui. *Environmental Pollution*, vol. 85, no. 3 (1994), p. 315-19.

A study of the pollution in the coastal waters off the United Arab Emirates, detailing the chemical composition of the water, composition of the sediments, the effects of wastewater discharge, and pollution from the oil industry.

438 **The petroleum geology of the United Arab Emirates.**
A. S. Alsharhan. *Journal of Petroleum Geology*, vol. 12, no. 3 (1989), p. 253-88.

A technical study of the petroleum geology of the United Arab Emirates and, in particular, the geology of the petroleum reservoirs, their formation, structure and reserves.

439 **Oil at the turn of the twenty-first century.**
Hooshang Amirahmadi. *World Future Society*, vol. 28 (June 1996), p. 433-52.

This examination of the interplay of market forces and politics in the world oil market to the year 2010 argues that oil demand will steadily increase, particularly in Asia. The proven reserves of the OPEC member countries, including the United Arab Emirates, would result in a substantially increased call on their oil production. However, declining investment in upstream projects could lead to supply constraints, increased prices, and an increasingly competitive market for Arabian Gulf oil, thus reinforcing the need for foreign investment to stabilize prices. The United Arab Emirates is considered to be one of the producers whose oil production levels and expansion plans will be restricted by shortages of capital.

440 **Arabs and their oil. Will they make it into petrochemicals?**
Earl V. Anderson. *Chemical and Engineering News* (16 Nov. 1970),
p. 58-72. maps.
A detailed article which looks at the various constituent parts of the petrochemical
industries and the prospects and problems for growth in the oil-producing states.

441 **The petroleum geology and resources of the Middle East.**
Z. R. Beydoun, H. V. Dunnington. Beaconsfield, England: Scientific
Press, 1975. 99p. maps. bibliog.
Deals with geology in general terms and then goes on to consider the conditions
specifically related to oil-bearing strata. The second part of the study discusses petroleum reserves in a global context, before examining the region specifically. In considering the UAE this work deals with the hydrocarbons of Abu Dhabi, Dubai and
Sharjah, which also have non-associated natural gas accumulations, and provides a
stratigraphical table for the area. Potential reserves are also considered, and in this
respect 20 per cent of the Abu Dhabi land area is thought to be highly promising.

442 **Middle East oil money and its future expenditure.**
Nicholas Fallon. London: Graham & Trotman, 1975; New York:
International Publications Service, 1976. 240p. maps. bibliog.
Begins by discussing the oil crisis of 1973-74 and its effects on oil prices and politics, and then projects these developments into the 1980s. The author examines the
major development and expenditure sectors and highlights problems and prospects
such as the lack of a middle-management resource. A country survey of development
plans is also given and the UAE is covered on pages 164-71. Fallon also considers
the banking system in the UAE (with a list of operating banks) and the role of Abu
Dhabi as an aid donor.

443 **Giant gas complex key to Abu Dhabi petroleum strategy.**
Oil and Gas Journal, vol. 94, no. 32 (1996), p. 27.
A description of the Bab/Hashan gas gathering and injection complex developed at a
cost of $1.35 billion. This is seen as a key element in a major investment programme
to bolster oil and gas production.

444 **Oil, the Persian Gulf States, and the United States.**
Vo Xuan Han. Westport, Connecticut: Praeger, 1994. 184p. map.
bibliog.
This work focuses on the post-Second World War relationship between the United
States and the member states of the Gulf Co-operation Council, including the United
Arab Emirates. The author concludes that this relationship will continue to strengthen
despite the end of the Cold War, largely because of the strategic nature of the region,
particularly in terms of oil supplies. His study of the economic realities of this relationship includes Arab investment in the United States, the politics of the petroleum
industry, and the complex nature of international business. The work is based on a
number of primary sources including United States government documents, OPEC,
International Monetary Fund, and United States Reports and Documents.

445 **Geology and development of Thamma Zone 4, Zakum Field.**
T. H. Hassan, Y. Wada. *Journal of Petroleum Technology*, vol. 33, no. 7 (1981), p. 1327-37.

The Zakum oilfield in Abu Dhabi is one of the six oil-bearing zones of the Thamma Group which consists of three well-defined, porous limestone reservoir units. Production from the zone started in 1967 and, to counter declining reservoir pressure, initially crestal water injection and later peripheral water injection was undertaken.

446 **Abu Dhabi branches out downstream.**
Angus Hindley. *Middle East Economic Digest*, vol. 39, no. 20 (1995), p. 30-32.

A report on the investment plans of Abu Dhabi for the oil town of Ruwais where $3,000 million are to be spent on new energy projects. The Supreme Petroleum Council announced plans to expand refining capacity and to develop a petrochemicals complex.

447 **Getting down to business at Ruwais.**
Angus Hindley. *Middle East Economic Digest*, vol. 40, no. 48 (1996), p. 16-17.

The Abu Dhabi National Oil Company (ADNOC) has formed a partnership with Borealis of Copenhagen to put together a petrochemical project at Ruwais, with the objective of producing 450,000 tonnes per year of polyethylene. This was planned as ADNOC's first venture into petrochemicals and the article discusses the setting up of the partnership, and the planned construction and capacity of the plants which are expected to be operational in 2000.

448 **OAPEC: an international organization for economic co-operation and an instrument for regional integration.**
Abdelkader Maachou, translated by Antony Melville. London: Pinter, 1983. 200p.

The Organization of Arab Petroleum Exporting Countries (OAPEC), of which the United Arab Emirates is a member, plays a crucial role in the oil industry, and in the economies of the member states. The work deals with OAPEC and its role in regional co-operation, as an institution for both sectoral economic co-operation and inter-Arab regional economic integration, and goes on to examine integration and the future of OAPEC. The appendices reproduce the Agreement of the Organization of Arab Petroleum Exporting Countries, and the Protocol of the Judicial Board of the Organization of Arab Petroleum Exporting Countries. The work also has a section of statistical tables relating to oil reserves, production, exports, and refining.

449 **The origin of oil and gas in onshore Abu Dhabi, UAE.**
Awad Mohamad, Ibrahim Ennadi. *American Association of Petroleum Geologists Bulletin*, vol. 79, no 8 (1995), p. 1236-37.

A study of the geological conditions which created the onshore oilfields in Abu Dhabi, including a consideration of the chemical composition of the rocks, the source rocks, spatial distribution of hydrocarbon deposits, and data interpretation.

450 **Power-play: the tumultuous world of Middle East oil, 1890-1973.**
Leonard Mosley. London: Weidenfeld & Nicolson; New York:
Random House, 1973. 369p. maps.
This work deals primarily with the development of the oil industry in the Middle East
and its inter-relationship with the politics of the area and international politics, from
the granting of the concessions and the interests of the various oil companies. Also
discussed are the political and economic changes, which took place after the transfer
of control from the oil companies to the producing nations. Chapter 25, entitled
'Tidying up' (p. 286-303), deals specifically with the British withdrawal from the
Trucial States and the steps leading to the establishment of the UAE.

451 **Operators close in on oil production goals.**
World Oil, vol. 215 (Aug. 1994), p. 97-106.
This report on the status of oil production in the Middle East in 1994 deals with the
pace of expansion in Abu Dhabi, the decline of offshore production in Dubai, and
prospects in Sharjah. In Abu Dhabi, expansion work was continuing at a rapid pace;
these changes are detailed in the article, though the latest projects were in the development of natural gas. Offshore production had declined in Dubai but some respite was
likely due to the drilling of two high-capacity horizontal wells in the existing oilfields,
and further exploration is still being undertaken. In Sharjah a third major field was
confirmed in the Emirate and production continued from the offshore Mubarak field.

452 **OPEC and the petroleum industry.**
Mana Saeed al-Otaiba. London: Croom Helm; New York: Halsted
Press, 1975. 192p. bibliog.
A significant study, by the UAE Minister of Petroleum and Mineral Resources, of the
beginnings and evolution of OPEC, dealing not only with its structure but also with
the oil industry in the member states, including the UAE. This study traces the development of the industry from the granting of concessions, and deals with the gradual
process that leads to transfer of power from the companies to the producing countries
through participation agreements. The author also explains the philosophy of the producing nations with regard to their reserves, the role of OPEC in the world at large,
and the political and economic significance of oil.

453 **Petroleum and the economy of the United Arab Emirates.**
Mana Saeed al-Otaiba. London: Croom Helm, 1977. 281p. map.
bibliog.
An extremely valuable work dealing with the petroleum industry in the UAE, its place
in the economy, and the wider role of the UAE economy in the region. The work deals
first with the economy prior to the discovery of oil, and then continues with a discussion of the petroleum industry, the legal framework within which it operates, the companies operating in the area, the development of the industry, and its position within
the international situation. The author goes on to discuss the economy following the
growth of petroleum revenues, the integration of the UAE economic structure, and the
setting up of the Abu Dhabi Fund for Arab Economic Development. The work concludes with an examination of the market for oil and future relationships between the
UAE government and the oil companies. Many statistics are included.

454 **Output expansions boost drilling.**
World Oil, vol. 217 (Aug. 1996), p. 107-21. map.

A review of oil industry activities and developments in the Middle East for 1995 and 1996, with forecasts for 1997. In terms of the United Arab Emirates the article examines the boosting of natural gas production by Abu Dhabi and plans to raise oil production to 2.5 million barrels per day by the year 2000, together with activity in Dubai's offshore facilities and drilling in the Mubarak field in Sharjah. The exploration activities of the various operating companies are also examined and forecasts made with regard to possible outcomes.

455 **Cross-border hydrocarbon reserves.**
David Pike. In: *Territorial foundations of the Gulf States*, edited by Richard Schofield. London: UCL Press, 1994, p. 187-99. maps.

An examination of cross-border hydrocarbon reserves. This is a global problem, but disputes in the Gulf are more numerous because of the size of the reserves and the number of small states. In terms of the United Arab Emirates the dispute between Sharjah and Iran over Abu Musa Island threatened operations in the Mubarak oilfield, and this was extremely critical because of the island's proximity to the tanker routes. However, the sharing of revenues between Sharjah and Iran has continued despite the tension over ownership of the island – the problem resurfaced in 1992, though the dispute has been going on for about a hundred years.

456 **Assessment of oil and natural gas resources in the Gulf Cooperation Council countries.**
M. Al-Ramadhan, A. M. R. Al-Morafie. *Energy*, vol. 15, no. 12 (1990), p. 1075-82.

An assessment of oil and gas reserves in the member states of the Gulf Co-operation Council, including the United Arab Emirates, based on production and an analysis of reserves for the period 1978-89.

457 **Geology and hydrocarbon potential of Dalma Island, offshore Abu Dhabi.**
M. G. Salah. *Journal of Petroleum Geology*, vol. 19, no. 2 (1996), p. 215-26. map.

An assessment of the potential for oil deposits at Dalma Island which dates from the Cambrian period. The article includes sections on the geological structure of the island, and the relation to oil-bearing strata.

458 **Arab oil policies in the 1970s: opportunity and responsibility.**
Yusif A. Sayigh. London: Croom Helm, 1983. 271p.

The objective of this work was to instil a greater understanding between oil importers and exporters through a study of Arab oil policies. It covers the process leading to national control of the oil industry; new policies and their implications for exploration, marketing, price structures, and downstream activities in petrochemicals and gas; oil as an engine for development in the oil-producing states; and the opportunities and responsibilities attached to Arab oil policies. There are references to the United Arab Emirates scattered throughout the text.

459 **Selected documents of the international petroleum industry, Abu Dhabi United Arab Emirates, Indonesia, Nigeria, 1979-1985.**
Vienna: OPEC, 1991. 168p.
Reproduces relevant documents on the United Arab Emirates petroleum industry covering exploration, extraction, commodity agreements, national legislation, and official documents.

Exploration and concessions

460 **Abu Dhabi fields and finds.**
Petroleum Times, vol. 37, no. 7 (1970), p. 245-47.
Reviews the current oil position in Abu Dhabi and discusses developments in production capacity, exploration, and concession awards.

461 **Petroleum agreements in the Arab and other oil producing countries.**
Mahmoud S. Amin.   *L'Egypte Contemporaine*, vol. 59, no. 332 (1968), p. 23-42.
Although not strictly related to the United Arab Emirates, this article is of relevance because of the coverage of the working relationships between the oil companies and the Middle East governments through concessions, partnership agreements and contract agreements. Each of the forms of relationship is discussed and illustrative examples are given.

462 **The Middle East: oil, politics and development.**
Edited by John Duke Anthony.   Washington, DC: American Enterprise Institute, 1975. 109p. maps.
These are the papers from a conference sponsored by the University of Toronto and the Canadian Institute of International Affairs. Papers of relevance are found throughout this work. The first part deals with the relationship between the international oil companies and the Arab governments, and covers concession agreements, profit sharing and participation agreements. In Part 4 the UAE receives specific coverage through a study of the impact of oil on political and socio-economic change, and here there is a contribution from the editor.

463 **The evolution of oil concessions in the Middle East and North Africa.**
Henry Cattan.   Dobbs Ferry, New York: Oceana Publications, 1967.
173p. maps.
The standard work on this very complex subject, and invaluable for an understanding of it. It is wider in coverage than the Gulf States, but extremely relevant because of the international nature of the oil industry and its inter-government relations which were adapted to local situations.

464 **Size and distribution of known and undiscovered petroleum reserves in the world, with an estimate of future exploration.**
Marcello Colitti. *OPEC Review*, vol. 5, no. 3 (Autumn 1981), p. 9-65.
The United Arab Emirates is considered as part of the world reserves, being classed in the 25-50 billion barrel bracket. In terms of future exploration, however, it is treated as part of the regional considerations of the Middle East. The text of the article is amplified by tables and statistics.

465 **A model for migration and accumulation of hydrocarbons in the Thamma and Arab reservoirs in Abu Dhabi.**
F. Hohamed Hawas, Hitoshi Takezaki. In: *Geo '94: the Middle East papers from the Middle East geoscience conference*, edited by Moujahed I. Al-Husseini. Manama, Bahrain: Gulf PetroLink, 1994, p. 483-95.
This paper presented a model designed to measure the movement and accumulation of hydrocarbons in oil reservoirs in Abu Dhabi and so to aid exploration techniques. The model was constructed to produce data on potential deposits of oil and gas, and was applied to the Thamma oilfields in Abu Dhabi.

466 **Exploration in the developing countries: trends in the seventies, outlook for the eighties.**
Francisco R. Parra. *OPEC Review*, vol. 5, no. 2 (Summer 1981), p. 22-38.
A consideration of the amount of oil exploration being carried out throughout the world, including the United Arab Emirates, and the prospects for the decade to 1981 [when Parra wrote the article]. It is pointed out that the activity in the less developed countries, even those with proven reserves, is less than in the industrialized world. However, events in the 1980s led to increased exploration activity in the 1990s.

467 **Oil and state in Arabia.**
Edith Penrose. In: *The Arabian Peninsula: society and politics*, edited by Derek Hopwood. London: Allen & Unwin, 1972, p. 271-85.
Deals with the relationship between the international oil companies and the producing nations, including Abu Dhabi, showing the development of this relationship from the early concession agreements, through partnership, to national control. Penrose also considers the development and significance of OPEC.

468 **Oil concession agreements and the evolution of the oil industry in the UAE.**
S. N. Asad Rizvi. *OPEC Review*, vol. 17, no. 4 (1993), p. 487-500.
A discussion of the historical development of the oil industry in the United Arab Emirates, beginning with a history of the oil concession agreements. The agreements are divided into old agreements, new agreements and participation agreements, and the nature of each is examined together with a comparative analysis. The history of oil discovery and production in the various Emirates is examined, as is the manner in which each of the states gained control of its oil industry.

469　**Petroleum politics: a five act drama reconstructed.**
Dankwart A. Rustow.　*Dissent* (Spring 1974), p. 144-53.

This examination of the oil industry 1951-74 looks at the change from a company-dominated operation to the concept of national control and the role of OPEC and OAPEC.

Energy

470 **Appraisal of wind-power generators in some Arabic countries.**
R. H. Abdel-Hamid. *Journal of Modelling, Measurement and Control*, vol. 45, no. 4 (1992), p. 17-28.

Assesses the potential of wind-power generators for energy production in Egypt and the United Arab Emirates, based on wind-speed distribution data compiled over a 13-year period. The author takes a judicious approach to the prediction of the optimum rating of wind-power generators required in order to avoid the uneconomic selection of wind-electric as a means of power generation.

471 **Abu Dhabi plant on track for major expansion.**
Oil and Gas Journal, vol. 95, no. 7 (1997), p. 52-55.

A description of the expansion of the Habshan gas-processing plant operated by the Abu Dhabi National Oil Company, some 150 km southwest of Abu Dhabi City.

472 **The Arabian Gulf: powerhouse of the future?**
Nitrogen, no. 221 (1996), p. 12-13, 15-18.

As assessment of the nitrogen and methanol industries situated in the Arabian Gulf countries, including the United Arab Emirates, in relation to the natural gas reserves in the region.

473 **EDSSF: a Decision Support System (DSS) for electricity peak-load forecasting.**
Masood A. Badri (et al.). *Energy*, vol. 22, no. 6 (1997), p. 579-89.

A description of a time-series-based decision support system (DSS) developed to provide near-optimal peak-load forecasting models for the United Arab Emirates. The system incorporates simulation, model base management, data management, statistical analysis, and graphic display capabilities. Short-term forecasts are generated by assessment of peak-load behaviour, and, when compared with human experts, the DSS yielded better results.

474 **Design requirements and associated performance of SVC plant for the Abu Dhabi power system.**
A. H. Al-Baya (et al.).   In: *Proceedings of International Colloquium on HVDC and Flexible AC Power Transmission* held in Wellington, New Zealand, 29 September-1 October 1993.   Wellington, New Zealand: CIGRE, 1993, p. 1-16.

Establishes the design requirements for static Var compensators in the power plants of Abu Dhabi aimed at resolving the problems experienced in providing reliable power supplies to the state, and at ensuring an acceptable level of reliability. The authors also discuss the cooling systems used in the power stations, together with voltage recovery techniques and the prevention of frequency drops. This is a specialist article.

475 **Skoda steam-turbine generating sets for United Arab Emirates.**
Z. Berny, J. Sladky.   *Czechoslovak Heavy Industry*, no. 8 (1979), p. 31-34.

Describes the design features and technical parameters of 64.5 MW steam turbines supplied by Škoda for the Umm Al Nar west power station in the United Arab Emirates. The turbines have controlled steam extraction which is passed to a nearby desalination plant for the production of fresh water.

476 **Enhancing control and protection for improved plant reliability.**
M. Elkateb, R. Subramarian.   In: *International Conference on Industrial Power Engineering* held in London, 3-5 December 1986.   London: Institution of Electrical Engineers, 1986, p. 59-64.

A consideration of the implementation and effectiveness of improved control and protection schemes to increase plant reliability within the Water and Electricity Department of Abu Dhabi. This is in response to disruptions in supply caused by plant being unreliable, a critical factor since the Department is the sole supplier for the whole Emirate.

477 **Wind energy production for some coastal sites in UAE.**
Y. H. Hamid, E. I. Eisa.   In: *Proceedings of the First World Renewable Energy Congress*, held in Reading, England, 23-28 September 1990.   Edited by A. A. M. Sayigh.   Oxford, England: Pergamon Press, 1990, p. 1680-85.

A survey of wind distribution for selected coastal sites in the United Arab Emirates to assess the potential for wind energy, and to explore suitable technologies for water pumping and power generation. The authors used data for the period 1982-88, provided by the meteorological office of the Department of Civil Aviation. A comparison is made with sites in Sudan.

478 **High spending in the race against time.**
Angus Hindley.   *Middle East Economic Digest*, vol. 39, no. 20 (1995), p. 54-55.

An assessment of the power industry in the United Arab Emirates. It has not been subjected to delays through lack of finance, as was evident elsewhere in the Arabian Gulf.

However, the UAE cannot afford to be complacent, especially in the northern Emirates where demand outstrips supply in the summer months thanks to a history of inadequate investment. The power utilities accept that increases are a fact of life, but they are adopting a policy of increasing prices to consumers in an endeavour to eliminate subsidies such that production costs are reflected in the selling price. Plans were also in hand to improve the distribution network in the northern Emirates, and to link them into the network of the rest of the federation.

479 **The desert blooms with power and water from Al Taweelah B.**
Klaus Jopp. *Modern Power Systems,* vol. 15 (July 1995), p. 3-4. map.
A report on the construction of the power and desalination plant in Al Taweelah in Abu Dhabi which would be the world's second-largest desalination plant built at a cost of $1700 million. The plant is designed to generate 17.5 million kWh per day, 346,000 m^3/day of drinking water designated for Abu Dhabi City, and to supply the farmland areas around Al-Ain. Once in full production the plant will increase Abu Dhabi's water supply capacity by 63 per cent.

480 **Experimental and theoretical investigation of global and diffuse solar radiation in the United Arab Emirates.**
A. Khalil, A. Alnajjar. *Renewable Energy,* vol. 6, nos. 5-6 (1995), p. 537-43.
The authors describe a detailed analysis of solar radiation monitoring in the United Arab Emirates. It covers the global, direct and diffuse components of solar radiation, as well as temperature, relative humidity and wind speed. The data are compared with the predictions of theoretical models, and showed measures of agreement within an 8 per cent maximum error.

481 **Installation of 132kV oil-cables in the United Arab Emirates.**
M. Laurent. *Kabel-Cables* (Switzerland), no. 18 (1992), p. 22-28.
Discusses a turn-key cable installation in Dubai by Cablex, which distributes power from the Dubai Electricity Company. Considers the technical, sociological and weather aspects of the installation.

482 **Solar radiation characteristics in Abu Dhabi.**
A. M. El-Nashar. *Solar Energy,* vol. 47, no. 1 (1991), p. 49-55.
This technical analysis of solar radiation in Abu Dhabi is based on instantaneous global and diffuse radiation measurements made in 1987. These showed variations according to the air mass and month of the year.

483 **Extension planning of the high-voltage system in the Abu Dhabi Emirate.**
J. Schlebbeck. *Elektrizitätswirtschaft,* vol. 88, no. 4 (1989), p. 170, 173-75.
This German-language article is a report of a study undertaken on the load carried by the high-voltage power system in Abu Dhabi and production of proposals for an extension of the network. The load demand varied throughout the year and it was considered that a static power compensation installation could raise the capacity of the existing system and be incorporated into a planned extension.

484   Further turboset for the United Arab Emirates.
V. Shamel, F. Patek.   *Skoda Review*, no. 4 (1985), p. 7-10.

A description of a successful consortium bid, of which Škoda was a part, to supply a new steam-driven power station at Umm al-Nar West, combined with a desalination station. The tenders were issued in 1980 as a result of increasing demands in Abu Dhabi for electricity and, particularly, on fresh water for domestic consumption and increased demand from the agricultural sector.

485   High-voltage interconnections in the Middle East.
A. M. Al-Sheri (et al.).   *Power Technology International*, no. 1 (1993), p. 53-57.

Discusses power-system development in the Middle East, including the United Arab Emirates, which concentrates on the access to large fossil fuel reserves in the country.

486   Spoilt for choice in gas quest.
Middle East Economic Digest, vol. 39, no. 48 (1995), p. 40-42.

Dubai has been experiencing an increasing demand for gas because of the need to expand electricity-generating capacity, and to fuel the re-injection programme for the declining oil reservoirs. The Emirate was providing 80 per cent of her needs, with the remainder being provided by Sharjah as part of a long-term agreement. Dubai has been offered a number of alternative supplies from Qatar, and from the Abu Dhabi National Oil Company who proposed running a pipeline into Dubai.

487   Towards Gulf power network.
Modern Power Systems, vol. 13 (Oct. 1993), p. 10.

A report on the linking together of electricity networks in the United Arab Emirates as a preliminary stage to the Arab Gulf Co-operation Council project. The project was designed to be in two phases, with the first phase linking Kuwait, Saudi Arabia, Qatar and Bahrain, and the second incorporating Oman and the United Arab Emirates. The whole project was expected to take ten years to complete at an overall cost of $2.4 billion, with the United Arab Emirates contributing 14.5 per cent.

488   H$_2$S-producing reactions in deep carbonate gas reservoirs: Khuff formation, Abu Dhabi.
R. H. Warden, P. C. Smalley.   *Chemical Geology*, vol. 133, nos. 1-4 (1996), p. 157-71.

An examination of the presence of hydrogen sulphide in the Permian Khuff formation of Abu Dhabi which is seen as limiting the economic viability of gas production from deep reservoirs. The authors discuss the chemical reactions responsible for its growth and the process of gas souring. These are not considered to be solely controlled by thermodynamics.

Industrial
Diversification

489   **Equipment for a new sugar refinery in Dubai: continuous crystallization of refined sugar massecuite.**
BMA Sugar Division.   Braunschweig, Germany: *BMA Information*, no. 34 (1996), p. 8-9.

Describes the equipment used in the Al Khaleej Sugar Company refinery in Dubai. It began operation in spring 1995 with a production capacity of 2,400 tons per day.

490   **New refinery in Dubai.**
BMA Sugar Division.   Braunschweig, Germany: *BMA Information*, no. 33 (1995), p. 10-11.

A description of a new sugar refinery built in Dubai by the Al Khaleej Sugar Company. It was designed to process 2,400 tons of raw sugar per day into EC2-grade white sugar.

491   **Policies for development: attitudes towards industry and services.**
Michael Chatelus.   In: *The Arab state*, edited by Giacomo Luciani. London: Routledge, 1990, p. 99-128.

This contribution investigates industrial structure and policies and the service sector in the Arab World, including the United Arab Emirates. In the UAE the government has favoured subsidies to private enterprise as a means of encouraging development within the industrial sector, but it is evident that there is still little co-ordination of activity between the member states. In the services area, the health service is considered, as is the significance of re-exports to the Dubai economy.

492   **Glass breaks new ground in Jebel Ali.**
Middle East Economic Digest, vol. 39, no. 48 (1995), p. 45-46.

A report on the Al-Tajir group which is used here as a case-study of the growing attractiveness of Dubai and its industrial infrastructure. The company has a major expansion programme planned, having spent much of its recent past investing in the

United States, Europe and the Far East. The company planned to open a glass-container plant in Jebel Ali, at a cost of $50 million, with the objectives of reducing the level of such imports and providing quality products for export.

493 Energy analysis and conservation prospects in the UAE cement industry.
O. A. Hamed, W. E. Abdalla. *International Journal of Energy Research*, vol. 16, no. 1 (1992), p. 75-83.

A report on an energy audit performed on the cement industry in the United Arab Emirates. The industry consumes annually the equivalent of 467,000 tons of oil. The authors assess energy conservation possibilities such as changing over to natural gas and the modification of energy-consuming systems.

494 Dubai smelter prepares for start-up.
E. Jeffs. *Energy International*, vol. 16, no. 9 (1979), p. 39-41.

Describes the aluminium smelter at Dubai which is powered by the largest gas turbine in the UAE and is notable for being the first Middle East application of the Frame 9 gas turbine.

495 OR in practice: results of a survey in the United Arab Emirates.
B. J. Kemp, D. A. Yousef. *European Journal of Operational Research*, vol. 20, no. 1 (1995), p. 25-33.

Discusses the policy of industrial diversification in the United Arab Emirates and the probable increasing role of operational research (OR) in this process. The survey investigated the levels of awareness and usage of operational research in the UAE and the factors affecting its use.

496 Still hope where there is scope.
Liz Kirkwood. *Middle East Economic Digest*, vol. 39, no. 20 (1995), p. 28-29.

The main construction boom in the United Arab Emirates peaked in 1993 but in 1995 there was still enough business around to keep companies busy, although consultants were starting to feel the effects of a slowdown. Profitability was due to greater competition, for companies were moving in to tender for contracts as a result of a slowdown in Oman and Saudi Arabia. Amongst the projects announced were the $500 million Abu Dhabi grand mosque and the $300 million Dubai airport expansion.

497 Economic assessment of the UAE's development strategy: the effectiveness of government expenditure in stimulating industrial development.
Robert E. Looney. *Journal of Developing Societies*, vol. 6, no. 2 (1990), p. 182-202.

Examines the industrial development of the United Arab Emirates from the early 1970s with an economy based on oil and gas. However, it concludes that diversification from oil has been largely unsuccessful, primarily as a result of government policies, and the high rates of investment required for industrialization. Tables are included to amplify the text.

498   **Industrialisation in the Middle East: obstacles and potential.**
Ragaei el-Mallakh. *Middle East Studies Association Bulletin*, vol. 7,
no. 3 (1973), p. 28-46.

A discussion of the whole of the Middle East, including general studies by country
and a regional assessment. The article examines prospects which are enhanced by the
availability of cheap energy, guaranteed following participation agreements. However,
this must be measured against the shortage of trained manpower, and the lack of political stability in the region. A further problem is that the research necessary for sustained
industrial development has lagged behind the desire for, and interest in, that sector.

499   **Oil driven cranes.**
Cranes Today (July 1994) p. 30-33.

A focus on crane sales and usage in the Middle East as a reflection of activity in construction and development projects reveals that it has levelled off due to falling oil
prices. However, the United Arab Emirates is seen as the most buoyant market in the
Gulf thanks to its efforts to reduce dependence on oil. Dubai is cited as a case-study of
diversification, with tourism, banking and trade becoming major contributors to the
economy.

500   **Problems and prospects of development in the Arabian Peninsula.**
Yusif A. Sayigh. *International Journal of Middle East Studies*, vol. 2
(1971), p. 40-58.

Sayigh examines the problems associated with development, such as education, infrastructure and the lack of an industrial base on which to build. In the case of the UAE,
which had just come into being at this stage (1971), political fragmentation is seen as
a major difficulty.

501   **Sights are set on some new horizons.**
Middle East Economic Digest, vol. 39, no. 48 (1995), p. 43-44.

A report on the policy of the Abu Dhabi government to develop non-oil industries partially through the government-owned General Industry Corporation (GIC). After being
in existence for sixteen years, the GIC had expanded its horizons to aim at the regional
market and to develop closer ties with the private sector. The latter development is
evidenced by sales of GIC investments in some companies to the private sector, and
there are plans to build three new industrial areas for private sector investment.

502   **There's money to be made in the hills.**
Middle East Economic Digest, vol. 39, no. 48 (1995), p. 48-49.

Ras al-Khaimah does not have a great deal of oil or gas but the building industry has
provided a good economic base in the form of cement, aggregates, tiles, or rock from
the Hajjar Mountains in the Musandam Peninsula. The industry was enjoying steady
growth with investment in tile and cement manufacture. However, electricity supplies
are overstretched and companies have had to install generators in order to secure supplies. The situation has helped to create an environment in which only viable and sustainable projects get off the ground, but that is beneficial to all concerned.

503   **United Arab Emirates.**
International Mining, vol. 6, no. 8 (1987), p. 115-16.
A report on a mineral survey carried out in the United Arab Emirates to determine the presence, or otherwise, of commercially viable copper deposits.

Dissertations

504   **The development of the manufacturing sector in the United Arab Emirates.**
M. K. Khirbash.   PhD thesis, University of Exeter, England, 1990.
[n.p.]. (Available from the British Library, Boston Spa, Wetherby, West Yorkshire).
Manufacturing development was selected as the major option for income diversification but the sector is hampered by the absence of a clear and comprehensive industrial policy. The public sector took the lead in manufacturing by investing in export-oriented large-scale industries, whilst the private sector investment was confined to small- and medium-scale enterprises. The whole sector has also been restricted by the lack of natural resources except for oil, gas, and some non-metallic minerals.

505   **Viability of industrial integration within the Gulf Cooperation Council: the case of petrochemical industries.**
Mohammed Salem Al-Sabban.   PhD thesis, University of Colorado at Boulder, 1989. 288p. (Available from University Microfilms, Ann Arbor, Michigan, order no. AAD 83-17636).
A study of industrial diversification within the Gulf Co-operation Council (GCC), including the United Arab Emirates, in order to reduce reliance on oil, though limited natural resources are a major constraint. The main advantage exists in the field of petrochemicals, but it is stressed that joint production and marketing within the GCC is essential to long-term development, and to the environmental problems associated with these industries.

Patterns of Arab Gulf exports: implications for industrial diversification of increased inter-Arab trade.
See item no. 432.

Agriculture and Fisheries

506 **Use of date-fronds mat fence as a barrier for wind erosion control: effect of barrier density on microclimate and vegetation.**
M. A. Al-Afifi (et al.). *Agriculture, Ecosystems and Environment*, vol. 33, no. 1 (1990), p. 47-55.

Reports on the use of four different densities of date-frond mat fences between rows of trees for wind erosion control. The fences were erected in a checker-board manner between *Prosopsis spicigera* and *Acacia tortillis* and the results showed that their growth rate was linearly proportional to barrier density; those growing with the highest fence density provided significantly more good shade. Additionally, soil surface evaporation and the biomass of natural non-tree vegetation growing in the plants both vary according to the treatment.

507 **Survey of antibodies against various infectious disease agents in racing camels in Abu Dhabi, United Arab Emirates.**
M. Afzal, M. Sakkir. *Revue Scientifique et Technique – Office International des Epizooties*, vol. 13, no. 2 (1994), p. 787-92.

A study of the antibodies against *Brucella abortus* detected in six of 392 racing camels in Abu Dhabi. Other antibodies detected in the camels are also listed.

508 **Chemical composition of date varieties as influenced by the stages of ripening.**
I. A. Ahmed (et al.). *Food Chemistry*, vol. 54, no. 3 (1995), p. 305-9.

The authors present data on the chemical composition of twelve date cultivars, which are widely consumed in the United Arab Emirates. These show significant levels of glucose, fructose and sugar. The high sugar and low moisture contents encouraged resistance to fungal spoilage after harvesting.

509 **Disease and pest outbreaks. United Arab Emirates: first record of** ***Fusarium*** **crown rot on tomato in UAE.**
M. Al-Ahmed. *Arab and Near East Plant Protection Newsletter,* no. 18 (1994), p. 19-20.

This disease affected 5-100 per cent of the tomato plants in the United Al-Ain agricultural area. Different levels of susceptibility were found, according to the location and the age of the farm, with the worst cases being on old farms.

510 **Analysis of minerals in date palm fruit under different nitrogen fertilization.**
H. J. Aljuburi. *Fruits* (Paris), vol. 50, no. 2 (1995), p. 153-58.

This English-language article, with summaries in French and Spanish, deals with the mineral content of developing fruits of date palms following annual applications of ammonium nitrate during the growing seasons of 1988-90. Tests showed that the applications had no effect on the fruit nitrogen content, except during later stages of development in the second season. There was also little effect on potassium and zinc content.

511 **Evaluation of response to agricultural resource problems in main ecological zones in the ECWA region.**
I. H. El-Bagouri, S. A. El-Arifi. New York: United Nations Social and Economic Council, 1981. 55p.

An analysis of agricultural resources in a number of Arab states, including the United Arab Emirates. In the case of the UAE, there is little agriculturally productive land and water resources are a major constraint, especially as groundwater irrigation has increased salinity. However, production has increased because of subsidies paid to farmers for equipment, materials and development.

512 **Forestry development strategy for the ECWA region.**
T. M. Eren, B. Ben Salem. New York: United Nations Social and Economic Council, 1981. 13p.

Discusses the importance of forestry to Western Asia where only 1.7 per cent of the land area is classified as forest or woodland. The authors examine the importance of afforestation, particularly in relation to protection of the soil, provision of nutrients and protection of crops. They conclude that in arid areas such as the United Arab Emirates these programmes are possible only with extensive irrigation and large capital investments.

513 **Multiple-infected diagnostic specimens from foot and mouth disease endemic regions.**
N. P. Ferris (et al.). *Revue Scientifique et Technique – Office International des Epizooties,* vol. 14, no. 3 (1995), p. 557-65.

Produces results from tests carried out in the United Arab Emirates. They were initially diagnosed as being a single foot-and-mouth virus, but were subsequently found to contain an additional virus type.

514 **Determination of gliotoxin in samples associated with cases of intoxication in camels.**
M. Gareis, U. Wernery. *Mycotoxin Research*, vol. 10, no. 1 (1994), p. 2-8.

Hay samples and specimens from camels in the United Arab Emirates with suspected mycotoxicosis were investigated for the presence of mycotoxins. It was suggested that gliotoxin was one causative agent of the disease.

515 **Study on some helminth parasite larvae common in Arabian Gulf fish: a comparison between west and east coasts of UAE.**
S. M. Al-Ghais, M. M. Kardousha. *Arab Gulf Journal of Scientific Research*, vol. 12, no. 3 (1994), p. 559-71.

A total of 610 fish belonging to four species were collected from the west and east coasts of the United Arab Emirates, Dubai and Khor Fakkan, during the period September 1991 to May 1992. Helminth parasite larvae were collected and it was determined that the prevalence was greater on the east coast than the west, the figures being 42.7 per cent and 29.4 per cent respectively.

516 **Improvement of effluent quality for reuse in a dairy farm.**
M. F. Hamoda, S. M. Al-Awadi. *Water, Science and Technology*, vol. 33, nos. 10-11 (1996), p. 79-85.

The study of the chemical treatment of wastewater from a dairy farm in the United Arab Emirates was undertaken in order to improve effluent quality and to assess the reuse of effluent water for irrigation. Tests showed that the wastewater pollutants could be reduced to obtain good effluent for reuse in irrigation by using alum as a coagulant. The authors propose a system based on the results of this year-long study that could be of benefit for the irrigation of farmland.

517 **Studies on the physico-chemical characteristics of date fruits of five UAE cultivators at different stages of maturity.**
S. Al-Hooti (et al.). *Arab Gulf Journal of Scientific Research,* vol. 13, no. 3 (1995), p. 553-69.

An examination of fruit samples of five date cultivars from the United Arab Emirates which evaluates their physical and chemical composition at various stages of maturity. The fruits were found to be reasonably good sources of some important minerals but were low in nitrogen.

518 **Response of safflower to different nitrogen levels in United Arab Emirates.**
Y. M. Ibrahim. *Annals of Arid Zone*, vol. 33, no. 1 (1994), p. 77-78.

A report of field trials on the effects of nitrogen on safflower grown on sandy loam soil in the 1990-91 growing season with different levels of fertilizer being applied. Ibrahim presents the results of improvements in seed yields, numbers of capsules/plant and seeds/capsule, and in stalk yields.

519 **Foot and mouth disease: surveillance and control in the Middle East.**
E. Istanbulluoglu. In: *Comprehensive reports on technical items presented to the International Committee or to Regional Commissions.*
Paris, France: Office International des Epizooties, 1994, p. 137-42.

This report is based on information provided by the Food and Agriculture Organization (Animal Health and Production Division), the World Reference Laboratory for Foot and Mouth Disease and various countries including the United Arab Emirates. Amongst the topics covered are: the position regarding foot-and-mouth disease; prevention and control; status of animal production; and animal health in the region.

520 **Present state of the genetic control of tomato yellow leaf curl virus and of the EEC-supported breeding programme.**
H. Laterrat. In: *Proceedings of the XIIth Eucarpie meeting on tomato genetics and breeding,* held in Plovdiv, Bulgaria, 27-31 July 1993.
Edited by L. Stomova. Plovdiv, Bulgaria: MARITSA Vegetable Crops Research Institute, 1993, p. 19-24.

A study of the spread of tomato yellow leaf curl, which is a problem mainly in Africa and South East Asia. However, in the Middle East generally and in the United Arab Emirates a particularly resistant F1 hybrid is available for commercial growing. The hybrid can be grown in open fields without staking or in greenhouses with stakes.

521 **Effect of Triggrr applications on snap bean and squash fruit quality.**
A. A. Al-Masoun. *Emirates Journal of Agricultural Sciences,* vol. 7, no. 1 (1995), p. 100-8.

Describes an experiment to measure the effects of applying Triggrr, a commercial seaweed extract, on beans and fruit. No significant effect was recorded on the number of fruits, fruit length, or bean and fruit weight.

522 **Productivity of six forage legumes at different sowing dates in the United Arab Emirates.**
R. S. Modawi (et al.). *Legume Research*, vol. 18, no. 2 (1995), p. 117-20.

Reports on a series of field trials between 1991 and 1992 in which pigeon peas and cowpeas were sown at Al-Oha in the United Arab Emirates. The trials showed that forage production was highest with sowing dates in early October.

523 **Milk production characteristics in the first two locations of Friesian cattle in the United Arab Emirates.**
A. A. Nigm (et al.). *Egyptian Journal of Animal Production*, vol. 31, no. 2 (1994), p. 235-49.

A study of milk production characteristics in the United Arab Emirates, based on the 1,020 lactation records of 636 German and Dutch Friesian cows from two farms at Al-Ain and Ras Al-Khaimah. The results showed that the imported cows were able to maintain their production standards under local conditions.

524 **Manipulation of vegetable communities on the Abu Dhabi rangelands. I. The effects of irrigation and release from long-term grazing.**
M. P. Otham (et al.). *Biodiversity and Conservation*, vol. 4, no. 7 (1995), p. 696-709.
Reports on the use of an enclosure system established eleven years previously to test the effects on vegetation communities of release from grazing by camels and goats. The authors also investigated the effects on the desert vegetation of sprinkler irrigation when grazing was stopped. Although species richness was not affected the percentage cover of vegetation was greater inside the enclosure and, within the enclosure, there was little difference between the irrigated and non-irrigated areas. The experiment was conducted in the Baynunah region of Abu Dhabi.

525 **Manipulation of vegetation communities on the Abu Dhabi rangelands. II. The effects of topsoiling and drip irrigation.**
M. P. Otham (et al.). *Biodiversity and Conservation*, vol. 4, no. 7 (1995), p. 710-18.
Reports on a study of the effects of topsoiling on the vegetation of coastal desert rangelands in Abu Dhabi using sand from an inland area which supported different vegetation. The study was carried out on Ghanada Island, an inshore desert island, which had been topsoiled for five years and partly drip irrigated. It was found that perennial vegetation on topsoiled areas was markedly different from the non-treated areas, as was the richness of the vegetation. Percentage cover was also greatest on areas that had been topsoiled and drip irrigated.

526 **Regional fishery survey and development project, Bahrain, . . . United Arab Emirates. Illustration identification guide to commercial fishes.**
E. Randall, G. R. Allen, W. F. Smith-Vaiz. Rome: Food and Agriculture Organization, Fisheries Department, 1978. 226p. (FAO Access, no. 40565).
A report in Arabic and English on the fishing potential in the region, with illustrations of fish considered to be commercially viable. In the case of the UAE, however, the economic viability of such a venture is doubtful because of the booming oil industry and acute manpower shortages.

527 **Recent developments in the agricultural sector in Western Asia.**
Agriculture and Development in Western Asia, no. 15 (1994), p. 1-20.
This publication from the United Nations Economic and Social Commission for Western Asia reviews and assesses the most salient developments in the agricultural sector of the member nations, which include the United Arab Emirates.

528 **The performance of imported and locally born Friesian cows in a herd located in the United Arab Emirates.**
R. R. Sandek. *Egyptian Journal of Animal Production*, vol. 31, no. 2 (1994), p. 221-33.

The productive and reproductive records of imported Friesian cows and their locally born female herd mates were compared on a farm at Ras Al-Khaimah. The records covered the period 1987-89 and the study examined age at first calving, total milk yield, and days in milk and calving intervals. Sandek found that imported cows calved initially at a younger age and had a higher milk yield in the first three lactations.

529 **Nomadismus im Niedergang: 'desert-farming' mit Perspektiven? Wendel im ländlichen Raum des Emirates Dubai, Vereinigte Arabische Emirate.** (Nomadism in decline: 'desert farming' with prospects? Change in the rural area of the Emirate of Dubai, United Arab Emirates.)
F. Scholz. *Erdkundliches-Wissen*, no. 90 (1988), p. 188-203.

This German-language article considers the traditional economy of Dubai with the emphasis on trade, fishing, and Bedouin pastoralism. The Bedouin have maintained a semblance of their former nomadic lives but are increasingly turning to desert farming for their income. The Gulf States are concentrating on food production and the Bedouin are growing fruits – dates and citrus fruits – and field crops – alfalfa, tobacco and vegetables.

530 **Changing agricultural practice in an Arabian oasis: a case study of the Al'Ain Oasis, Abu Dhabi.**
J. H. Stevens. *Geographical Journal*, vol. 136, no. 2 (1970), p. 410-18. maps.

The al-Ain oasis in Abu Dhabi was a traditional, predominantly subsistence-oriented unit, before being replaced by one that is more commercial in nature. This change has been caused by the growth of a market for produce due to both population increases and the development of a modern communications network. The changes are seen as an admirable example of development, but future expansion must be measured in relation to the availability of water resources. This latter aspect has assumed even more significance since this article was written because of increased consumption in the region as a whole.

531 **Salinity management in irrigated agriculture.**
N. K. Tyagi. In: *Sustainability of irrigated agriculture. Proceedings of the NATO Advanced Research Workshop*, held at Vimeira, Portugal, 21-26 March 1994. Edited by L. S. Pereira (et al.). Dordrecht, The Netherlands: Kluwer Academic, 1996, p. 345-58.

Salinity is a serious problem for irrigated agriculture anywhere, but it is a major problem in the United Arab Emirates, where the presence of excess soluble salts affects plant growth, and results in poor permeability and tilth of soil. The situation is manageable, but Tyagi stresses that programmes for the prevention of waterlogging and salinity must have institutional support and economic incentives, such as water pricing, subsidized technology, and drainage taxes.

532 UAE: towards agricultural self-sufficiency.
Arab Economist, vol. 14, no. 153 (1982), p. 23-24.

Discusses the problems related to the expansion of agricultural production in the UAE. The article concentrates on the two main factors: the increasing population and the adverse climate. However, it is estimated that by 1990 the UAE should attain self-sufficiency in fish and poultry and be producing three-quarters of its fruit and vegetable consumption needs. A water conservation policy, improved growing techniques and sophisticated marketing should contribute towards an improved agricultural sector.

533 Agriculture and water resources in the United Arab Emirates.
Jim Unwin. *Arab Gulf Journal*, vol. 3, no. 1 (1983), p. 75-85.

An analysis of changes in agriculture since 1971 covering production, large-scale agricultural projects, and forestry projects and their impact on the environment. Unwin concludes that, unless immediate efforts are made to cut back on the pumping of groundwater for agricultural use, a major environmental crisis will be inevitable. The point is made that water, like oil, is a finite resource, and that in the longer term water is more important and, if wasted at the current rate, the agricultural future will be bleak.

534 Infectious disease of camels.
U. Wernery, O. R. Leaden.   Berlin: Blackwell Wissenschaft, 1995. 133p.

A report on the experience gained from a study of 22 bacterial and 15 viral diseases of camels in the United Arab Emirates. Further studies were carried out at the Institute for Medical Microbiology at Munich University, and reports carried in the literature are also summarized. The work has 50 illustrations, mainly in colour, and 30 pages are devoted to references.

535 Characterization of the mycoplasma-like organism associated with witches'-broom disease of lime and proposition of a *Candidatus* taxon for the organism 'Phytoplasma aurentifolia'.
L. Zreil (et al.).   *International Journal of Systematic Bacteriology*, vol. 45, no. 3 (1995), p. 449-53.

A study of the witches'-broom disease of small-fruited acid lime which was caused by a mycoplasma-like organism. The disease was particularly acute in the United Arab Emirates and Oman.

Dubai's wealth and the greening of the Emirates.
See item no. 34.

Diterpene glycosides from *Iphioni aucheri*.
See item no. 160.

The desert blooms with power and water from Al Taweelah B.
See item no. 479.

Use of date-fronds mat fence as a barrier for wind erosion control. 1. Effect of barrier density on sand movement stabilization.
See item no. 596.

Tourism

536 **Dubai travel and tourism sector.**
M. M. Ali. *Trade and Industry* (Dubai), vol. 14, no. 163 (1989),
p. 10-16.
An assessment of Dubai's tourism industry which has a well-developed infrastructure,
good weather to offer, and is competitively priced. Hotel occupancy is high, travel and
tourism agencies have flourished, and continued growth of the sector is envisaged. Ali
also assesses the general economic growth of Dubai, particularly in the trade sector.

537 **Hotel industry in Dubai.**
M. M. Ali. *Trade and Industry* (Dubai), vol. 14, no. 157 (1989),
p. 12-19.
The hotel industry in Dubai had grown to cater for expansion in the commercial and
industrial sectors of the economy but had now adopted strategies aimed at the tourism
market. The article looks at occupancy by area of origin and revenue by hotel
classification, and includes an outline of a proposed hotel classification scheme.

538 **The Arab Gulf travel market.**
Melbourne, Australia: Australian Travel Commission, 1983. 90p.
This study of the tourist industry focused on the members of the Gulf Co-operation
Council (GCC), including the United Arab Emirates. The market brief provides information that will assist in understanding the potential of the GCC for Australia's
travel/tourism products. Details are provided about the economy, political and social
structures, geography, the structure of the travel industry, the main features of the
tourism sector, and there is advice on selling to the area.

539 **Arabian Peninsula (Saudi Arabia, Kuwait, UAE, Oman, Bahrain, North Yemen, South Yemen). Regional report no. 16.**
International Tourism Quarterly, no. 4 (1985), p. 50-60. maps.
Incoming vacation tourism is considered insignificant due to the climate, lack of attractions, high prices, and discouragement by some countries. The United Arab Emirates accounts for a significant section of the Peninsula total, which is largely dominated by external travel from the expatriate population. Inbound tourism is expected to show only gradual growth whilst external travel is expected to show a rapid increase.

540 **Arabian Gulf outbound.**
S. Balasubramanian. *Travel and Tourism Analyst*, no. 6 (1992), p. 26-46.
An assessment of the travel industry in the Gulf States, including the United Arab Emirates, which peaks during the summer months, with families avoiding the hot period, and expatriates visiting home for the long summer break. The region's travel industry is expected to remain untouched by the recession elsewhere and major improvements are planned to airport facilities, but large increases are not expected, only a period of steady growth. However, it is pointed out that the volatile political nature of the region could affect all forecasts.

541 **United Arab Emirates.**
S. Balasubramanian. *International Tourism Reports*, no. 3 (1993), p. 29-54.
Tourism has been targeted as a development sector to counter the declining world oil prices. The sector is small-scale and was badly affected by the Gulf War but is being marketed as an exclusive winter destination. The commitment of the federal government to the industry is demonstrated by a huge investment in tourism infrastructure and aviation facilities, including extensive hotel construction.

542 **Deluxe in the desert.**
Caterer and Hotelkeeper, vol. 187, no. 3814 (1994), p. 14-15.
A description of the five-star Royal Abjar hotel in Dubai which cost more than $100 million to build. The hotel is environmentally friendly; it has a computerized building management system and is designed to service a growing tourist industry.

543 **Dubai: bracing for tourism boom.**
Trade and Industry (Dubai), vol. 15, nos. 175-176 (1990), p. 46-54.
Tourism is one of the fastest-growing industries in Dubai and the country is being actively promoted as an international destination. The work of the Dubai Civil Aviation Department, the National Travel Agency, and the Emirates Airline in attracting tourists is also discussed.

544   **Turning in a high-class performance.**
Angus Hindley. *Middle East Economic Digest*, vol. 40, no. 20
(1996), p. 32-33.
A review of the increasingly high profile of Dubai as a tourist centre. The article is preceded (p. 31) by a report on the progress of the Chicago Beach tourist development.

545   **An expensive alternative catches on.**
Liz Kirkwood. *Middle East Economic Digest*, vol. 39, no. 20 (1995),
p. 37-38.
An assessment of the tourist industry in the United Arab Emirates which was [in 1995] about to make a significant development step – the opening of a major beach front development at Jumairah in Dubai. The sector is also being encouraged in Abu Dhabi, when there was a doubling of visitors in the 1995-96 season largely as a result of an advertising campaign in Europe. The typical tourist is aged 40 or over and in the well-off bracket.

546   **Tourist destination management: issues, analysis and policies.**
E. Laws.   London: Routledge, 1995. 224p.
An introduction to the key issues involved in developing and managing tourist destinations. Laws considers, amongst other topics: tourist satisfaction and customer care; impacts of tourism; tourism policies; marketing and planning; differing importance of tourism for residents, investors and tourists. Dubai is used as one of the case-studies.

547   **The making of Dubai's success story.**
Middle East Economic Digest, vol. 39, no. 14 (1995), p. S6-S8.
Reports on the increase in tourist traffic to Dubai and its significance to the post-oil economy of the Emirate. This is the result of a deliberate policy which had been in place for a decade aimed at making the city a centre for international shoppers and for the leisure industry. The infrastructure for these developments is provided by Dubai Commerce and Tourism Promotion Board through seven offices throughout the world, and has the backing of a range of state-owned and state-sponsored institutions.

548   **Peace pacts stimulate long-haul incentives.**
Marketing (16 Feb. 1995), p. S9-S11.
A report on the incentive travel industry which was expected to make a big comeback in 1995, with Dubai seen as a country with potential in the incentive market.

549   **United Arab Emirates.**
J. Seckings. *International Tourism Reports*, no. 2 (1988), p. 37-49.
The United Arab Emirates, especially Dubai, was beginning to develop an interest in the tourism sector. It is accepted that business visitors would always predominate, but leisure tourism is seen as a significant minor activity that would help to justify some of the expensive infrastructure investment. Dubai and Abu Dhabi are both adopting competitive tourism policies aimed at attracting visitors during the winter months, though Sharjah is concerned at the potential damage to the traditions of Islam. The reduction in refuelling stops by long-haul carriers has given a new impetus to the promotion of tourism.

550 **Tourism development potential in the southern ECWA sub-region.**
Baghdad: UN Economic and Social Council for Western Asia,
Transport, Communications and Tourism Division, 1982. 123p. maps.

This study deals with the tourism development potential of the southern sub-region of
the United Nations Economic and Social Council for Western Asia (ECWA), which
includes the United Arab Emirates. Amongst the topics studied are: the geographical
and socio-economic features of the sub-region; the main characteristics of existing
tourism resources and attractions; present tourism development potential; tourist
movements, payments, facilities and policies; problem areas affecting tourism development; and recommendations for the development of tourist potential and facilities.

551 **Tourism sector in Dubai.**
Trade and Industry (Dubai), vol. 10, no. 10 (1985), p. 17-27.

A brief review of the tourist attractions of Dubai, together with statistics on air pas-
senger traffic, climate, number and classification of hotels, hotel occupancy, and travel
and tourism agencies.

552 **Arabian delights.**
Penny Wilson. *Caterer and Hotelkeeper*, vol. 187, no. 3813
(Feb. 1994), p. 49-50.

A survey of the hotel sector in Dubai which, at the time of writing, had 157 hotels
with a further expansion programme planned over the following five years. The majority of hotel staff are expatriate workers, as nationals do not choose to take up job
opportunities in the sector. In 1994, 75 per cent of the population of Dubai were expatriates and represented 90 per cent of the total workforce.

Transport and Communications

553 Update on the electronics industry in the Arabian Peninsula.
B. Baronian. *Electronics*, vol. 29, no. 5 (1983), p. 43-44.

Analyses the market for communications equipment in the Middle East, with the United Arab Emirates identified as one of the major growth markets. The area is seen as a showcase for state-of-the-art communications technology used to streamline operation in the oil-rich economy. Baronian points out that underdeveloped infrastructures mean that the constraints of ageing or incompatible systems are not problems that have to be faced.

554 Rural telecommunications using ARABSAT.
S. Ganeswaran, M. Richharia. In: *International Conference on Rural Communications*, held on 23-25 May 1988, at London. London: Institution of Electrical Engineers, 1988, p. 142-46.

Examines the possibility of using the ARABSAT satellite to provide telecommunications services to remote areas of the United Arab Emirates. A digital network has been designed, using an ARABSAT transponder in order to investigate the possibility.

555 A job in the life of a cableship.
R. Gribble. *Middle East Electronics*, vol. 7, no. 6 (1984), p. 24-25.

Describes the work of the cableship *Iris* in laying submarine cables for a telecommunications link between Bahrain, Qatar, and the United Arab Emirates. The project was a joint British/Japanese venture, and was developed and implemented over a number of years.

556 PV-diesel hybrid power for Etisalat.
C. T. McCloskey (et al.). *Modern Power Systems*, vol. 11, no. 9 (1991), p. 25-28.

Discusses the use of Remote Area Power Supply Units, which are photovoltaic–diesel hybrid power plants, by Etisalat, the national telecommunications company in the United Arab Emirates, particularly in relation to the cellular telephone network at Salabik.

557 Mobile in the Persian Gulf.

H. Mueller. *Telecom Report International*, vol. 18, no. 3 (1995), p. 14-16.

Describes the expansion of mobile communications within the Gulf Co-operation Council. These are based on the GSM standard with Siemens and Motorola building three radio communications networks in Qatar, Kuwait and the United Arab Emirates.

558 Gaining stature (Gulf Aircraft Maintenance Co.).

Douglas Nelms. *Air Transport World*, vol. 33, no. 3 (1996), p. 83-85.

The Gulf Aircraft Maintenance Company began operations in 1987 as a 60-40 partnership between Gulf Air and the Abu Dhabi government. After seven years of loss-making activity the company began to make profits, largely as a result of a five-year programme designed to provide the company with a clear strategy: to establish a customer base; joint partnerships; and new third-party business.

559 Aviation in the Arabian Gulf.

P. Sheppard. *Travel and Tourism Analyst*, no. 4 (1991), p. 5-19.

Prior to the Gulf War the region's airports and carriers were developing strategies to promote the area as a refuelling stop for long-haul carriers, but it was in danger of being left behind by the development of long-range aircraft. Dubai was the most successful of the destinations, but Abu Dhabi was also hoping to develop its air transportation business. Sheppard also examines the broad tourism strategies of the Gulf States, and points out that the development of aviation within and to the Gulf is necessary to replace the declining transit business.

560 A maintenance management system for highways and urban streets.

W. Uddin. In: *Proceedings of the 4th International Conference on Microcomputers in Transportation,* held in Baltimore. Maryland, 22-24 July 1992. Edited by J. Chow (et al.). New York: American Society of Civil Engineers, 1993, p. 572-83.

A description of a comprehensive management system for highways and urban streets in Dubai resulting from a United Nations project. The system utilizes local expertise and microcomputer systems in order to ensure self-reliance within a period of two years. A comprehensive database of road and street networks was compiled using Dbase IV software, together with software for implementing pavement distress analysis, budget analysis, and management reports generation.

Dissertation

561 **The role of transportation networks in the development and integration of the seven emirates forming the United Arab Emirates, with special reference to Dubai.**
J. M. Al-Mehairi.   PhD thesis, University of Durham, 1993. [n.p.].
(Available from the British Library, Boston Spa, Wetherby, West Yorkshire).

Uses the transport sector as an indicator of development across sectors of the state and various aspects are examined in order to evaluate the integration of the Emirates into one state. The rapid expansion of the transportation network has come about largely as a result of the federal state and the need to link the major centres of population. The modern road routes follow the caravan routes which themselves had evolved as a result of topography and other physical features. However, it is pointed out that the lack of maintenance and the absence of an integrated roads policy has consequences for the comprehensive integration of the state.

Carbon monoxide exposure from motor vehicles I. United Arab Emirates.
See item no. 587.

The United Arab Emirates and the Internet: cultural and social implications for higher education.
See item no. 615.

Employment and Manpower

562 **Expatriates and host country nationals: managerial values and decision styles.**
Abbas J. Ali, Ahmed A. Azin, Krish S. Krishnan. *Leadership and Organization Development Journal*, vol. 16, no. 6 (1995), p. 27-34.
Reports on a study of the work value systems and decision styles of indigenous and Arab and non-Arab expatriate managers in the United Arab Emirates. The results revealed that indigenous and expatriate managers had significantly different value systems. Arab expatriates were found to be more conformist, whilst non-Arab expatriates were inclined to be more manipulative and egocentric. In terms of decision-making styles, indigenous and Arab expatriate managers opted for participative or pseudo-participative styles, whilst non-Arab expatriates were more consultative.

563 **Relationship between job satisfaction and organizational commitment among employees in the United Arab Emirates.**
Ahmad A. Alnajjar. *Psychological Reports*, vol. 79, no. 1 (1996), p. 315-21.
The author presents the results of a survey of 171 employees aged 26-35 years with regard to job satisfaction and job commitment. It was based on two questionnaires. The first questionnaire assessed job security, job status, relations with managers and with colleagues. The job commitment survey assessed the desire to fulfil commitments using the Organizational Commitment Scale, measuring discipline, concern, and updating of skills. In terms of job commitment there was a correlation between relationships with managers and colleagues and job status. The scores on job security were not correlated with job commitment.

564 **Labour migration from Pakistan: trends, impacts and implications.**
Farooq Azam. *Regional Development Dialogue*, vol. 12, no. 3 (1991), p. 53-71.
This article concentrates primarily on the impact on the labour-exporting country's economy and society of labour migration from Pakistan to the United Arab Emirates and Saudi Arabia. The migrant outflow figures are studied in order to compare migrant workers' earnings, consumption and expenses, remittances, savings and investments, and the impact on the Pakistan economy. The workers in the UAE are mainly unskilled labourers and the Pakistan economy is not able to reintegrate returning workers into the rural economy from which they came. In addition, the success of labour migration has meant that Pakistan has not tackled problems of population control or made any attempt to strengthen the employment structure, with the result that decline in Gulf employment placed the labour market under great strain.

565 **Arab manpower.**
John Stace Birks, C. A. Sinclair. London: Croom Helm, 1980. 391p. maps. bibliog.
The first part is introductory to the case-studies and considers the process of development in the Arab world since 1970, a process which has resulted in mixed progress and a widening gap between rich and poor. The authors also consider the size of the indigenous labour population and the levels of educational attainment. The UAE is specifically dealt with in Section 2, 'The capital rich states', and is cited as probably the 'best example of a capital rich state suffering from severely limited indigenous human resources, but experiencing spectacular economic growth. The development plans of the Emirates are dramatically ambitious on the agricultural, financial and industrial fronts . . .' The treatment is broken down into the supply of labour, the demand for labour, the labour market and foreign workers in the UAE. The study is backed by a series of statistical tables.

566 **Internal migration and development in the Arab region.**
John Stace Birks, C. A. Sinclair. London and Geneva: International Labour Organization, 1980. 186p.
The work examines the question of international migration for employment to, from and between the Arab states of the Middle East, and includes an analysis of the underlying factors. The pattern is examined in relation to the advantages and disadvantages to the employing country and, in the latter context, the long-term prospects of employing labour from the Indian subcontinent are discussed. The UAE is considered as an employer of such labour from the Indian subcontinent, the Far East, and other Arab states such as Oman, Jordan and Palestine.

567 **Labour migration in the Arab Gulf States: patterns, trends and prospects.**
J. S. Birks, I. J. Seccombe, C. A. Sinclair. *International Migration* (Switzerland), vol. 26, no. 3 (1988), p. 267-86.
The analysis of changes in non-national migration in the Gulf States, including the United Arab Emirates, examines the nature of the labour force and migrant worker flows and outflows resulting from the decline in oil prices and production in 1986.

568   **Labour migration to the Middle East: from Sri Lanka to the Gulf.**
Edited by F. Eelens (et al.).   London: Kegan Paul International, 1992.
259p.

A study of the living conditions of migrant labour in the Gulf, based largely on a study
of migrants from Sri Lanka. The work is not restricted to the United Arab Emirates,
but covers the Gulf as a region. Amongst the topics covered are: recruitment
processes; the policies of the Gulf States towards migrant workers; social mobility; the
socio-economic conditions of migrant workers; and the impact of migrant workers on
the Sri Lankan economy.

569   **Manpower nationalization in the United Arab Emirates: the case
of the banking sector.**
A. M. Elhussein.   *Journal of Developing Societies*, vol. 7, no. 2
(1991), p. 282-92.

The United Arab Emirates' indigenous labour market has failed to satisfy the needs of
an expanding economy and the country has been heavily dependent upon expatriate
labour from Asia, Europe, and other Arab states. The government has launched a programme of labour nationalization, but the effort has been frustrated by the highly frag-
mented nature of the policy-making system, as illustrated by the banking sector.

570   **UAE: sun goes down on illegal workforce.**
Peter Feuilherade.   *Middle East*, no. 262 (Dec. 1996), p. 29-30.

A study of the problems of the illegal workforce in the United Arab Emirates which
had been the object of a clampdown, with severe penalties for those caught working
illegally. About 20,000 workers, or between 15 and 20 per cent of the workforce had
left the country to avoid prosecution but it is considered that the move could backfire
if, as thought, illegal immigrants formed the backbone of the labour force.

571   **UAE weeds out its labour force.**
Angus Hindley.   *Middle East Economic Digest*, vol. 40, no. 40
(1996), p. 2-3.

A report on the mass exodus from the labour market of illegal migrant workers during
an amnesty period of three months granted by the federal government. It was clear
from publicity in the mass media that the federal government was intent on finding a
final solution to the problem of illegal immigration and it was anticipated that some
200,000 migrant workers would leave the federation before the amnesty expired – it
was due to expire on 30 September 1996. Hindley considers that every aspect of the
economy would be affected by the resultant labour shortage and that labour costs
would rise because of regulation of the market.

572   **Labour exodus takes the edge off expansion.**
Middle East Economic Digest, vol. 40, no. 49 (Dec. 1996), p. 37-39.

A report on the downturn in the economy of the United Arab Emirates despite a rise of
$3 a barrel in the price of oil. This was largely accounted for by the exodus of illegal
migrant workers during the period of amnesty granted by the federal government. It
thus created a shortage in the labour force which was unable to meet market demands.

573 **International migration, Arabisation and localisation in the Gulf labour market.**
Ian J. Seccombe. In: *The Arab Gulf and the Arab World*, edited by B. R. Pridham. London: Croom Helm, 1988, p. 153-88.

An examination of the relationship between the Gulf Co-operation Council states and the rest of the Arab world, based on the migration of Arab nationals to the Gulf for employment. This was of considerable importance to both the labour-importing and labour-exporting countries as, by 1975, non-national Arabs represented 36 per cent of the total workforce. In the case of the United Arab Emirates, Arab migrant workers amounted to a major section of the migrant labour force and represented 89 per cent of the workforce. The contribution provides a wealth of statistical data on migrant labour, work permits, arrivals and departures of migrant workers, origins of migrant labour, and workers' remittances from the Middle East.

574 **Pakistani workers in the Middle East: volume, trends and consequences.**
Nasra M. Shah. *International Migration Review*, vol. 17, no. 3 (1983), p. 410-24.

Examines the impact of migration from Pakistan to the Gulf States, particularly the United Arab Emirates, in terms of the labour-exporting and the labour-importing societies. The non-Arab population in the UAE exceeded 70 per cent in 1983 and it is estimated that by 1985 half a million Pakistani workers will be employed in the Gulf States.

Dissertations

575 **Management development in the industrial sector in the UAE.**
A. H. Ali. PhD thesis, University of Swansea, Wales, 1991. [n.p.]. (Available from the British Library, Boston Spa, Wetherby, West Yorkshire).

A study of management development in the non-petroleum industries in the United Arab Emirates – the sector had been identified as a significant area in the policy of industrial diversification. Ali used a questionnaire to survey a sample of factories in the sector, in order to establish knowledge of, attitudes to, and existence of management development plans in those factories. The results indicated that active management development was weak, in many cases non-existent, and that a more positive and active approach to management development was needed.

576 **The dilemma of ultra rapid deployment: reliance on migrant
labour in the oil rich Gulf states.**
Lubra Ahmad Al-Kazi.   PhD thesis, University of Texas at Austin,
1983. (Available from University Microfilms, Ann Arbor, Michigan,
order no. AAD84-4335).

In the case of the United Arab Emirates, reliance on migrant labour in the development process was critical, such that by 1980, only 24 per cent of the population were
nationals. The need for labour was the result of a push towards modernization of the
economy and the provision of extensive welfare services. Parallel labour market sectors were created as the importation of labour for the capitalist sector resulted in an
expansion of the social services which, in turn, required further importation of labour.
Society is also undergoing cultural change because of rapid development, not all of
which is planned or welcome, as it is the desire of UAE society to become commercially modern whilst preserving the traditional religious and authority structures.

Statistics

577 Annual Statistical Abstract.
  Abu Dhabi: UAE Ministry of Planning, 1971- . annual.
This official publication provides statistical data on the planning activities of the United Arab Emirates, covering economic data, social statistics, building development, industrial statistics, government infrastructure, and financial data.

578 Dubai External Trade Statistics.
  Dubai: Dubai Statistics Office. annual.
Gives full details of the export trade of the Emirate.

579 Statistical Bulletin.
  Abu Dhabi: Abu Dhabi Department of Planning. monthly.
Provides the full range of governmental statistics relating to the Emirate of Abu Dhabi.

580 Statistical Review.
  Abu Dhabi: UAE Ministry of Planning, Central Statistical Department, 1978- . annual.
Published in English and Arabic, the *Review* provides statistics on all aspects of the Emirates, from agricultural production to the hotel industry.

581 Statistical Yearbook.
  Abu Dhabi: Abu Dhabi Department of Planning. annual.
A summary and compilation of the monthly *Statistical Bulletin* (q.v.), covering all the governmental statistics relating to the Emirate.

582 **National Basic Intelligence Fact Book.**
United States. Central Intelligence Agency. Washington, DC:
US Government Printing Office. irregular.

An irregularly updated publication giving a few data on each country of the world. Coverage is restricted to a brief outline of the country, with a section on military capability. The UAE is always covered because of the strategic significance of the region.

Environment

583 Assessment of tar pollution on the United Arab Emirates beaches.
A. H. Abu-Hilal, H. K. Khordagui. *Environment International*,
vol. 19, no. 6 (1993), p. 589-96.

The pollution effects of the Gulf War demonstrated that there was inadequate information regarding stranded tar balls on the beaches of the Arabian Gulf and Oman. An
investigation was instigated to provide information on the nature, location, and levels
of stranded tar balls on the beaches of the United Arab Emirates – the numbers were
found to be higher than expected or previously reported. Little of the oil released
during the Gulf War reached these beaches as the distribution and degree of weather-
ing indicated that the pollution was from oil-tanker spills or ballast water.

**584 Sanitary conditions in three creeks in Dubai, Sharjah and Ajman
emirates on the Arabian Gulf.**
A. H. Abu-Hilal (et al.). *Environmental Monitoring and Assessment*,
vol. 32, no. 1 (1994), p. 21-36.

Monitoring of the creeks showed that Dubai and Sharjah creeks have occasional high
nutrient levels, with sharp fluctuations and wide spatial and temporal variations. This
indicates the presence of an anthropogenic source of pollution near the monitoring
sites, which include wastewater outlets and recreational areas. Ajman Creek showed
much lower nutrient levels. The authors conclude that there were no major pollution
problems, but make recommendations to prevent deterioration in the future.

**585 The environmental impact of ships traffic in and out of the Dubai
Creek.**
J. Almehairi. *Urban Transportation and the Environment II
(Computational Mechanics)*, 1996, p. 265-72. maps.

The different stages of development of the Creek for ship traffic are described – from
1955 to date – and the environmental impacts of shipping are determined. The environmental problems have arisen from: the movement of commercial vessels; the

movement of small ferries; and changes in land use along the Creek. In terms of the shipping activity the main areas of concern are the disposal of solid and oily wastes, traffic congestion, and air pollution.

586 Microbial and nutrient pollution assessment of coastal and creek waters of northern UAE.
I. M. Banat (et al.). *Environment International*, vol. 19, no. 6 (1993), p. 569-78.

An examination of the bacteria was made over a period of twelve months in order to determine the pollution levels in the coastal waters and creeks of the northern United Arab Emirates. The results showed a distinct pattern for the microbial populations. Nutrient levels were generally normal for seawater, but there were sharp fluctuations in ammonia concentrations and therefore totally dissolved nitrogen. Pollution was also affected by the presence of nearby drains, wastewater outlets, or recreational areas. The study found a small degree of microbial pollution in these areas and more stringent measures are recommended to prevent further pollution.

587 Carbon monoxide exposure from motor vehicles. I. United Arab Emirates.
M. A. Darbool (et al.). *Journal of Environmental Science, Health-Environmental Science Engineering Toxic Hazard Substances Control*, vol. A, 32, no. 2 (1997), p. 311-21.

Reports on a study of carbon monoxide emissions from cars in Al-Ain City as a forerunner to the establishment of emission standards. The study took place over a three-month period at three locations in the city. The levels of carbon monoxide emissions were significantly influenced by the age, model and size of the car, the number of cylinders, and the fuel used.

588 Getting serious about safety and survival.
Middle East Economic Digest, vol. 40, no. 49 (1996), p. 55-57.

A preview of the first federal environment law due to be approved in 1997. The government hopes it will create a framework to raise environmental awareness and cut down on air and marine pollution, as well as industrial and domestic waste. In parts of the United Arab Emirates, air quality has deteriorated because of: an increase in traffic, increased emissions of nitrogen oxides and sulphur oxides, enormous increases in industrial and domestic waste, and suspended dust particles. The Gulf's marine environment is also under constant threat from oil spills and illegal dumping by ships. Some of the individual states have already taken some action, but this is the first attempt to introduce a federal regulatory framework.

589 Post-Gulf War nutrients and microbial assessments for the coastal waters of Dubai, Sharjah, and Ajman emirates (UAE).
E. S. Hassan, I. M. Banat, A. H. Abu-Hilal. *Environment International*, vol. 21, no. 1 (1995), p. 23-32.

Water pollution after the Gulf War was measured on the shores and in the creeks of Dubai, Sharjah and Ajman through the monitoring of selected chemical nutrients and microbial communities. The levels were found to be similar to pre-war records and it was found that there was no significant nutrient or microbial pollution in any of the creeks.

590 **Dustfall rate and composition in Al Ain City: United Arab Emirates: a preliminary study.**
K. T. Hindy, A. R. Baghdady. *Environment Education and Formation*, vol. 14, no. 3 (1995), p. 303-14.

The authors report on a study of dust-fall rate and its water-soluble and insoluble composition in Al-Ain City. The study was carried out between October and November 1993, using samples collected up in five different districts in the city. It revealed that wind-blown dust and sand from the south-west was the major contributor to the dust-fall rate in Al-Ain, which was measured at double the limit set for residential areas. Combustible matter within the dust was found to be from man-made sources emanating from the commercial centre of the city. Tarry matter was also detected in the samples.

591 **Coastal environmental sensitivity mapping for oil spills in the United Arab Emirates using remote sensing and GIS technology.**
J. R. Jensen (et al.). *Geocarto International*, vol. 8, no. 2 (1993), p. 5-13.

Discusses the implications of both accidental and intentional oil spills on the ecologically sensitive areas of the United Arab Emirates shoreline. The results of spills can be compounded if there are no effective clean-up plans. The authors consider that an environmental sensitivity index database – developed with the aid of remote sensing and geographical information systems (GIS) – can be an effective tool in clean-up operations. The shoreline sensitivity of Abu Dhabi was assessed and classified using three Landsat Thematic Mapper scenes.

592 **Man-made litter on the shores of the United Arab Emirates on the Arabian Gulf and the Gulf of Oman.**
H. K. Khordagui, A. H. Abu-Hilal. *Water, Air and Soil Pollution*, vol. 76, nos. 3-4 (1994), p. 343-52.

A survey of the environmental pollution along the coastline of the United Arab Emirates resulting from human activity, in terms of industry, domestic pollution, and recreational activities.

593 **Tides of war: eco-disaster in the Gulf.**
Michael McKinnon, Peter Vine. London: Boxtree, 1991. 192p. maps. bibliog.

A study of the effects of the Gulf War on the ecosystem of the Arabian Gulf, with oil slicks and poisonous smoke from oil wells combining to create an environmental disaster affecting both people and wildlife. However, it is pointed out that the area had already suffered because of both the pace of modern development based on hydrocarbons, and also the reliance on the Gulf by the inhabitants for their economies and societies. Birdlife was a major sufferer from the Gulf War as was the turtle population and, in some instances, species were brought to the edge of extinction. The disaster has caused a change in individual and governmental attitudes to the environment which gives the authors some confidence for the future. They point out that this work was written whilst the ecological damage was at an early stage and would continue to unfold over a number of years. The work is profusely illustrated with coloured photographs, and there are references to individual Emirates throughout the text.

594 **Bottom sediments of the Arabian Gulf. 2. TPH and TOC contents as indicators of oil pollution and implications for the effect and fate of the Kuwait oil slick.**
M. S. Massoud (et al.). *Environmental Pollution*, vol. 93, no. 3 (1996), p. 271-84.

An analysis of 77 core samples taken from the Arabian Gulf to determine the total petroleum hydrocarbon (TPH) concentrates in the sediments and to determine their distribution. It is suggested that offshore pollution in the United Arab Emirates is almost certainly directly related to the Kuwait oil slick. The authors use the data to try to determine the movement and fate of the oil slick, especially the oil floating from the impacted tidal flats along the Saudi Arabian coastline which could move further down the Gulf.

595 **Mycoflora of dust particles accumulated on filters of air conditioning systems in United Arab Emirates.**
A. A. Mougith. *Indian Journal of Mycology and Plant Pathology*, vol. 23, no. 3 (1993), p. 260-66.

This analysis of air-borne dust particles which had accumulated on the filters of air-conditioning units in the United Arab Emirates identified more than fifty species belonging to nineteen fungal groups. These are identified and listed in descending order of dominance.

596 **Use of date-fronds mat fence as a barrier for wind erosion control. 1. Effect of barrier density on sand movement stabilization.**
H. Murai (et al.). *Agriculture, Ecosystems and Environment*, vol. 32, nos. 3-4 (1990), p. 273-82.

Reports on the results of a trial using four wind-barrier systems constructed of four different densities of date-frond mat fences as a means of controlling wind erosion. These barriers were erected in a staggered pattern between rows of two locally culti-vated trees, *Prosopis spicigera* and *Acacia tortillis*. The efficiency of the systems was assessed, using the amount of drifting sands, changes in wind speed and variations in ground surface level. The effectiveness of the barrier increased with fence density and it was successful in retarding the encroaching sand. The results improved with tree growth.

597 **Accidental release of chlorine and its impact on urban areas.**
H. A. El-Sheikh (et al.). In: *Proceedings of 30th Intersociety Energy Conversion Engineering Conference*, held at Orlando, Florida, 30 July – 4 August 1995. Edited by D. Yogi Gaswani (et al.). New York: ASME, 1995, vol. 2, p. 37-42.

Uses Al-Ain City in the United Arab Emirates as a case-study to apply an animation technique to the effects of a possible accidental release of chlorine from high-pressure cylinders. It is possible thus to predict the size and location of the toxic cloud at ground level, the period of decay, and the effects of meteorological conditions on the size of the cloud. The simulation also produced data on the population and environ-ment for the affected area.

Petroleum hydrocarbons in the nearshore marine sediments of the United Arab Emirates.
See item no. 437.

Use of date-fronds mat fence as a barrier for wind erosion control: effect of barrier density on microclimate and vegetation.
See item no. 506.

Education

598 **The historical development of the Middle Eastern university: the effect of the American model in the Islamic context.**
Shafika Ebrahim Abbas. *Journal of Educational Administration and History*, vol. 21, no. 2 (1989), p. 46-54.

Examines the establishment of the University of the United Arab Emirates which was influenced by American patterns of academia. The author makes a comparison with American institutions, focusing on administration, academic freedom, and state involvement in the governance of the university.

599 **Dimensionality of burnout: testing for invariance across Jordanian and Emirati teachers.**
Maker M. Abu-Hilal. *Psychological Reports*, vol. 77, no. 3, pt. 2 (1995), p. 1367-75.

Reports on tests carried out on two samples of female teachers from the United Arab Emirates and Jordan, using the Maslach Burnout Inventory. Burnout scores are compared in order to measure the legitimacy of the results across two countries. Results suggested that the burnout factor might be the same for both countries and that the Inventory appeared to be valid for both Western and non-Western countries.

600 **An Arabic version of the Study Process Questionnaire: reliability and validity.**
Mohamed A. Albaili. *Psychological Reports*, vol. 77, no. 3, pt. 2 (1995), p. 1083-89.

A report on a study to assess the reliability and validity of the Arabic version of the Study Process Questionnaire as a measure of the learning and study processes of 246 college students aged 19-31 years in the United Arab Emirates. The author describes how the questionnaire was administered, and concludes that it can be used to assess learning and study processes of students from different traditions, practices, and educational systems.

601 **Informed hemispheric thinking style, gender, and academic major among United Arab Emirates college students.**
Mohammed A. Albaili. *Perceptual and Motor Skills*, vol. 76, no. 3, pt. 1 (1993), p. 971-77.

Reports on the results of a test conducted amongst 86 male and 104 female undergraduates in the United Arab Emirates in order to examine the relationship between the informed hemispheric thinking style, gender and academic major. Form A, 'Your Style of Learning and Thinking' was used. Although endorsements of an integrated style were highest, men tended to indicate endorsement of the right-hemispheric style items in processing information, whilst women tended to endorse items of an integrated style. In terms of academic majors, applied science students appeared to endorse items of a more right-hemispheric style in processing information than social science majors.

602 **Learning processes and academic achievement of United Arab Emirates college students.**
Mohamed A. Albaili. *Psychological Reports,* vol. 74, no. 3, pt. 1 (1994), p. 739-46.

An examination of the relationship between scores in the learning process assessed by the Inventory of Learning Processes and academic achievement assessed by high-school average.

603 **Psychometric properties of the Inventory of Learning Processes: evidence from United Arab Emirates college students.**
Mohamed A. Albaili. *Psychological Reports,* vol. 72, no. 3, pt. 2 (1993), p. 1331-36.

Investigates the reliability and validity of the Arabic version of the Inventory of Learning Processes, using 166 undergraduates from the United Arab Emirates. The test was conducted over a four-week period and provided satisfactory estimates of internal consistency and stability. The two scales used proved to be moderately predictive of academic performance.

604 **A two-stage multi-objective scheduling model for (faculty-course-time) assignments.**
M. A. Badri. *European Journal of Operational Research*, vol. 94, no. 1 (1996), p. 16-28.

Discusses the application of a model to maximize faculty course preferences in assigning faculty members to courses, and then to maximize faculty time preferences in allocating courses to time blocks. Badri reports on the success of the mathematical matrix-based model at the United Arab Emirates University.

605 **Surviving the war – a college counsellor's journal.**
Philip L. Clinton. *Journal of College Admission*, no. 133 (Fall 1991), p. 7-10.

A presentation of entries from the journal of a college counsellor at a United States school in Egypt which records the problems faced by students from United States and international schools in the Gulf States, including the United Arab Emirates. The students had been transferred to Egypt as a consequence of the Iraqi invasion of Kuwait.

606   **Women and public relations education and practice in the United Arab Emirates.**
Pamela J. Creedon (et al.).   *Public Relations Review*, vol. 21, no. 1 (1995), p. 59-76.

Reviews the history of public relations education in the United Arab Emirates and surveys research on public relations practice. The progress of establishing a public relations degree programme in the United Arab Emirates and the selection of a curriculum model is also examined. In addition, the authors give some consideration to the status of women in UAE society, and their future in public relations.

607   **Student and faculty perceptions of the characteristics of an ideal teacher in a classroom setting.**
Mondiras Das, Farouk El-Sabban.   *Medical Teacher*, vol. 18, no. 2 (1996), p. 141-46.

The results of a study which was carried out amongst students in the Faculty of Medicine and Health Sciences at the United Arab Emirates University in order to determine the characteristics of an ideal teacher in a classroom setting. A descriptive research approach was used to collect data from students and faculty members who were using conventional teaching and learning approaches in an integrated curriculum. There were large areas of common ground between students and faculty members but the students identified different characteristics, which, if present, would encourage student learning. These were 'build skills of self-learning', 'promote student interest in independent learning', and 'create an atmosphere for discussion'.

608   **Attitudes towards counselling in the Middle East.**
Richard C. Day.   *International Journal for the Advancement of Counselling*, vol. 6, no. 2 (1983), p. 143-52.

Reports on two questionnaires administered to assess the attitudes of nationals to counselling at both a governmental and an individual level in various countries of the Middle East, including the United Arab Emirates. The first questionnaire dealt with the status and future of counselling in the countries which recognized that counselling services were important and likely to increase in the future. The second questionnaire was aimed at undergraduates who had undergone an experience of counselling; 80 per cent of those surveyed expressed satisfaction with the services received and would recommend their use to a friend. The article also presents arguments for the expansion of counselling services in the Middle East.

609   **Educational Abstract.**
Abu Dhabi: UAE Ministry of Education and Youth, 1971- . annual.
The statistical details of education in the UAE.

610   **Developing a quality teaching force for the United Arab Emirates.**
William E. Gardner.   *Journal of Education for Teaching*, vol. 21, no. 2 (1995), p. 289-301.

The acquisition of a quality teaching force has been a major problem for development and this is a survey of the implementation of a teacher supply policy in the United Arab Emirates. The policy has three main goals: to supply enough teachers; to employ more nationals; and to raise the quality of the teaching force. Thanks to the benefits of oil revenues there has been no problem in employing sufficient numbers of teachers and more nationals have been trained, but expatriates still dominate the teaching sector and there are concerns about quality.

611 **Professional development schools: how well will they travel?**
William E. Gardner, Abdalla Abu Libde. *Journal of Education for Teaching*, vol. 21, no. 3 (1995), p. 303-15.

The concept of the professional development school advocating active partnerships between universities and schools is the main feature of the North American teacher education reform movement. However, it is maintained that the principles behind the concept need some modification if it is to be implemented in the United Arab Emirates. Four major aspects of the professional development school are identified as needing modification to reflect UAE culture: the decision-making process; the need to build autonomous institutions; equity and reciprocity between school and university; and the preferred classroom teaching method.

612 **Communication skills training early in the medical curriculum: the UAE experience.**
A. Harrison, T. Townsend, M. Glasgow. *Medical Teacher*, vol. 18, no. 1 (1996), p. 35-41.

A study of the effectiveness of a five-day communication skills training course held during the second year of a six-year medical teaching programme.

613 **How effective is self-directed learning at generating successful learning experiences, and what is its role within higher education?**
Reginald S. Hubbard. Paper presented at the Annual Meeting of the Teachers of English to speakers of other languages, held on 8-12 March 1994 at Baltimore, Maryland. 10p. refs. (Available from Educational Development Research Service RIE Mar 95).

The survey used a group of 720 first-year students from the United Arab Emirates University to determine if self-directed learning experiences produced higher levels of achievement than traditional learning experiences. The findings showed that 94 per cent of self-directed learning and 83 per cent of Independent Learning Centre students passed the first-year exams, but only 73 per cent of all first-year students passed.

614 **The admission and academic placement of students from: Bahrain, Oman, Qatar, United Arab Emirates, and Yemen Arab Republic.**
Edited by K. Johnson. Washington, DC: National Association for Foreign Student Affairs, 1984. 129p. bibliog.

This publication is designed to assist United States colleges and universities with the placement of students from the listed countries. The report covers the educational systems, society and population, education at all levels, vocational education, military education, teacher education, and English-language teaching. Sample documents are included from each country, including transcripts and diplomas.

615 **The United Arab Emirates and the Internet: cultural and social implications for higher education.**
A. M. E. Jones. *Information Development*, vol. 12, no. 1 (1996), p. 16-19.

Assesses the impact that the Internet could have on educational institutions and information centres in the United Arab Emirates, particularly in terms of social and cultural implications. Jones concludes that the use of this facility needs to be accompanied by appropriate curriculum development which takes into account cultural perspectives, language needs, and a diverse level of skills in likely users of the Internet.

616 **A comprehensive review of the status of early childhood development in the Middle East and North Africa.**
Mohammad Salih Kattab. Amman, Jordan: United Nations Children's Fund, 1995. 127p.

This review of the status of early childhood education programmes in the Middle East and North Africa region includes the United Arab Emirates. Information was collected by questionnaire sent to UNICEF country offices and from other sources. The report reviews the regional literature on early childhood education; profiles early childhood education in the surveyed countries – with data on programmes, background, cost, curricula, and constraints; historical background and data on staff, programme quality, institutions and buildings; cost of programmes; input and output data for evaluation; and recommended actions. English and Arabic versions of the questionnaire are appended.

617 **The transfer of psychological knowledge to the Third World countries and its impact on development: the case of five Arab Gulf oil-producing states.**
Levan H. Melikian. *International Journal of Psychology*, vol. 19, nos. 1-2 (1984), p. 65-77.

Examines the psychological knowledge transmitted in five universities in the Arabian Gulf, including the United Arab Emirates, and identifies some of the socio-cultural roots. The courses offered are similar to those in the United States, and almost all are taught in Arabic and located in the Faculty of Education. In terms of resources it was determined that laboratories were well stocked with both Arabic and English material, with research directed towards educational-psychological issues. Psychological tests are widely used but lack standardization, though there are attempts to develop locally based tests. However, top students are not being attracted to the subject and expatriates undertake most of the teaching. The major impact of the subject is in special education and the media but there is only a small impact in the areas of management and planning.

618 **Vocational guidance for equal access and opportunity for girls and women in technical and vocational education: UNEVOC Studies in Technical and Vocational Education 6.**
Juliet V. Miller, Louise Vetter. Paris: Unesco, 1996. 121p.
Examines the relevance of vocational information and guidance to the equal access of girls and women to technical and vocational education in a range of countries including the United Arab Emirates. Case-studies were conducted using a questionnaire covering national legislation policy, implementation plans and programmes; these were completed by in-country collaborators. Findings showed that equal employment and education for girls and women were national policies, and efforts had been made to implement structures and develop strategies to increase female participation.

619 **Knowledge and attitude of university female students towards obesity.**
Abdulrahman O. Musaiger. *International Quarterly of Community Health Education*, vol. 14, no. 4 (1994), p. 337-43.
Reports on a survey of 203 female students which was aimed at assessing knowledge of, and attitudes towards, obesity. The results showed that 53 per cent of the students believed that overeating and inactivity were the main causes of obesity, but half of the students had no knowledge of the dangers of obesity. Magazines and television were the main sources of information about nutrition.

620 **Improving education in the Arabian Gulf region.**
Mohammed A. Rasheed, Herbert R. Hengst. *Journal of Thought*, vol. 18, no. 2 (1983), p. 97-103.
Discusses the impact of the Arab Bureau of Education for the Gulf States on the development of education in the region, including the United Arab Emirates. The Bureau, which was established in 1976, had focused on obtaining information on education programmes from member states, educating citizens about their own culture, and promoting the establishment of a multinational university.

621 **Struggling for power and respectability in the Arab economic field.**
Mohammed Sabour. *International Social Science Journal*, vol. 45, no. 1 (1993), p. 107-18.
This examination of the status and power of academics in Arab academia uses case-studies from a number of countries, including the United Arab Emirates. The article explores academia's representation of self, ways in which academics compete for power, and the process by which respectability is acquired. However, Sabour shows that, owing to the realities of Arab academia, social status may yield only an uncertain degree of respectability.

622 **Restructuring the electrical and computer engineering curriculum at the UAE University.**
H. S. Shahein, A. Ismael. In: *Proceedings of the IEEE Frontiers in Education Conference*, held in Washington, DC, 6-9 December 1993. Edited by L. P. Grayson. New York: Institution of Electrical Engineers, 1993, p. 663-69.

Outlines plans for the restructuring of the electrical and computer engineering curriculum of the United Arab Emirates University which would emphasize the development of human resources and not just course content. Amongst the objectives are to: encourage graduates to think across a variety of disciplines; couple experience with abstract description; develop and implement novel ideas; understand the functional core of the engineering process; experiment with design and research and understand their synergy; analyse and synthesize; formulate problems and solve them; act both independently and as a team member.

623 **Higher education and development in the lower Gulf States.**
K. E. Shaw. *Higher Education Review*, vol. 25, no. 3 (1993), p. 36-47.

An examination of the expansion of higher education in the lower Gulf States, including the United Arab Emirates, which considers the providers of higher education and the motivation, cultural versus national identity, the role of mass education, and the difference between growth and development.

624 **Higher education in the Gulf: problems and prospects.**
Edited by K. E. Shaw. Exeter, England: Exeter University Press, 1997. 240p. bibliog.

This work considers the question of higher education in the Gulf States, including the United Arab Emirates, and stresses the need for engagement with the problems of the region as developing countries. It particularly stresses the significant role that locally based research should play in promoting balanced self-reliant development. One of the main objectives of the work is the promotion of further research into the topic and its importance to the development process.

625 **United Arab Emirates University students' attitudes towards the handicapped.**
Ahmed A. Smadi, Abdel Aziz M. Sartawi. *European Journal of Special Needs Education*, vol. 10, no. 3 (1995), p. 242-48.

Reports on the results of the use of the College Students' Attitude Scale with 313 students at the United Arab Emirates University to measure attitudes towards the handicapped. The findings showed significantly more positive attitudes by females versus males; single versus married students; residents versus non-residents; families with children having disabilities; students having previous contact with the disabled; and urban versus rural groups.

626   **The role of the College of Education at UAE University in manpower development.**
M. Touq.   Paper presented at the World Assembly of the International Council on Education for Teaching, held at Eindhoven, Netherlands, 20-24 July 1987. 22p. (Available from Education Development Research Service RIE March 88).

The College of Education was amongst the first of four colleges established at the United Arab Emirates University in 1977 and, in terms of enrolment, is now the second-largest college. The significant role of the college is examined, covering both qualitative and quantitative aspects, together with its participation in the university's development through transformation of programmes and study plans based on the needs of teachers and administrators. The structure of the college is based on eight undergraduate programmes, two diploma programmes and six master's programmes. Emphasis has been placed on both academic study and practical training, and a centre for research, development and educational services has also been established.

Dissertations

627   **The roles of administrators and faculty in university governance: a comparative study of a State University in the U.S. and the University of the United Arab Emirates.**
Shafika Ebrahim Abbas.   PhD thesis, Claremont Graduate School, California, 1986. 187p. (Available from University Microfilms, Ann Arbor, Michigan, order no. AAD86-07817).

A study of university governance, focusing on the role played by administrators and faculty at two universities: the University of the United Arab Emirates and California State University, Dominguey Hills. The comparison is made because the American model of higher education has shaped the growth of universities in the developing world, but indigenous values can have an effect on the way governance actually functions. The survey showed that a more open style of government was practised in the United States whilst the UAE governance was dominated by the administration. It was also found that there was more agreement between faculty and administrators at California State University over curriculum, departmental affairs, administration in general, and matters of academic freedom. It is evident that the UAE University has developed its own system of governance which is highly centralized and influenced by governmental and cultural factors.

628 **An investigation into students' academic achievement in the United Arab Emirates.**
A. S. A. Ali.   PhD thesis, Swansea University, Wales, 1991. [n.p.]. (Available from the British Library, Boston Spa, Wetherby, West Yorkshire).

An investigation to determine whether United Arab Emirates and non-UAE students differ in their academic achievement in the science curriculum of the third year of secondary education. It was based on a questionnaire sent to 300 students and an examination of the Ministry of Education records of achievement for those students. Ali found that the non-UAE students had significantly higher academic achievements and tended to have better-educated parents, fathers with higher levels of occupation, and more positive attitudes towards school and future career prospects.

629 **A needs analysis study for the establishment of a Community College educational system in the United Arab Emirates.**
Hussain M. Joma.   EdD thesis, Western Michigan University, Kalamazoo, 1982. 139p. (Available from University Microfilms, Ann Arbor, Michigan, order no. AAD83-05551).

An analysis of the training and educational needs of the United Arab Emirates in the areas of technical and middle management by means of a study of high-school students and presidents of banks and factories. The objective was to produce a needs analysis for the establishment of a community college educational system in the UAE. The conclusions drawn from the study were that: all areas of business expressed a growing interest in technical-level education beyond high school; sufficient interest was shown by students in the community college for transfer-credit courses; there was evidence of interest by students because the college would be close to home and a place to spend a few years in a transfer programme.

630 **Factors contributing to the drop-out rate from adult evening elementary school centers: Sharjah City, Sharjah Emirate of the United Arab Emirates.**
Nurah Abdulrahman Al-Medfa.   EdD thesis, University of Southern California, Los Angeles, 1984. [n.p.]. (Available from Micrographics Department, Dohemy Library, USC, Los Angeles, CA 90089).

Investigates the relationship between selected demographic variables and the perceived importance of selected institutional variables on the one hand, and the dropout phenomena among fifth- and sixth-level adult evening students in the United Arab Emirates, on the other. Data were collected from evening students in Sharjah, based on a sample of 100 dropouts and 100 non-dropouts. It was discovered that dropout was likely to increase: with age; with increased domestic responsibility; if subjects live in rural areas; and as perceptions of the importance of teachers' attention to students increases. The author concludes that the dropout rate could be reduced through an improvement in the level of teaching abilities and increased financial support for those students with family responsibilities.

631 **Personnel administration of education in the United Arab Emirates.**
Najat Abdulla Al-Nabeh.   PhD thesis, Claremont Graduate School, California, 1982. 255p. (Available from University Microfilms, Ann Arbor, Michigan, order no. AAD82-28737).
The education system in the United Arab Emirates was established only in 1953. It is still evolving and must be improved if development plans are to be sustained. However, a profound problem standing in the way of advancement is identified as the lack of qualified administrators and teachers, resulting in a dependence on expatriate labour. The objective of the study was to develop a new model staffing procedure to provide the best recruitment, selection and placement process for teachers and administrators in the education system.

Faculty evaluation of educational strategies in medical schools.
See item no. 259.

Learning preferences of medical students.
See item no. 282.

The effectiveness of sentence combining practice on Arab students' overall writing quality and syntactic maturity.
See item no. 639.

Language and Literature

632 Second language acquisition notes and topics: a newsletter for researchers and teachers.
Edited by Judith Chun.   San Francisco, California: San Francisco State University, 1978. 80p.

This newsletter covers research in Canada and an article on second-language acquisition in the Middle East, including the United Arab Emirates. The conclusion is that progress in the region is very slow in terms of second-language education.

633 English Teaching profile: United Arab Emirates.
London: British Council, English Language and Literature Division, 1986. 14p.

Reviews the status of English Language teaching in the United Arab Emirates, including a review of the role of English in society, and the status of English use and instruction at all levels. Topics covered include: characteristics and training of English Language instructors; type and availability of instructional materials; educational administration and planning of language teaching; English instruction outside of the educational structure; and British support and commercial opportunities relating to English instruction. Concludes that the teaching force is neither stable nor highly competent, and that the educational approach is inflexible and conservative. However, the Ministry of Education is supportive of English instruction and in-service teacher education.

634 Dubai tales.
Muhammad al-Murr, translated by Peter Clark.   London: Forest Books, 1991. vi+154p.

This translation presents twenty stories written by Muhammad al-Murr, a native of Dubai, between 1982 and 1989. They have been selected to illustrate different aspects of life in the Gulf region. One of the major themes underlying the stories concerns the status of women within society and, in particular, the difficulties faced by the younger generations exposed to other ways of life through the media, and the realities of their own culture.

635 A basic course in Gulf Arabic.

Hamdi A. Qafisheh. Tucson, Arizona: University of Arizona Press, 1975. 482p.

A text for a basic course in Gulf Arabic as used by the educated indigenous population in the United Arab Emirates. The work provides a linguistic sketch of the UAE and forty-two units of study each consisting of a narrative, grammatical structure, vocabulary, pronunciation exercises, and grammatical drills. Guidance is given on the use of the text and an explanation of the transcription system is provided.

636 A short reference grammar of Gulf Arabic.

Hamdi A. Qafisheh. Tucson, Arizona: University of Arizona Press, 1977. xxii+274p.

This work presents an outline of the structure of Gulf Arabic based on the dialect of Abu Dhabi and is intended for linguists, dialectologists, and teachers and students of Gulf Arabic. Parts 1-3 cover the phonology, morphology and syntax of Gulf Arabic; Section 9 contains five texts which relate to daily life, accompanied by English translations. The appendices contain details of phonological variations between literary Arabic and Gulf Arabic.

637 Language development in the Gulf: lexical interference of English in the Gulf dialects.

J. R. Smart. In: *Arabia and the Gulf: from traditional society to modern states*, edited by Ian Richard Netton. London: Croom Helm, 1986, p. 202-12.

The author studies the borrowing of English words into Gulf dialects. It is not considered surprising because of: the commercial and political history of the area; oil exploration and production being English-language based; and the rapid development and commercial expansion resulting from oil wealth. The varieties of English language studied are British, American and Indian, the latter being the lingua franca of the large numbers of workers from the Indian subcontinent. The article covers the literature on the subject, including material on the dialects of Abu Dhabi and Dubai.

638 Pidginization in Gulf Arabic: a first report.

J. R. Smart. *Anthropological Linguistics*, vol. 32, nos. 1-2 (1990), p. 83-119.

Smart's examination of the modern Arabic used in the Gulf States considers the various dialects in use and the pidginization of the spoken language.

Dissertations

639 **The effectiveness of sentence combining practice on Arab students' overall writing quality and syntactic maturity.**
Shaker Rizk Aki El Din.   PhD thesis, Indiana University of Pennsylvania, 1985. 157p. (Available from University Microfilms, Ann Arbor, Michigan, order no. AAD86-21576).

A study aimed at determining the effectiveness of sentence-combining practice, integrated in an EFL (English as a Foreign Language) composition course, on the overall writing and syntactic maturity of students at the United Arab Emirates University, Al-Ain. The study was based on two groups: one experimental consisting of 63 students, and a control group of 67 students. This was a preliminary investigation, and various problems were recognized in the design of the study: institutional constraints, lack of control over the instructor variable, and lack of control over gender population.

640 **A glossary of the dialect of the United Arab Emirates transcribed and arranged according to the English alphabet.**
F. Handahl.   PhD thesis, Exeter University, England, 1987. [n.p.]. (Available from the British Library, Boston Spa, Wetherby, West Yorkshire).

A presentation of eight years of fieldwork carried out in the United Arab Emirates. The work began in 1969 and resulted in a lexicon of the dialects of the UAE presented in the form of a glossary. No one specific dialect is covered, but a range from the several hundred present in the federation. The glossary is designed to assist future scholars who wish to specialize in narrower fields. Information is also provided on folk customs and literature, mainly from the camel-rearing bedouin and the pearlers and seafarers – the era of these two groups is passing, making it necessary to do the research before it is too late.

Culture and Customs

641 **Falconry in Arabia.**
Mark Allen. London: Orbis, 1980. 143p. bibliog.
An illustrated book written by an expert on the art of falconry which sets the sport in the cultural background of Arabia, but with particular concentration on the UAE.

642 **Modernization in the Arabian Gulf States: a paradigm of cultural changes.**
Ghaus Ansari. *The Eastern Anthropologist*, vol. 38, no. 3 (1985), p. 189-205.
An examination of modernization in traditional societies which includes the United Arab Emirates as one of the case-studies. Prior to the discovery of oil, the economy of the UAE was limited and the process of modernization was slow in terms of education and the status of women, but both aspects were accelerated by oil revenues. The media also expanded rapidly, as did urbanization, largely through the growth of migrant labour. The process has also had an impact on the culture, by making the indigenous population more aware of their cultural heritage.

643 **Towards ethnographic cartography: a case study.**
Walter Dostal. *Current Anthropology*, vol. 25, no. 3 (1984), p. 340-44. maps.
A case-study of ethnographic documentation in Ras Al Khaimah designed to record traditional culture before it is lost in the development process. The United Arab Emirates is regarded as an area marked by a lack of ethnographic knowledge and rapid cultural change. The article discusses aspects of the data-gathering process, including the use of field studies and questionnaires to determine general topographical data, economic data, and information about material culture.

173

644 Rites of hospitality and aesthetics.

Aida S. Kanafani. In: *Everyday life in the Muslim Middle East*, edited by Donna Lee Bowen (et al.). Bloomington: Indiana University Press, 1993, p. 128-35.

This contribution provides a brief insight into the rites followed by a Muslim in the United Arab Emirates, with particular reference to the role and rites of hospitality within the culture, and to their Bedouin origins.

645 Arab socio-political impact on Gulf life-styles.

Levon Melikian. In: *The Arab Gulf and the Arab World*, edited by B. R. Pridham. London: Croom Helm, 1989, p. 112-28.

A study of the influence of the Arabs from the northern part of the Arab World on the socio-political life-styles of the Gulf Arabs, primarily in the period following the discovery of oil. Melikian considers that the Gulf States needed the Arabs from the north as they were better educated, more skilled, more sophisticated, and better able to handle the complexities of modern life. These attributes were needed by the oil-producing states, including the United Arab Emirates, to build and develop all sectors of society, and, luckily, the impact of oil led to an influx of northern Arabs into the oil-producing states. In this context, life-style is regarded as the manner in which an individual adapts to his environment and meets his security needs. The contribution considers the traditional life-styles of the region, political life-styles, the impact of education, religion, socio-political life-styles, and the significant role and influences of the expatriate population. In two major areas no impact has been made, that of names and dress, a fact which is seen as pointing to the relative stability of the identity of the Gulf Arab.

Sport and Recreation

646 **Public parks in Dubai.**
S. Elsabaa. *Trade and Industry* (Dubai), vol. 19, no. 220 (1994),
p. 10-18.

Elsabaa's examination of the various parks in Dubai traces their development since
1980 when only two parks, Al Safa and Mushrif, were in being. In the ensuing decade,
the creation of parks has been a major feature of development in Dubai, planned
according to a set of specifications and criteria which are amongst the most advanced
in developing countries. Public parks are considered to be a vital asset to the city, as
both cultural and aesthetic attractions, but they are also crucial in terms of the environment as they assist in purifying the air and increasing the oxygen component.
Parks are also seen as providing opportunities for recreation and entertainment, and as
a feature which attracts tourists from within the Gulf and elsewhere.

647 **Camel racing in the United Arab Emirates.**
J. Haydn-Evans, W. Wernery. *Journal of Camel Practice and
Research*, vol. 2, no. 2 (1995), p. 135-37.

Describes the evolution of camel racing in the United Arab Emirates. It was first performed by bedouin who used to race camels for fun. The sport has evolved into a serious pastime for the wealthy, and the resultant financial investment has meant that
regulations have had to be introduced. These included restrictions on the age of
jockeys and drug testing of camels.

648 **Arabs still look for help.**
K. Radnedge. *World Soccer*, vol. 19, no. 11 (1978), p. 36-37.

Assesses the need for assistance from expatriate experts with the administration of
association football in the United Arab Emirates, Saudi Arabia and Iran.

649 Name of the game is petrosports: in the Persian Gulf, oil is funding lavish facilities for sports, from camel racing to soccer, falconry to ice hockey.
J. D. Reed. *Sports Illustrated*, vol. 53, no. 21 (1980), p. 90-94, 96-98, 100, 102, 104.

A study of recreational facilities in the Gulf States, including the United Arab Emirates. They have been heavily subsidized by oil revenues, enabling facilities to be provided which would normally be environmentally impossible.

650 Preserving cultural identity by outdoor recreation and domestic tourism: the case of the Gulf Arabs.
W. Ritter. In: *Towards appropriate tourism: the case of developing countries*, edited by T. V. Singh (et al.). Frankfurt, Germany: Peter Lang, 1989, p. 311-23.

Ritter's study of the recreational behaviour of the Gulf Arabs, including those in the United Arab Emirates, examines the internal needs of the indigenous population for family-centred recreation. The families have a need to withdraw from the daily exposure to foreigners who do not understand local traditions and sensibilities. They do so through the use of secondary homes, such as houses in inland capitals, amenity farms, and coastal chalets. Such family-based recreation is largely at the instigation of women, which is somewhat surprising in a supposedly strictly patriarchal society.

651 The dromedary derbies of Dubai.
Mary Roach. *Reader's Digest* (US edition), vol. 150, no. 897 (1997), p. 169-76. map.

Describes the camel racing events in Dubai, but points out that the spectacle has lost much of its attraction with the popularity of four-wheel-drive vehicles.

652 The flowering of hockey in the desert.
Barbara Wickens. *Maclean's*, vol. 109 (7 Aug. 1996), p. 13.

A brief description of the success of three hockey teams that have flourished in the United Arab Emirates and the search by the Mighty Camels team for a Canadian coach.

GPS-augmented live television coverage of Persian Gulf boat races.
See item no. 654.

Mass Media

653 Arab Gulf Journal.
London: MD Research and Services, 1981- . bi-annual.
Published in April and October of each year and devoted exclusively to the Gulf States.

654 GPS-augmented live television coverage of Persian Gulf boat races.
R. D. Cooper, D. Earl.   *GPS-World*, vol. 4, no. 7 (1993), p. 40, 42.
Describes the use of GPS [Global Positioning System] to enhance coverage of dhow races in the Persian Gulf over public television. The races are a major sporting event, with over 100 boats taking part, and covering over 30 nautical miles from the offshore islands to Abu Dhabi. GPS enabled continuous coverage of the race to be provided.

655 Emirates News.
Abu Dhabi: UAE Ministry of Information and Culture, 1971- . daily.
A semi-official newspaper in English, with local news and material taken from the international press agencies. Available from the Ministry of Information and Culture, PO Box 791, Abu Dhabi.

656 Gulf States Newsletter.
London: International Communications, 1 Dec. 1980-   fortnightly.
(Formerly *Middle East Newsletter*).
Specialist coverage of economic, financial and political affairs throughout the Gulf. Aimed at the senior business executive, politicians and others involved in decision-making regarding the area.

657 Gulf Weekly Mirror.
Manama, Bahrain: Gulf Weekly Mirror, 1971- . weekly.

An English-language newspaper published on Sundays and covering the whole of the Gulf, but with a special Lower Gulf edition based on news from Abu Dhabi and Dubai. Available from Gulf Weekly Mirror, al-Moayyed Building, Government Road, PO Box 455, Manama, Bahrain, or from PO Box 290, Dubai.

658 The flow of foreign news into six Arab Gulf countries.
Abdulraham Ibrahim Al-Habib.   Paper presented at the Annual Meeting of the Association for Education in Journalism and Mass Communication held in Washington DC, 10-13 August 1989. 33p. (Available from Educational Development Research Service RIE Feb 90).

This study of the foreign-news coverage of newspapers in the Arab Gulf States is based on an examination of one paper from each of six countries, which in the case of the United Arab Emirates was *Al-Ittihad*. Each selected newspaper was considered prestigious and had the highest circulation in its country. Stories were separated into foreign and domestic categories, and measured by length. Findings indicated that: foreign news occupied more than half of the total news space; Latin America and the Eastern bloc received scant coverage; conflict and defence topics dominated the foreign news; international agencies emphasized conflict at the expense of more positive news; there was a strong imbalance in the regional coverage and subject category distribution of foreign news.

659 Software protection in the UAE.
A. Kelman.   *Computer Fraud and Security Bulletin*, vol. 4, no. 9 (1982), p. 2-3.

Kelman assesses the problems of protecting software in the United Arab Emirates. It will be difficult because of the lack of legislation to build on – there is not even a basic copyright law. The only safeguard is to use hardware protection to deter piracy.

660 The literal text of the Gulf Information Honorary Covenant which has been acknowledged from the GCC leaders in the summit conference which took place in the state of the UAE.
Journal of the Gulf and Arabian Peninsula Studies, vol. 8, no. 50 (1987), p. 279-87.

Reproduces the text, dating from December 1986, of the covenant on ethics in communication. It was signed by the leaders of the Gulf Co-operation Council (GCC) at the summit meeting held in the United Arab Emirates. The media would adhere to the values of Islam and Gulf co-operation, and all information transmitted would be objective, exact and authentic, without provocation or personal attacks. The media also agreed to support social development in the Gulf, and to oppose anything that might harm the Arab identity in the GCC.

661 **Advertising agencies and media in the lower Gulf.**
R. A. Middleton, Tariq Almoayyed.   Manama, Bahrain: al-Hilal
Bookshop, 1977. vi+133p. map.
A list of agencies and media throughout the lower part of the Gulf, including the UAE.

662 **Ras al Khaimah Magazine.**
Sharjah: Sharjah Department of Information. bimonthly.
An English-language magazine.

663 **The Recorder.**
Sharjah: The Recorder. daily.
An English-language paper, with local news and international news from Reuters
Press Agency. Available from the publisher at PO Box 597, Sharjah.

Libraries

664 Resource sharing in Gulf academic libraries '95.
A. A. Bukhari. *Library Hi-Tech News*, no. 130 (March 1996), p. 9-12.
A report on the Annual Conference of the Special Library Association, Arabian Gulf
Chapter, held at Al-Ain between 15 and 17 March 1995. Papers presented at the conference covered: information policy and resources; international, regional and national
perspectives; standards for resource sharing; technology and resource sharing; databases and systems for resource sharing; and inter-library loan and document delivery.

665 University libraries in Arab countries.
M. M. Dyab. *International Library Review*, vol. 15, no. 1 (1983),
p. 15-29.
Describes the holdings, including manuscripts, of university libraries in the Arab
world, including the United Arab Emirates.

666 Coordinated economic development and the information network.
D. K. Easton. Arlington, Virginia: Education Resources Information
Center, 1977. 9p.
A discussion of the major problems to be faced by the Advisory Organization for Gulf
Industries which was being set up to: organize an information centre for the Gulf
States, including the United Arab Emirates; compile an indigenous databank that
could supply comprehensive economic information and statistics about the member
states; and index data.

**667 United Arab Emirates – outline for a National Documentation and
Information Centre.**
A. H. Helal. Paris: Unesco, 1975. 25p. (FMR/COM/DND/75/135).
A report on a consultant's visit to Abu Dhabi to advise on the establishment of
documentation, libraries and information services to the federation. The report recom-
mended a ten-year development plan and stressed the need to: establish priorities;

allocate funds for priority areas; locate and train staff; encourage co-operation at national, regional and international level; and develop a research and training programme. A centre was established as a result of the consultancy.

668 **Medical libraries and their services to the health sector in the United Arab Emirates (1971-1993).**
M. S. Jaffar. In: *Information and libraries in the Arab world*, edited by M. Wise, A. Olden. London: Library Association Publishing, 1994, p. 214-39.
A review of medical libraries and information services in the United Arab Emirates between 1971 and 1993. Concentrates on the libraries of: the Faculty of Medicine and Health Sciences of the United Arab Emirates University; the National Medical Library; the Female Private Medical College Library, Dubai; and the Ministry of Health hospital libraries. Brief notes are provided for other medical libraries in the federation.

669 **Economic and social change in the Emirates: is the information provision adequate?**
M. B. A. Karim. In: *Information and libraries in the Arab world*, edited by M. Wise, A. Olden. London: Library Association Publishing, 1994, p. 240-59.
Begins with a description of the economic and social background to the United Arab Emirates and the extent to which information services serve the needs of the country. Karim considers the public, academic, school and special libraries, together with the Chambers of Commerce as providers of business information. The Arab Information Bank on-line database is also described and the telecommunications policies affecting information provision are examined. Brief mention is also made of the role of the government in: information technology; printing and publishing; the book trade; the press; censorship; and copyright.

670 **On your MARC, get set, go.**
F. A. Khalid. *Information Technology and Libraries*, vol. 15, no. 2 (1996), p. 99-103.
This paper presents a summary of machine-readable bibliographical control in the Arab Gulf States, including the United Arab Emirates, and details measures to be taken to establish standards for Arabic machine-readable data.

671 **Exploring the Emirates: a visit to the National Medical Library, Al-Ain, Abu Dhabi Emirate.**
Philip Thomas. *Focus on International and Comparative Librarianship*, vol. 23, no. 1 (1992), p. 4-5.
Thomas's report on a visit to the National Medical Library of the University of the United Arab Emirates covers: the building; the collections; on-line database facilities; funding; inter-library loans; and segregation of male and female students.

Bibliographies

672 **The contemporary Middle East, 1948-1973: a selective and annotated bibliography.**
George N. Atiyeh. Boston, Massachusetts: G. K. Hall, 1975. 664p.

A very useful bibliography with brief annotations of some 6,500 entries, covering monographs, pamphlets and periodical articles, primarily in Western languages. The material is selective and orientated largely towards the social scientist, with items on history, politics, social conditions, economics and education. One section deals specifically with the UAE, citing some fifteen items, but other references can be found in the general subject sections.

673 **Some Western views of the Arab Gulf.**
Paul Auchterlonie. In: *Arabia and the Gulf: from traditional society to modern states*, edited by Ian Richard Netton. London: Croom Helm, 1986, p. 43-56.

A survey of works by Western writers on the Gulf States in the areas of historical, bio-graphical and political writings, but excluding specialist economic and anthro-pological studies, collective works and journal literature. Auchterlonie makes the point that literature on the Gulf, in any language, is scarce and that there is no real evi-dence to support the area as a geopolitical concept prior to Britain adopting the view of the region as an entity, particularly after the signing of a series of treaties with the ruling Sheikhs after 1880. Western scholars have only recently become interested in the Gulf States for two main reasons: the Gulf States have not supported an extensive vernacular literature in history, the Islamic sciences or *belles-lettres*; the theme of the impact of modernity on traditional societies which has dominated much of Western writing on the Third World is not relevant to the Gulf States until the late 1950s. The work deals primarily with the standard historical texts on the Gulf States, which were largely produced by the British Political Agents and issued through the Government of British India, as a prime source of information. The author then goes on to review the significant contemporary works on the Gulf States.

182

674 **Bibliography of population literature in the Arab world, part 1: non-Arabic literature.**
Beirut: United Nations Economic Commission for Western Asia, 1980. 274p.

This listing of the greater part of recent population research dealing with the Arab world, is arranged by the following subjects: size, growth and structure, morbidity and mortality, reproduction and family formation, distribution and internal migration, internal migration and multi-variable population research. The work has an author index and each entry has an annotation in the margin to indicate the geographical area of coverage.

675 **Arab regional organizations.**
Frank A. Clements.   Oxford, England: Clio Press, 1992. 198p.

An annotated bibliography of selected Arab regional organizations. The sections of relevance to the United Arab Emirates are: the Organization of Arab Petroleum Exporting Countries; the Gulf Co-operation Council; and the Abu Dhabi Fund for Arab Economic Development.

676 **Kuwait.**
Frank A. Clements.   Oxford, England: Clio Press, 1996. rev. ed. 340p. map.

This bibliography is primarily about Kuwait, but it is included because some references in the sections on 'Environment' and the 'Gulf War' are of relevance to the United Arab Emirates – they are not, however, significant enough to be separately annotated within the present work.

677 **Ports of the Arabian Peninsula: a guide to the literature.**
H. Dodgeon, A. M. Findlay.   Durham, England: University of Durham, Centre for Middle Eastern and Islamic Studies, 1979. 49p. (Occasional Papers Series, no. 7).

A briefly annotated list of books, articles and reports, with a large number of references to the UAE and the new ports in Abu Dhabi and Dubai.

678 **Middle East information online: the Arab Information Bank.**
L. M. Ellis.   *Online*, vol. 15, no. 2 (1991), p. 44-46.

A description of the data provided by the Arab Information Bank (AIB) through the Dialog online system. The file provides access to newspaper, periodical and radio sources about the Arab World and Middle East affairs. AIB is provided from Abu Dhabi and covers, amongst other topics, politics, economics and international relations. The article also provides tips on searching and relevant techniques.

679 **Analytical guide to the bibliographies on the Arabian Peninsula.**
L. Geddes.   Denver, Colorado: American Institute of Islamic Studies, 1974. 50p.

A listing of some seventy bibliographies in European languages on the Arabian Peninsula, together with annotations as to coverage, content, limitations, etc. Those dealing solely with the Trucial States are numbers 59, 60 and 62.

680 The Third World: Saudi Arabia, Organization of Petroleum
   Exporting Countries, Kuwait, United Arab Emirates, Qatar,
   Oman, Yemen People's Democratic Republic, Yemen Arab
   Republic: a bibliography.
   E. W. Miller, R. M. Miller.   Washington, DC: Vance Bibliographies,
   1989. 41p.

Provides a listing of 415 English-language articles, books and other publications
dating from 1981. The arrangement is alphabetical by author within countries and subject sections, and includes: political developments; foreign relations; defence; economy; society; and natural resources. There is also a section of 143 references on the
Organization of Petroleum Exporting Countries.

681 Index Islamicus, 1906-1958.
   Compiled by J. D. Pearson.   Cambridge, England: Heffer, 1958. 897p.
   new ed., London: Mansell, 1972. (Distributed in the USA by
   International Scholarly Book Services, Forest Grove, Oregon).

A catalogue of articles on Islamic subjects in periodicals, *Festschriften*, congresses
and other collective works. The work is arranged by subject, dealing first with general
material, and then with specific topics under headings such as art, religion and literature. Further sections are devoted to area studies, subdivided by subject. Entries are
not annotated, but give author, title, bibliographical details, and cross-references to
other entries. It includes an index of authors and subjects. There are supplements
1956-60; 1961-65; 1966-70; 1971-75; 1976-80 (2 vols), and quarterly updates with
quinquennial cumulations, now edited by Geoffrey Roper.

682 Arabia in early maps: a bibliography of maps covering the
   peninsula of Arabia printed in western Europe from the invention
   of printing to the year 1751.
   G. R. Tibbetts.   Cambridge, England; New York: Oleander Press,
   1978. 175p. maps.

Useful for a study of the very early cartography of the area, compiled mainly before
detailed exploration of the area began, and with full attribution and assessment for
each map. The compiler's introductory essay on the cartography of the Arabian
Peninsula is also very informative.

Internet Sites

The following are a representative sample of Internet sites related to the United Arab Emirates. Guides to other links will be found at most of these sites.

683 **Higher Colleges of Technology Home Page.**
   http://www.hct.ac.ae/
Provides information about the Higher Colleges of Technology, and includes employment opportunities, a welcome from the Chancellor, links for students and a live picture of the Abu Dhabi corniche.

684 **United Arab Emirates.**
   http://trave.state.govt/united_arab_emirates.html
Provides information on the federal government and the government of the individual Emirates.

685 **The United Arab Emirates and the ECSSR Page.**
   http://www.ecssr.ac.ae/
Provides information and news about the Emirates Centre for Strategic Studies and Research (ECSSR).

686 **United Arab Emirates (UAE) Government.**
   http://www.arab.net/uae/govt/uae_govt.html
Provides a general description of the government of the United Arab Emirates and the status of women in the federation.

687 United Arab Emirates Home Page.
http://www.emirates. org/

A guide to the United Arab Emirates which gives a considerable amount of information on the federation and, in particular, the development processes in all sectors of the economy and society.

688 United Arab Emirates Libraries.
http://www.arab.uacu.ac.ae/library.html

The United Arab Emirates University Library's resources information service.

689 United Arab Emirates Online Yellow Pages.
http://www.onlineyellow.com/

This is an online service to yellow pages which covers the United Arab Emirates and other Gulf Co-operation Council states.

690 United Arab Emirates (UAE) Sharjah Government Customs Department.
http://www.sharjahcustoms.gov.ae

This site provides details of customs regulations for the Emirate of Sharjah and includes some statistical data.

Indexes

There follow three separate indexes: authors (personal and corporate); titles; and subjects. The numbers refer to bibliographical entry rather than page number. Title entries are italicized.

Index of Authors

Belgrave, Charles Dalrymple 177
Bener, A. 257
Bernier, P. 86
Berny, Z. 475
Beydoun, Z. R. 441
Bidwell, Robin 64, 73
Bingham, Annette 189
Birks, John Stace 217-18, 565-67
Blair, Edmund 400
Blake, Gerald 330
Blatter, E. 146
Blum, Charlotte 388
BMA Sugar Division 489-90
Boltzer, F. 87
Boucharlot, R. 166
Boustead, Hugh 190
Bowen, Dona Lee 644
Braun, Ursula 350
Bray, Frank 46
Brent, Peter 74
Bristow, C. 88
Bukhari, A. A. 664
Bulloch, John 5
Bundy, Rodman R. 332
Burrell, R. M. 191
Burrows, Bernard 192
Busabir, A. A. 271
Busch, Briton Cooper 45, 193
Bushrod, Howard Jnr 201
Busit, O. S. 320
Buttiker, W. 155, 162-63

C

Casey, Paula 40
Cattan, Henry 463
Chandler, Patricia M. 423
Chatelus, Michael 491
Chow, J. 560
Chubin, Shahram 296, 370
Chun, Judith 632
Cicak-Chand, Ruzica 219
Clark, Peter 634
Clements, Frank A. 675-76
Clinton, Philip L. 605
Codrai, Ronald 6
Colitti, Marcello 464
Comair-Obeid, Nayla 311

Constable, Robin 8
Cooper, R. D. 654
Cooper, R. T. 147-48
Cope, T. A. 157
Cordes, Rainer 227
Cordesman, Anthony H. 351
Costello, F. 238
Cottrell, Alvin J. 46
Coz, Percy Z. 75
Creedon, Pamela J. 606
Crystal, Jill 220
Cuddington, J. T. 384
Cunningham, Andrew 402
Cunningham, Michael 333

D

Dalongeville, R. 89
Daniels, John 7
Daradekeh, T. K. 258
Darbool, M. A. 587
Das, Mondiras 259, 607
Davey, B. J. 105
Davies, Charles E. 178
Dawson, K. P. 260
Day, Richard C. 608
Deakin, Michael 8
Demir, Soliman 369
Derevensky, Jeffrey I. 216
Dib, G. 261
Din, S. S. El 290
Din, Shaker Rizk Aki El 639
Dixon, A. 403
Dodgeon, H. 677
Dostal, Walter 643
Dowdy, William Leroy 304
Duncan, Andrew 47
Dunnington, H. V. 441
Dyab, M. M. 665

E

Earl, D. 654
Easton, D. K. 666
Ebraheem, Hassan Ali Al-334
Eelens, F. 568
Ehteshami, Anoushiravan 9
Eisa, E. I. 477

Elhussein, Ahmed Mustafa 569
Elkateb, M. 476
Ellis, L. M. 678
Elsabaa, S. 646
Elschami, F. 116-17
Ennadi, Ibrahim 449
Eren, T. M. 512
Etaibi, Ghalib Tulhab 360
Evans, Kathy 11

F

Fairservice, Ian 12
Fallon, Nicholas 442
Farzin, Y. H. 405
Fenelon, Kevin 13
Ferrara, F. 163
Ferris, N. P. 513
Feuilherade, Peter 570
Field, Michael 14, 370
Findlay, A. M. 677
Fitterman, D. V. 118
Fitzsimons, Mathew A. 196
Formen, Werner 15
Fredericks, Brian E. 352
Friedman, G. M. 90
Frifelt, Karen 167-68

G

Gallagher, E. B. 262
Gallagher, M. D. 155
Ganeswaran, S. 554
Gardner, William E. 610-11
Gareis, M. 514
Gaswani, D. Yogi 597
Gause, F. Gregory III 16
Geddes, C. L. 679
Ghais, S. M. Al- 148, 515
Ghanayem, Mohammad A. 397
Ghazanfor, S. A. 263
Ghorab, K. E. 406
Ghubash, R. 264-65
Glasgow, M. 612
Glasgow, M. J. 266
Gohil, V. S. 267-68
Goodall, T. 88
Grant, Gillian 27

Grayson, L. P. 621
Graz, Liesl 17
Great Britain. Admiralty,
  Naval Intelligence
  Division 48-49
Great Britain. Foreign and
  Commonwealth Office
  50, 202-3
Greenwald, J. 408
Gribble, R. 555
Grieve, Chuck 12
Groom, N. 133
Guazzone, Laura 353
Gunatilaka, A. 97
Gush, Hilary 18

H

Habib, Abdulrahman
  Ibrahim Al- 568
Habib, F. I. Al- 409
Habibullah, J. 276
Hacker, B. R. 91
Haerinck, E. 169-71
Hajri, K. R. Al- 120
Hakim, Ali A. El- 204
Hall, Marjorie 314
Halliday, Fred 297
Hamadi, Abdulkarim
  Mohamed 213
Hamdi, E. 264
Hamed, O. A. 494
Hameed, Mazhar A. 354
Hamid, Y. H. 477
Hammadi, A. A. A. Al- 237
Hamo, Ishrek 269
Hamoda, M. F. 516
Han, Vo Xuan 444
Hanafi, A. 121
Handahl, F. 640
Harman, J. 427
Harrison, A. 270-71, 612
Harrison, Ann 272
Hassan, E. S. 589
Hassan, M. A. 92
Hassan, T. H. 445
Hawas, F. Mohamed 465
Hawley, Donald 19
Hay, Rupert 205
Haydn-Evans, J. 647
Heard-Bey, Frauke 197,
  221, 228

Helal, A. H. 667
Hengst, Herbert R. 620
Higgins, Kevin 33
Hillingworth, J. A. 250
Hills, Nicholas 364
Hinchcliffe, Doreen 232,
  307
Hindley, Angus 371, 388,
  411-12,
  446-47, 478, 544, 571
Hindy, K. T. 590
Hiro, Dilip 51, 335
Hofmeier, R. 302
Hooti, S. Al- 517
Hopwood, Derek 188, 191,
  222, 467
Hosni, Sayed M. 315
Hossain, M. M. 273
Howlett, J. C. 149
Hubbard, Reginald S. 613
Hudson, Michael C. 298
Husain, T. 106

I

Ibrahim, Y. M. 518
Imes, Jeffrey L. 110
India Office, Political
  Department 194-95
Indian Government,
  Foreign and Political
  Department 179-80
Ishvi, K. 124
Ismael, A. 622
Istanbulluoglu, E. 519
Izzard, Molly 52

J

Jackson, C. C. E. 107
Jaffal, A. A. 275
Jaffar, M. S. 608
Jassin, S. M. Al- 372
Jeffs, E. 494
Jennings, Michael C. 150
Jensen, J. R. 591
Joffe, George 299
Johnson, K. 614
Joma, Hussain M. 629
Jones, A. 151-52
Jones, A. M. E. 615

Jopp, Klaus 479
Jorgensen, D. G. 122

K

Kadhim, Mihssen 379
Kalidar, Abbas 244
Kanafani, Aida S. 644
Kardousha, M. M. 515
Karim, F. M. 153-54
Karim, L. 258
Karim, M. B. A. 669
Karti, Isamdar 373
Kattab, Mohammad Salih
  616
Kazi, Lubra Ahmad Al-
  576
Kechichian, Joseph A. 355,
  361
Kelly, John Barrett 53-55,
  198, 206-8
Kelman, A. 659
Kemball, Donald Burrowes
  181
Kemp, B. J. 495
Kemp, Peter 374-75, 413
Kendall, C. G. St. C. 93
Kenig, F. 94
Kennet, Derek 20
Khalid, F. A. 670
Khalifa, Ali Mohammed
  21
Khalil, A. 480
Khashan, Hilal 336
Khattab, M. M. 95
Khirbash, M. K. 504
Khordagui, H. K. 437, 583,
  592
Kinsman, D. J. J. 96
Kirby, R. P. 134
Kirkwood, Liz 239, 376-77,
  430, 496, 545
Koury, Enver M. 300
Koutouby, A. 276
Krishnan, S. 562
Krupp, F. 155, 162-63
Kubursi, Atif A. 431
Kuher, P. 250
Kumar, Ravinder 182
Kupchan, Charles A. 356
Kuwari, Ali Khalifa Al-
  378

Index of Titles

199

Index of Subjects

213

chemical nutrients
  water pollution
    monitoring 589
Chicago Beach
  development
  Dubai tourist project
    544
child obesity
  influencing factors 278
children
  Al-Ain obesity study 278
  incidence of anaemia
    290
  of parasites 290
  malnutrition 249
  marasmus 249
  obesity and blood
    pressure 277
  patterns of paracetamol
    prescription 260
  undernutrition 249
*Chlamydotis undulata
  macqueenii see*
  houbara bustards
chlorine discharge
  predicted effects on Al-
    Ain city 597
chloroform
  use in traditional
    medicine 252
citrus fruits production 529
city planning 239
civic improvements 239
Civil Code 314
civil companies
  legal aspects 315
civil construction projects
  588
Civil Law
  Code of Civil Procedure
    312
Civil Service 16
climate 28, 63, 107, 157
  effects on agriculture
    532
  late Quaternary 110
climatic change
  effects on coastline 86
climatology
  use of mathematical
    modelling 109
Clinical Interview Schedule
  use of 285

clinical teaching
  simulation in Skills
    Laboratory 269
coalition forces
  Gulf War presence in
    UAE 335
coastal area
  environmental sensitivity
    591
  mapping by remote
    sensing 132
coastal pollution law 309
coastal waters
  pollution 437, 583, 586
coastline
  effects of climatic
    change 86
  mapping 132
  nautical charts 137-38
  sediment migration 86
Code of Civil Procedure 312
cognitive style
  undergraduate analysis
    601
College of Education
  courses 626
  student programme 626
college students
  achievements 602
  learning strategies 600
  relationship between
    learning process and
    academic achievement
    602
colonialism
  contribution to political
    dependency 303
commerce
  arbitration rules 312
  contracts 308
  economic significance of
    international visitors
    547
  historical developments
    54, 64
  international airport
    facilities 31
  law 308
  legal developments 316
  shopping facilities 31
  significance of Dubai
    423, 547
  of regional access 434

commercial companies
  legal aspects 315
Commercial Directory
  Internet site 689
communications
  development 13, 530
  plans 36
communications sector
  growth 374
communications skills
  programme 612
Community College system
  proposals for 629
companies
  directory of 396
computer engineering
  curriculum
    UAE University 622
computer simulation
  emergency hospital
    services 250
computer software
  protection 659
concession agreements
  oil industry 211, 450,
    452, 459-63, 466-69
conservation
  flora 157
  groundwater 129
  law 309
  Sharjah 243
  water supply measures
    113
constitution 305
  relationship with
    regional authorities 36
  structure 36
construction industry 391,
    502
  buoyancy 411
  crane sales as barometer
    499
  growth 373-74
  levels of business 496
  profitability 496
  public sector investment
    388
  statistics 577
Consultative Council
  role 351
consultative process
  role of Federal National
    Council 377

217

Jebel Ali Free Zone
381, 423
re-exports 491
slowdown 375-76
stability 393
statistics 39, 375-76, 577
traditional 529
water supply demands
113
ed-Dur
antiquities 173
archaeological
excavations 169-72
graveyard relics 169
education 13, 25
Abu Dhabi 7
bibliography 672
cultural programmes 620
development 36, 358
problems 500
early childhood 616
English Language
teaching 614
establishment under
British control 214
female access to 234,
618
employment in 234
Gulf Co-operation
Council 339, 358
higher education
provision 623
impact 645
on agriculture 221
implications of Internet
615
influence of Arab Bureau
of Education for the
Gulf States 620
levels of attainment 565
medical students'
learning preferences
282
military 614
role of missionaries 248
statistics 39, 609
status of women 235
teacher 614
UAE University, College
of Education 626
university–school
relationships 611
vocational 614

education programmes
information 620
education services
achievements 305
educational administrators
lack of indigenous
personnel 631
educational development
342
influence of Arab Bureau
of Education for the
Gulf States 620
educational system 614
administrative failings
610, 631
reliance on expatriates
631
effluent
use for irrigation 516
Egypt
relations with 342
electricity
consumption of
desalination plants 127
demand 478, 484
distribution 481
federal power network
487
high-voltage network
extension, Abu Dhabi
483
potential for wind-power
utilization 470
price structure 478
provision 36
subsidies 478
supply–demand
forecasting 473
supply problems 478
electricity consumption
peak-load forecasting
473
electricity supply
disruption to 476
electromagnetic mapping
Al-Jaww Plain 118
Emirates Airline
tourism role 543
Emirates Centre for
Strategic Studies
Internet site 685
employment
banking sector 569

equal opportunities
policies 618
female employment in
education 234
in health services 234
in social services 234
impact of oil industry
227
labour demands 565
lack of trained
manpower 228
national percentage of
labour force 217, 351
nationalization policy
569
psychiatric patients'
potential 258
public sector 323
role conflict of women
237
role of missionaries 248
women 232, 235-36
significance of expatriate
labour 36, 218-19,
351, 573, 576
state sector 72
statistics 573
status of women 233-34
employment commitment
survey 563
employment satisfaction
survey 563
energy 10, 391
power system
development 485
energy conservation
cement industry 493
engineering curriculum
UAE University 622
English language
development 637
impact on dialects 637
role in society 633
English Language
instructors
competence 633
training 633
English Language teaching
614
British support 633
materials 633
Ministry of Education
support 633

geochemical
characteristics 92
geological structure 98
Oman ophiolite
data from UAE 91
geology 91, 95
Oman Peninsula
external relations 174
online database
Arab Information Bank
678
OPEC
bibliography 680
development 467
establishment452
membership 51
price regulation 384
quota system 384
role 469
in oil production 384
significance 467
Operational Research
role in industrial
development 495
ophiolite belt
geology 95
ophiolites
Al-Fujairah 92
Organizational
Commitment Scale
use in employment
survey 563

P

Pakistan
economic impact of
migrant labour 564,
574
Pakistani migrant workers
spending patterns 564
Palestine
GCC reaction to 361
migrant labour supply
566
policy towards 327
Palestine Liberation
movements
relations with 327
paracetamol
danger for children
260

prescription patterns in
children 260
paramilitary forces 351
parasites
incidence in bustards 151
in children 290
in houbara bustards
152
in rufous-crested
bustards 158
parks
Dubai 646
environmental
significance 646
participation agreements
oil industry 452, 461-63,
467-68, 498
patents
intellectual property law
316
patients
attitudes towards
smoking 272
evaluation of health-care
consultations 270
pearl fisheries 64
pearl fishing
attractions to migrant
labour 221
importance 7, 13
traditions of 640
pearl trade
decline of 22
pearling
economic significance
178
social significance 178
peritidal settings
Abu Dhabi 90
Persian Gulf
charts 137-38
India Office
administration 195
secret agreements, India
Office 194
superpower interests 356
see also Arabian Gulf
Persian Gulf States
British treaties with 176
personal loans
banking sector
development 400
personal status laws 307

petrochemical industries
399
petrochemicals
development of sector
458
environmental problems
505
marketing 505
production 351, 505
prospects for growth 440
Ruwais complex 446
phonology
Gulf Arabic 636
photogrammetry
desert terrain 134
photographs
collections 33
early 27
pidginization
Gulf Arabic 638
piracy
Arab activities 183
Arabian Gulf 178
British perceptions of
183
myth of 185
threats from 177
pirated goods
legislation 319
problems of 319
planning
effects of state size on
cohesiveness 385
policies 39
urban 239
planning bodies 36
planning process 391
planning strategies
evaluation of 324
plant extracts
medicinal properties
252-54, 292
plant growth
effects of salinity
531
plants
chemical composition
140
political aggregation
dynamics of 327
political boundaries
resolution by
urbanization 240

shari'a law
  influence on agency laws
    318
  status of women 232
Sharjah
  agriculture 35
  archaeological
    excavations 172
  archaeology 166
  banking sector 415
  blasphemy case 313
  conservation 243
  customs regulations
    Internet site 690
  debt problems 368
  dispute with Iran over
    Abu Musa Island 328-
    29, 331-32, 337, 343,
    345, 351, 455
  dropout rates from adult
    education 630
  economic revival 368
  gas finds offshore 368
    reserves 41
    supplies for Dubai 486
  infrastructure projects
    368
  loss of Abu Musa Island
    to Iran 341
  maritime boundary with
    Iran 330
  Mubarak field drilling
    454
    production 451
  Oasis Agricultural Farm,
    Dhaid 35
  oil production 451
    reserves 441, 451
  shared zone with
    Fujairah 330
    with Iran 330
    with Oman 330, 345
  tourism concerns 549
  urban conservation areas
    243
  urbanization 243
Sharjah Creek
  pollution monitoring
    584
  water pollution 589
Sharjah Customs
  Department Internet
  site 690

Sharjah Ports Authority
  annual report 435
  statistics 435
Sheikh Zaid (1855-1909)
  rule 22
Shii community
  role in politics 244
  standards 244
Shi'ite minority
  impact of Iranian
    policies 355
    Iranian revolution 360
shipbuilding traditional 64
shipping
  investment in 398
  pollution from 585
shoreline oil pollution 437,
  583, 586
Skills Laboratory
  use in medical training
    269
skin infections
  treatment by traditional
    medicine 251
skin tests
  stings from Samsum ants
    261
slave trade 57, 433
  India Office documents
    195
  Royal Navy role in
    suppression 54, 178-79
  slave trade suppression
    attempts 183, 194
  suppression of 176, 179,
    181-82
slavery
  treaty agreements 22
smoking
  attitude of doctors 272
    of patients 272
  incidence amongst health
    professionals 257
smuggling
  arms 57
  historical 433
  suppression agreements
    176, 194
social background
  description 669
social change
  effects on female
    morbidity 264

  on mental health of
    women 256
  impact of oil 450, 462
  of urbanization 238
  problems 231
  relationship to Islam 47
    to *shari'a* law 47
social development 17, 351
  policies 380
social groups
  impact on political
    dependency 303
social sciences
  research opportunities
    220
social services 12
  female employment in
    234
  maintenance of 358
social structure 52, 56, 70,
  327, 538
  Abu Dhabi 22
  Al-Liwa oasis 221
  bibliography 672
  expatriate community
    645
  impact of Gulf war 229
    modernization 229
    oil wealth 348
    urbanization 238
  position of migrant
    labour 223
  pressures for democracy
    229
  relationship to political
    structure 302
social welfare
  development 36
  statistics 39
society 15, 27, 37, 59, 62,
  387, 391, 614, 687
  bibliography 680
  change in 55
  characteristics 60
  cultural change 576
  decline of tradition
    231
  development 13, 36
    process 274, 385
  effects of development
    229
  of migrant workers
    226

242

wind strengths
  winter *shamal* 109
winds
  analysis of 104
witches'-broom disease
  acid lime trees 535
women
  access to technical
      education 618
    to vocational
      education 618
  education policies 235
  educational access 234
  effects of social change
    on mental health 256
    on morbidity 264
  employment 235
    and role conflict 237
    status 232, 234
  equal employment
      opportunities 618
  government employment
      233
  health services provision
      237
  incidence of anaemia
      273
    of morbidity, Al-Ain
      285
  issue of 16
  legal status 232, 235, 237
  marriage contract 235
  neo-conservative
      movements 233

political role 233
psychiatric survey
    264-65
role 23, 222
role conflict from
    employment 237
role in labour market 237
  in public relations 606
  in society 47, 237
social change 233
status in society 222,
    235, 606, 634, 642,
    686
welfare services
    provision 237
Women's Federation
  government funding for
      236
  legal autonomy 236
  role of 236
women undergraduates
  future role in public
      relations 606
  hemispheric thinking
      style 601
World Health Organization
  report on 'health for all'
      programme 274

X

Xanthidae
  distribution 148

Xeromphis nilotica
  treatment of jaundice
      255
  use as a fish poison
      255

Y

Yellow Pages
  Internet site 689
yoghurt
  presence of *Listeria*
      267

Z

Zaid, Sheikh (1855-1905)
  rule 22
Zakum oilfield
  declining reservoir
      pressure 445
  geology 445
  use of water to aid
      production 445
Zayed, Sheikh
  assessment of 300
  investment in BCCI
      408
  ownership of BCCI
      408
  recompense to BCCI
      depositors 401

248

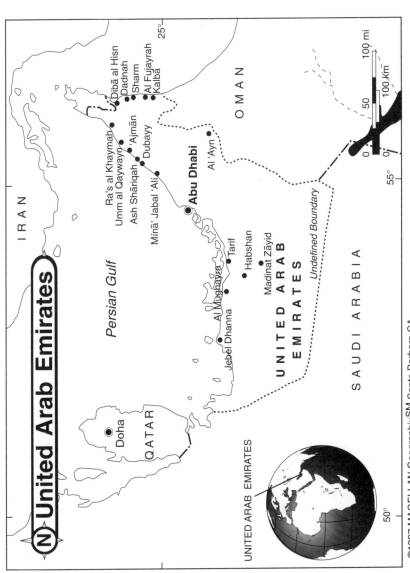

United Arab Emirates

IRAN

Persian Gulf

Doha
QATAR

Ra's al Khaymah
Umm al Qaywayn
Ash Shāriqah 'Ajmān
Dubayy
Minā' Jabal 'Alī

Dibā al Hisn
Dadnah
Sharm
Al Fujayrah
Kalbā

25°

OMAN

Abu Dhabi

Al 'Ayn

Tarif
Habshan
Madinat Zāyid

55°

Al Mughayra
Jebel Dhanna

UNITED ARAB
EMIRATES

Undefined Boundary

SAUDI ARABIA

50°

UNITED ARAB EMIRATES

0   50   100 mi
0   100 Km

©1997 MAGELLAN GeographixSM Santa Barbara,CA

ALSO FROM CLIO PRESS

INTERNATIONAL ORGANIZATIONS SERIES

Each volume in the International Organizations Series is either devoted to one specific organization, or to a number of different organizations operating in a particular region, or engaged in a specific field of activity. The scope of the series is wide-ranging and includes intergovernmental organizations, international non-governmental organizations, and national bodies dealing with international issues. The series is aimed mainly at the English-speaker and each volume provides a selective, annotated, critical bibliography of the organization, or organizations, concerned. The bibliographies cover books, articles, pamphlets, directories, databases and theses and, wherever possible, attention is focused on material about the organizations rather than on the organizations' own publications. Notwithstanding this, the most important official publications, and guides to those publications, will be included. The views expressed in individual volumes, however, are not necessarily those of the publishers.

VOLUMES IN THE SERIES